IN SEARCH OF THE ELUSIVE PEACE CORPS MOMENT

Destination: Estonia

5203-WELL

IN SEARCH OF THE ELUSIVE PEACE CORPS MOMENT

Destination: Estonia

Douglas Wells

To order additional copies of this book, contact:
Xlibris Corporation
1-888-7-XLIBRIS
www.Xlibris.com
Orders@Xlibris.com

CONTENTS

To my lovely wife Kairit,
who was my biggest and best Peace Corps "project", to my
mother and father, who raised me with the right values and
instilled in me a desire to help make the world a better place,
and to the mystical island of Hiiumaa.

ACKNOWLEDGEMENTS

I would like to thank those people who encouraged me to write this book and kept me going through doubts, frustration and writer's block. Without their help, these memories never would have made it onto paper and this book would have never made it into your hands.

First of all, I must pay tribute to the late author James Herriot, whose books about being a country vet in Yorkshire, England brought me such pleasure in my childhood, and later provided inspiration for a book of my own. He was often on my mind when I was striving to find a way to adequately portray the complex, close-knit island society I lived in.

I would like to thank Tunne and Mari-Ann Kelam, who, on a rainy, late night drive through an oncoming hurricane in Virginia, motivated me to finally get off my tail and start writing. Also, I wouldn't have been able to finish this book without Joel Waters, who kept encouraging me to keep going when I faltered and, at the same time, explored ways to bring the book to market when I couldn't be bothered with the business aspect of being an author. Most importantly, his experience with the subject matter I was writing about, gained while serving as one of my Peace Corps contemporaries in the Baltics, was invaluable in making the stories accessible to a wider audience. Joel's suggestions and constructive criticisms had an effect on virtually every page of this manuscript. I owe him a huge debt of gratitude for helping me turn a dream into reality.

I am also grateful to Tõnu Naelapea of the Estonian newspaper "Meie Elu" in Toronto. His motivational E-mails kept me encouraged and on track during those dark times behind the computer in West Virginia, when I started to doubt if my book was ever going to see the light of day. In addition, his tireless editing and attention to detail gave me my first workable manuscript. With regards to editing, Jenna Robbins was the one who really gave a professional touch to this manuscript. With her help we were able to put short stories that had been published individually into a single book that would be easy for the reader to follow. She went above and beyond the call of duty to give us something we could actually put into print.

Lastly, I have to thank those in Estonia who provided me with the true-life experiences that can be found inside this book. Whether they helped me or hindered me during my time on Hiiumaa Island, their personalities, mannerisms, deeds and misdeeds fill the pages of this book and are what make it a special, heartwarming treat for the reader.

FORWARD

In the early 1990's Estonia achieved what just a short time earlier had seemed an impossible dream, a revolution without bloodshed resulting in its regaining independence from the Soviet Union. Dubbed the "Singing Revolution", it is appropriate that our first hint about a special American in Estonia also came in the form of a song, which topped the Estonian pop charts in 1994. Intriguing stories about its American composer-performer led us to meet with Douglas Wells soon afterwards at his Peace Corps post on Hiiumaa Island. As Hiiumaa is one of our favorite vacation spots, we probably would have visited the tourist information center in Kärdla that summer anyway. But certainly the wish to meet the young American man who not only speaks, but also sings, in Estonian was an added incentive. We looked forward to making the young man feel welcome in Estonia and as Mari-Ann is Estonian-American, she thought she might be of help in bridging possible culture gaps. So, one sunny afternoon we chatted with a friendly Douglas Wells, admired the Information Center and drove around the island with his now famous "Lighthouse Tour" booklet to guide us—all without much idea of the struggles behind each of these achievements.

We are very happy that Doug took the advice of his fans and wrote this book memorializing his Peace Corps adventures. He has chronicled a unique time in Estonia's history, giving us glimpses of what was involved in making the transition from communism to democracy and freedom. The impact of the Soviet system was more insidious than many people either in Estonia or in the West want to acknowledge. It involved more than mass executions and deportations, more than the destruction of the landscape, more than the blighting of careers and the stifling of lives. It involved the deformation of minds and souls. While recovery has been amazingly swift, fifty years of occupation cannot be wiped out overnight.

Douglas is a talented humorist, reminiscent of noted American outdoor writer Patrick McManus. He has a knack for telling a good tale. Douglas' modesty and self-deprecating humor keep his stories, which are deadly accurate, from being cruel. The reader finds himself laughing *with* Douglas and not really *at* anyone. His stories ring true because he spent time in Estonia, living with ordinary people, sharing their daily lives, learning about Estonian history and culture and trying to do his best as a Peace Corps Volunteer.

Over the six years that Douglas spent in Estonia, our friendship grew. We admired his enthusiasm and shared his frustration as we tried to help him overcome bureaucratic inertia and other obstacles. After finishing his Peace Corps stint, Douglas went to work for the Estonian Tourist Board where he almost singlehandedly created its information network on the Internet. Always looking for new ways to introduce and promote Estonia, he initiated and intensified cooperation between the Tourist Board and Estonia's Embassies overseas.

During Estonia's 50 years under Soviet occupation hundreds of thousands of citizens of Russia and other Soviet Republics came to live in Estonia, but many never learned the Estonian language. For this reason Estonians are all the more impressed that Douglas became such a master of our language. On one occasion, I recall, he was approached by a young Russian woman who was curious as to why anyone would bother to learn Estonian. "Why don't you learn a real language like Russian?" she asked. Douglas' answer was perfect: "Because I am living in this country and it is natural to learn the local language. I want to show respect."

Before we lost this bright and talented man to the United States Foreign Service, Douglas also made new friends for Estonia while working at our Embassy in Washington, D.C. Everyone seemed to know about the energetic and helpful Douglas Wells who, in addition to his regular duties, converted an unused basement area into a sophisticated Information Center.

We are convinced Douglas has enough post-Peace Corps material for at least one more book. We strongly urge him to write it!

-Tunne and Mari-Ann Kelam

The Kelams are the only married couple serving together in the Riigikogu (the Estonian Parliament). With the exception of one year, Tunne Kelam has been the Vice-President of the Riigikogu since 1992. He was a leading candidate in the 2001 Estonian Presidential elections.

INTRODUCTION

"You should write a book!" That is what I heard over and over again when I told stories about my Peace Corps service in Estonia. I had a few good yarns, like every volunteer, but nothing that seemed to warrant writing an entire book. But then I began to think, how many volunteers have had a number one song in their country of service, received a commendation from the President for finding a national treasure, and fallen in love—all in the same tour? Or how about fishing with a hammer, catching sheep with a net, or driving across the frozen sea in a car?

No volunteer I know of has been stalked by the local cop, armed with a new radar gun received as humanitarian aid from Texas!

Furthermore, as I kept in contact with my former colleagues and friends back in Estonia, I came to understand that the Estonian island of Hiiumaa in the early 1990s wasn't simply a place; it was a unique period in time. The island was a coming together of a special set of circumstances that had never before existed and would likely never occur again. Estonia, a country that enjoyed but twenty years of independence between the two World Wars, was free again after fifty years of Soviet occupation. The Cold War had ended, Communism had been discredited as an ideology, and now this tiny nation of 1.5 million people had to find a place for itself in a democratic, free-market Europe. Nobody was going to show them the way. They had to make it on their own. The initial turmoil that I witnessed, the "Wild West" element of a complete change in government, economic system and social structure, is now mostly a thing of the past.

During my time in Estonia, I watched the last remnants of the Cold War being swept away in the form of the Russian Army finally packing up and going home. I pulled down barbed wire with my own two hands, helping the Estonians reclaim beautiful landscapes that had been off-limits, even to those who had lived there in peace just a few decades before. The Soviet Union is just a memory now and, God willing, that tortured history won't repeat itself.

Another unique aspect of my Peace Corps service was that I was part of the first group of Volunteers to serve in the former Soviet Union. We were Group One, a respected title among former Peace Corps Volunteers. I was proud to be a part of that first group, being there as Peace Corps experienced its growing pains in Estonia right along with the rest of the country. And what growing pains we had! Our ill-fated agricultural program was cancelled three months after we were at post. Peace Corps told us flat out that we shouldn't expect much out of our tour and that we could go home if we wanted to. No one did.

Through our efforts—some successful, some not—we helped blaze trails into various fields of expertise and laid a solid base for the other groups that followed. Most importantly we showed the Estonian people, who had no idea what Peace Corps was (save for it possibly being some branch of the CIA), that we were there to help them and work alongside them. Not only will there never be another Group One, but by 2002, Peace Corps will have left Estonia entirely, no longer needed and never to return. Estonia will have joined the ranks of those few countries that have "graduated" from their Peace Corps programs.

In the years after I finished my tour of duty, I realized I really should write down my Estonian adventures, if not to write a book, at least to record them before they faded from memory. It would also save me the trouble of having to constantly repeat the same story until I myself became bored, never again to speak of the events that took place. But most importantly, this book provides a way for me to share my respect for the people of the Baltic States. They were confronted with an entirely new game; a completely different set of rules and told to get on the field and start competing with those who had been playing for years. Many doubted they would even survive, but not only did they learn to play the game, they excelled and for better or worse, this process changed their country's society from top to bottom. Of one thing I am sure, being in Estonia after the fall of Communism was a one-of-a-kind experience. Even if I went back and lived in the very same village where I served as a volunteer, it wouldn't be the same. Everything–and I mean everything–has changed: people, technology, infrastructure, etc. In the decade since I first arrived, it has all changed, almost beyond recognition.

This book is a collection of true stories that are both humorous and moving. Some were published previously and some are available to read here for the first time. In summary, the following Peace Corps tales are a compilation of successes and failures that a disillusioned young man from America's heartland experiences when he ventures behind the former Iron Curtain in an attempt to make good as a Peace Corps Volunteer and experience that elusive "Peace Corps Moment".

1–NOT YOUR FATHER'S PEACE CORPS

Sometime during the fourth hour of our journey, as we bounced along in the aging Soviet bus, I noticed that we weren't on the main highway anymore. As a matter of fact, I was beginning to doubt we were even going the right way. After all, how could this bumpy forest road be the way from the Latvian capital of Riga to Tartu, the second-largest city in Estonia? We had been driving for what seemed like forever and now it was starting to grow dark. I already felt a little uneasy about leaving the relative security of our Latvian training site and this wasn't helping one bit. Something was amiss, I was sure, but our driver didn't speak enough English to explain what was going on and I seemed to be the only one concerned by our predicament. I had this dreadful premonition that we were going to stop in some deserted clearing and a bunch of KGB thugs would step out of the forest and arrest us, or beat us, or worse. Then again, maybe we were just lost. I tried to shake off the feeling of impending doom by concentrating on the conversations of my fellow Peace Corps Volunteers, who were seemingly oblivious to our predicament.

Most of them were talking about home and why they had joined the Peace Corps. The year was 1992 and we were SED (Small Enterprise Development) Volunteers, a relatively new breed in the Peace Corps as evidenced by our demographics. Instead of a bunch of idealistic twentysomethings headed off to teach English in the Horn of Africa, the average age of our group was around 40, half of us had MBA's, and we were going to put our skills to work improving agriculture in the dense forests of northeastern Europe—

so far north, in fact, that we would be serving out our two years just 800 miles from the Arctic Circle. Idealism was a fairly scarce commodity among this crew with years of experience in various business sectors. Instead of singing "Kum-Ba-Yah" and talking about the latest bands, the conversations on the bus dealt more with interrupted careers, problems regarding renting out townhouses, and the difficulties of managing financial assets back in the States. Still, we were all there by choice and everyone, including me, was anxious to pitch in and make a difference in the re-emerging Baltic democracies.

When the inevitable question of why we each had joined the Peace Corps came up, everyone in our group seemed to have a different answer. Mine sounded a little corny compared to the others and the telling of it drew more than a few groans, but it was genuine. I was raised in a family with strong religious faith. We went to church every Sunday and, as a child, I went to Wednesday night classes to be confirmed in the Presbyterian Church. There, we were taught a very simple truth: God has a plan for everyone. My parents always told me and my siblings—all sixteen of us— that we were each born with certain gifts, and that it was our job to figure out what those gifts were and what to do with them in order to make the world a better place. Most importantly, the more you had or were born with, the more that was expected of you. In my late 20's, chasing unsuccessfully after various dreams and schemes, I was starting to think I had been born with a good position on the starting line of life but had gotten a little short-changed in the gifts department. Sure, I had a decent job as a bookkeeper and made a good salary, but it made me uneasy looking at the other professionals around me getting older and richer but still whining about cracks in their swimming pool or the poor service at the Lexus dealership. I began to see how ridiculous it was just to accumulate the biggest pile of "stuff" that you could and then complain about how complicated your life was. Plus, I just wanted to give something, to do something that wouldn't just benefit me. I just couldn't shake the feeling I should be somewhere else, doing something else.

Coincidentally, about the time I was going through this tortured, self-examination process, the Soviet Union started to break apart. I remember very well how I was sitting in a bar in Omaha, watching the Berlin Wall come down in 1989. Less than two years later, in another Nebraska bar, I watched with others in shock and anger as CNN showed footage of the 1991 crackdown on the Baltic States. As we quaffed our beer, we cursed at the "commie stormtroopers" we saw parading about on the screen. Americans hate nothing more than to see a big guy picking on a little guy, and I was no different. After all, the U.S. had made such a big deal about not officially recognizing the Soviet occupation of the Baltics in World War II and we had always encouraged them to break free of the Soviet Union. But now, it seemed like we were leaving these little countries hung out to dry. These distant political events, coupled with my dissatisfaction with my life, pushed me to action. Over the next several months I pondered my choices. I didn't think I could cut it as a missionary, I was too old for the Army, and getting into the U.S. Foreign Service was a long shot at best. Finally, following in the footsteps of one of my uncles who did the "real" Peace Corps in the '60s, I picked up the phone and called the local recruitment office.

The first thing I did when they answered the phone was to rail at them for not supporting the folks in the Baltic States, for being a tacit accomplice to President Bush, who I saw as going back on his word about supporting new democracies in Eastern Europe, etc., etc. I told them that I would be ready to go anywhere as a volunteer, a requirement for any applicant, but I had a pretty good idea about where I wanted to serve. The woman at the receiving end of my tirade let me finish without interruption, then calmly informed me that by coincidence, they were just in the process of putting together a group to go to the Baltics: Estonia, Latvia and Lithuania. I was welcome to try and get into that group but it wouldn't be easy, she informed me, as there were only thirty spaces available and already hundreds of people had shown an interest in being a part of this "new mission" for the Peace Corps. If I didn't make it into the Baltic group I would have to go wherever they wanted to send me. "Sign me up!" I said, and thus began my process of becoming a Peace Corps Volunteer. A few interviews, medical exams and police background checks later, I miraculously made the cut and was on a plane out of Omaha about fourteen weeks after my first phone call.

Following the initial culture shock of arriving in the Baltics on a rickety Russian Aeroflot plane and being greeted at the airport by a giant Soviet helicopter—complete with a menacing red star—I set about getting used to my surroundings at our first training site in Latvia. It was to be our home while we prepared to go to our respective countries. We volunteers lived three to a room in an old railroad school dormitory where to take a "shower", we had to heat up water in a kettle and ladle it over our heads. At mealtimes, we ate strange food at the cafeteria located in an abandoned factory next door, where it seemed everything was made with dill sprinkled on it. I learned to traverse our building's stairwells, littered with cigarette butts and smelling of urine, without even holding my breath. This was all part of the Peace Corps "experience" we had signed up for and I was determined to be tolerant and not complain. After all, we were the first group of SED volunteers, ten for each of the three Baltic Republics, to enter the former Soviet Union, so we felt like pioneers of a new frontier. A few rough edges were to be expected.

As a matter of fact, I took these hardships as a badge of honor, another step on the way to experiencing the "Peace Corps Moment" my Uncle had told me about. He had said that at some point, you are no longer just a former student or engineer or whatever you were in your former life. You actually go through a transformation of sorts. After that, your answer to someone who asks what you are doing in their country isn't a stammering explanation of what you are supposed to be accomplishing, you simply answer, "I am a Peace Corps Volunteer," and that suffices. The moment can come during times of extreme hardship or danger, or it can come with some great accomplishment, just like on the recruitment posters where the Peace Corps Volunteer is surrounded by smiling villagers and standing next to a new bridge or well. It doesn't happen to everyone and you won't know exactly what your own Peace Corps Moment will be, but you'll know when it happens and that is when you know you have succeeded in becoming a real volunteer.

I kept my Uncle's words in mind and after three weeks of training and acclimation in Riga, I had more or less become accustomed to everything except for a nagging feeling of being watched. Being born in Omaha, a few miles from the headquarters of the U.S. Strategic Air Command, I knew all about the Cold War and who the enemy was. I grew up on movies that invariably pitched the Russians against the Americans, and as hard as I tried to get over it, those red stars and the hammer and sickle emblems still raised the hair on the back of my neck. As far as I was concerned, my main mission was to help my assigned country, Estonia, stay out of the clutches of the "Evil Empire." I was very suspicious of the post-Soviet military still in the Baltics, and the folks in our group liked to tease me about how I would watch the groups of soldiers like a hawk whenever they came near. There weren't that many Russian soldiers right around where we lived, but we saw them quite often and the whole place still had the feeling of an armed camp. After all, the Baltics had regained their independence less than a year before and there was still a lot of tension in the air.

Some of the locals that we met told us that the Russians where just waiting for a provocation to take over again, and that they weren't above starting something themselves. According to them, the Russians wanted revenge after the humiliating collapse of the Soviet Union. There certainly had to be those who resented Americans coming on their turf and setting up shop, Peace Corps or not—but maybe that was just me, coming from the other side of the Iron Curtain. Some of our group went exploring on the second day, and they came back raving about some of the nicer parts of Riga, but I had to deal with my fear and loathing one step at a time. The first week I wouldn't even leave the dorms by myself. Then, gradually, I took excursions farther and farther afield, one block at a time. Sometimes I sat down by the railroad tracks behind the school and recorded cassette tapes of commentary to send home to my friends. I merely watched as the other volunteers, in groups of three or four, took the tram downtown to explore the wild and woolly open air market. Gradually though, at my own pace, I built up a feeling of security, and in the process made some friends before we were split up into our ten-member country groups and sent to our respective independent republics. With the division of our 30-person Baltic contingent into separate country groups, we were taking one step further away from home and towards the time when we would be on our own. As we said our good-byes and piled onto waiting buses, I felt my fragile sense of well-being eroding away.

* * *

I peered down the aisle and through the windshield but could barely make out the road ahead in the gathering darkness. I soon spotted a light, then two, and then a whole series of floodlights set atop barbed wire. The bus ground to a halt and suddenly all was quiet. We waited silently in the darkness for whatever would come next. A few people laughed nervously and whispered amongst themselves, but all talking ceased when the door of the bus slammed open. I could just make out the outlines of two dark figures boarding the bus and heard them speak a few words in Russian to the driver. As they turned to face us, they were silhouetted against the windshield and I could clearly see the outlines of their AK-47 automatic rifles. We were dead quiet. I could feel fear and panic rising in my throat. Finally, one of them took out a flashlight, turned it on and held it under his chin. For a minute, he enjoyed the spooky effect it had on us before he broke into a grin. "Welcome to Estonia!" he said proudly in English. "May we see your passports?" My introduction to the Estonians was only the first of my many experiences with their strange brand of humor.

2—TARTU

After leaving our initial training site in Riga, the first stop for our ten-member Peace Corps group was Estonia's university town. Located in the south, Tartu, dating back to at least the 1100's and billed as the oldest city in Estonia, had a population of about a hundred thousand. Its other claim to fame, besides the 400 year-old Tartu University, was its role as the home of a major Soviet air base. Before Estonia regained its independence, foreigners were not even allowed to spend the night in the city, which added to the feeling of adventure and mystery surrounding our arrival. The base had been scaled down by the time we arrived, but there were soldiers and planes that still flew missions, mainly shipping equipment back to Russia. You can't truly appreciate what modern technology has done to make airplanes quieter in the U.S. until you've heard one of those monster Soviet transports take off. Their passing caused windows to rattle in our classroom, despite the fact it was a good three miles from the airport.

Tartu was a beautiful old city, built on the banks of the Emajõgi (Mother River) and blessed with many parks, the largest of which was located on the top of the ancient earthen fortifications built by Estonians before the beginning of the second millennium. Whenever I felt lonely, I would take a walk up to a hill where there was an old observatory that had been turned into a museum. The hill provided a quiet place to look out over the city and think about friends and family back home in Nebraska. After an hour or so of this, I was ready to walk back down to the bustling city center and immerse myself once again in Estonian life. The Old Town's cobblestone streets were lined with shops and the outdoor market had all kinds of meat, vegetables and even fresh fish from the Emajõgi. The nice thing about the outdoor markets was that almost all the food was from local producers—eggs right from the chicken and milk in huge metal canisters, fresh from the cow. Of course, we were told by the Peace Corps medical office to avoid these homegrown goods like the plague, but there wasn't a lot else available to eat at that time. Tartu also had its own brewery, which was another reason to be envious of the students at Tartu University, whom I considered among the luckiest in the world to be able to study in such a place.

It was in this town that we were to spend three months, August through October, learning about the intricacies of Estonian language and culture. We were placed with Estonian host families and we had to come to class every day by whatever means we saw fit. Some of the lucky ones in our group were staying in houses within walking distance, but I was way across the river in a roach-infested first-floor apartment, nestled in a huge forest of the ubiquitous Soviet concrete-slab high-rises called Annelinn (Anne's Town). My location required that I roll out every morning and join the masses of commuters taking the bus into town. One of my fellow commuters was a Russian officer who lived upstairs. We would usually end up leaving home at about the same time each morning–he with his sharp army uniform and briefcase, and I with my Nebraska Cornhusker jean jacket and backpack. We spent a considerable amount of time checking each other out at the bus stop but we never spoke. Even when jammed together chest-to-chest when the bus was especially crowded, we just eyed each other with mutual suspicion. I am not sure if he knew who I was, but he didn't seem too interested in striking up a conversation, even at a distance of six inches. Some days, after several minutes of staring into his silent, dour face, I fantasized about reaching out and plucking one of the medals off his chest—just to get a reaction. However, I figured I would have plenty of other—and possibly better—opportunities to abruptly end my budding Peace Corps career, so I opted to deny myself the instant gratification of causing an international incident.

As I mentioned, the bus was always crowded, but the patrons of our bus stop were relatively lucky, as our boarding point was near the beginning of the #17's run towards downtown. When it arrived at our stop, we still had to push and elbow our way up on board, but by the time we reached the later stops, the poor yellow bus was bursting at the seams, despite its unusually large size. It looked like two buses stuck together, with a black rubber connector between the front and rear sections and this round metal plate in the floor where they were joined that rotated every time the bus turned. God forbid that you should have one foot on the regular floor and one foot on the twisting floor when the bus decided to take a turn! I had learned this quickly after a few unintended attempts at doing the splits, so I always stationed myself away from the twisting section. The problem was, as people forced their way on the bus at the later stops, I was invariably forced halfway onto the dreaded metal plate. In that situation, you had two choices: either cram your feet together on the regular floor, or cram your feet together on the plate and ride around the corners. To add to the difficulties, as more and more people squeezed onto the bus, the amount of available breathable air lessened. Fortunately, the people of Tartu seemed to bathe more regularly than the people I had encountered in Riga, but there was still the rancid smell of garlic-breath and the suffocating fog of oxidized alcohol to deal with on some mornings. But nobody complained, at least out loud. Businessmen, soldiers, students, and old women headed to market all dealt quietly and calmly with this daily indignity.

The constant squeezing and the bad air always took its toll on me and I was usually light-headed by the time I bailed out of the bus near the town market. Next, after crossing a footbridge over the Emajõgi, I switched to the considerably more tolerable bus #5, which took me to the management institute where we studied. Before heading upstairs to language lessons, our group of volunteers usually met down in the coffee shop to exchange war stories from the previous evening. With ten of us Americans living in local Estonians' living rooms and spare bedrooms, there were plenty of cultural misunderstandings and mishaps to report.

Food always seemed to be one of our most favorite subjects of discussion. Estonians seemed to eat only bread, cheese, sausage, and these little open-face sandwiches with cucumbers and fish on them. For warm food they relied heavily on fried meats and potatoes. Between their culinary preferences, smoking habits and affinity for vodka, it was a real surprise that Estonian men even made it to their rather modest average life expectancy of 60. My own host mother, Tiina, served me a daily breakfast of eggs and slices of crispy fried fat—not bacon, which has at least a little bit of meat, but 100% pure slab-o-fat. I wasn't about to complain and hurt her feelings, so I simply reached for the salt shaker. She watched disapprovingly as I sprinkled a liberal amount on the glistening white morsels of pure cholesterol. "You probably don't know this in America," she said, "but you shouldn't put so much salt on your food. In Estonia, we know it's bad for your heart."

There were even more unusual things about the Estonian diet. For example, one of the things we had for breakfast was fresh milk—straight from the cow. Someone from a nearby farm came to the apartment buildings every morning and sold milk so fresh it was still warm and hadn't even had the cream separated from it. Next to that, store-bought milk seemed like water. Of course our Peace Corps doctor said we would drop dead if we drank non-pasteurized milk, so I only partook in moderation. Tiina really loved the milk, so I was surprised one day when she poured a full glass and put it down on the counter untouched. She usually kept the kitchen area pretty clean, so all the more puzzling to see the same glass of milk still standing in its place the next morning. On the third morning she came into the kitchen where I was drinking coffee and went straight for the glass, which by that time had taken on a sickening, yellowish tinge. She held it up to the light, swished it around and, before I could stop her, downed it in one gulp. I could only watch in horror as she completed this apparent suicide attempt and smacked her lips in satisfaction. Surprisingly, she didn't keel over right away and I headed off to work wondering what condition she would be in when I got home that evening. As it turned out, she was none the worse for wear and actually seemed invigorated by the evil concoction.

Even a simple trip to the grocery store proved interesting. The store in our apartment complex had a bunch of wire baskets by the door and you were required—and I do mean required—to take one before you came in. If all of the baskets were taken, you had to wait until somebody finished shopping, paid, then returned the basket to the table by the front door. Once when I just needed a bottle of beer, I slipped through the turnstile without a basket. I was immediately accosted by a short, fat, angrily sputtering old woman. This class of the population (the short, fat old woman class) seemed to have appointed themselves enforcers of the social mores, and I had seen them fearlessly berate everyone from a tiny two-year-old child to a huge lumbering drunk. I knew better than to argue, so I beat a hasty retreat to the end of the line. When I finally had my basket, I headed to the beer section. There I saw a group of people pulling out bottles, turning them upside down and holding them up to the light. Not wanting to stand out, I did the same but couldn't see what they were looking for. I pulled out a bottle and showed it to a fellow shopper who shook his head. When I presented him with the next bottle he nodded approvingly, so I took that one and headed for the counter to check out.

Standing in line, I notice that when people paid, they pulled their crisp, unfolded bills slowly out of their wallets, turned them over, held them up to the light, and almost reluctantly passed them to the cashier, who repeated the same process before sliding them carefully into the drawer. As I approached the cashier, I realized I had my bills stuffed in my pocket. I hurriedly pulled them out and tried to press out the wrinkles against my leg. When it came my turn to pay, I handed over my cash with apprehension. I had tried the best I could, but the cashier shook her head in disapproval and said something I didn't catch to the person behind me, who shrugged his shoulders in a "what-are you-gonna-do" fashion.

It was only later when I quizzed my Estonian teachers about this behavior that I learned that the new Estonian currency, an important symbol of independence, had replaced the ruble just a month before our arrival. For them, it was unthinkable that someone would take this symbol of free Estonia and wad it up in their pocket!

The Peace Corps had a fairly rigorous and well thought-out training program set up for us. Language was a big part of it, but we also had guest speakers from the Estonian government and visitors from artisan and cultural backgrounds. The stars of the training program were certainly our language teachers, Kairi and Linda, two women in their 20's. The hardest part of their job was putting up with all of our questions that invariably began with the word "why," which we soon learned was a question you just didn't ask when learning Estonian. No one in Estonia really had much experience in teaching the language to foreigners, so they had to start from scratch and put together a program that would meet the Peace Corps' rigorous standards for language instruction, which put a heavy emphasis on practical usage. For example, following exercises where we would learn how to buy a certain kind of food, we would be sent into town and were not allowed back in the classroom until we had the proper item in our hand.

One day we studied purchasing train tickets and, as usual, we were sent out to apply our skills in the real world. Our fictitious destination was Estonia's capital, Tallinn. I hung back and didn't go with the rest of the group right after class because I liked to take on these missions alone, mainly so the others wouldn't see how bad I usually screwed things up. I was not the shining star of our language class, but on that day I was determined to improve my standing. So after lunch in the coffee shop, I went over to the train station and patiently stood in line, silently rehearsing my sentence. When I got up to the window, I carefully sized up my adversary. I had learned to take some time before shocking the locals by speaking Estonian. The clerk behind the window was a short, overweight elderly woman whom I took to be about 60. She fingered some paperclips and stared silently down at some papers on her desk. I knew better than to wait for a "may I help you," so after a few moments I just dove in.

"*Tere!*" I said cheerfully, and patiently waited for an answer to my greeting

No response.

"I would like to buy a train ticket to Tallinn please," I said, using all the proper polite grammar and forms of address. The old woman looked up at me with no discernable expression and then went back to staring at her paperwork.

I went over the sentence in my head and tried again. "One ticket to Tallinn please."

No response.

I felt a flush beginning to creep up my neck as the people behind me in line began to shuffle nervously and whisper amongst themselves. I was at a loss as to what to do next, but then it hit me: the poor old woman was probably hard of hearing! I took a deep breath and posed my question at a significantly higher decibel level. This time I did indeed receive a reaction, but it wasn't quite what I expected. The old clerk made a strange growling sound, then stood up out of her chair and began screaming at me in a shrill voice. I tried to interrupt with an apology, but that seemed to make her even angrier. Finally, she slammed the ticket window shut and turned her back to me. No amount of pleading and cajoling could convince her to turn around. I eventually slunk away, cringing under the irritated stares of the other ticket line patrons.

I returned to class a little early, my head hung low, and searched out one of our teachers in her office. With a sigh, I slumped into the chair across from her desk. She put down her papers and gave me a puzzled look.

"What's the matter, Douglas?" she said kindly. "You look like you just lost your best friend."

"Kairi, I just can't seem to get it right," I said, my voice full of dejection. "I can't even buy a train ticket."

"Now, don't get frustrated. Tell me what you said in Estonian."

I repeated the sentence I used in the train station.

"Hmmm, sounds okay," said Kairi. "What happened next?"

"Well, I repeated the question and then she just stood up and started yelling."

"Just like that?"

"Yeah, just like that!"

"What did she say?"

"I don't know, it went by too fast."

"Come on, try to think. Think carefully. Can you even remember a few words?"

"Well . . . there were a couple that came up quite often, but I don't know what they mean."

"Try to repeat them."

I obliged and repeated as best I could the few words I could remember, emphasizing the ones that where repeated most often and at the highest volume. To my surprise, my teacher blushed a bright red and sat back in her chair with a horrified look on her face.

"Where . . . where did you learn those words?" she gasped.

"At the train station, I told you. What do they mean?"

"You . . . you don't need to know!" she stammered. "Those words . . . those bad words . . . Russian words . . . they....just forget it! You can get a ticket another time."

"But why did she scream at me in Russian? I was talking in Estonian."

"Uh, I'll explain it to you some day, we have to get to class."

It was during this phase of the training that I became familiar with the "other" residents of Estonia, the population of people from Russia and the other Soviet republics who had either moved or been brought here during the Soviet period. Honestly, I couldn't tell them apart either by language or by appearance and just assumed that anyone who had lived in Estonia could speak Estonian. The last thing I expected was open hostility. I got a quick education in the way things really were one day when I was coming home on the bus. I was itching to try out a few of the sentences we had learned that day in class. They seemed to be pretty innocuous and non-controversial sentences so I decided to use a couple on my fellow riders. This was pretty risky business, as people in Estonia generally didn't speak to strangers in public, but I figured with a polite tone of voice and a winning smile I would be all right. About halfway home, I turned to the woman next to me, who was wearing a big fur hat, and in Estonian tried out the new additions to my vocabulary.

"*Vabandage, mis kell on?*" I asked, politely inquiring about the time.

The woman shot me a strange look and kept silent.

I figured I had either botched the grammar or my accent was throwing her off, so I tried again. This time I smiled, leaned over and spoke a little louder, clearly enunciating every syllable.

"*VAAAAA-BAN-DAAAAAGE, MIS KELLLLLL ON?*"

The woman drew back and launched into a loud torrent of angry words. By this time, I had learned the difference between the way Russian and Estonian sounded, so I realized I had picked a non-Estonian and certainly not a local, considering how she didn't even understand a simple question. It seemed sort of strange that a foreigner would be visiting Tartu in the fall and riding on a packed commuter bus alone in the middle of rush hour. But no matter, I mumbled an apology and turned to the man sitting on the other side of me. I took a deep breath and proudly tried the other sentence in my rapidly growing arsenal.

"Pardon me, where is the post office?"

The man stared past me out the window.

"Post office?" I asked hopefully. "Where is it please?"

To my surprise, I found myself on the receiving end of another tirade. This time I even recognized some of the special words I had heard at the train station. Bad luck, another traveler and a grouchy one, too! I smiled apologetically, shrugged my shoulders and kept quiet for the rest of the trip.

When I got home to the apartment, my host met me at the door with a smile.

"Hi Douglas, how was your day?"

"Pretty good, but it seems there are all these tourists in town."

"Tourists?"

"Yeah, I was riding home on the bus and there were these two people who couldn't speak any Estonian at all. In fact, they got angry when I tried to talk to them."

"Uh, Douglas, I am pretty sure those weren't tourists."

"You mean they live here? Why don't they speak Estonian?"

"Uh . . . maybe you better sit down, this is a long story."

So it was in this way that I learned about the realities of the Soviet times, when the Russian language was king, and of the lasting effects this had on present-day Estonia. All the Estonians were required to learn Russian, but arrivals from other Soviet Republics had little if any interest in learning Estonian. As a matter of fact, many of them looked on Estonian as some sort of third-rate language, suitable only for peasants and uneducated people. It was hard to picture being forced to speak a foreign language when you went to the post office or talked to the police, but that's the way it was. For their part, the Russians couldn't understand why Estonians resisted assimilation into the wonderful Russian culture, the culture of those who saved them from Hitler. The basic bone of contention was that the Russians believed that Estonia had joined the Soviet Union voluntarily in 1940 and the Soviets had saved Estonia from the Nazis. The Estonians knew that they were forced to join the USSR and that they had desperately struggled towards the end of the conflict to restore the independence they had during the '20s and '30s. On the street there was no real noticeable hostility, but when you were sitting around Estonians in a private room with a couple of beers, you learned that they felt they were now much better off having broken the tie with Moscow. All of them were waiting for the Soviet troops, the last symbol of occupation, to leave.

This is not to say that there were not problems in the new, free Estonia. There were shortages to deal with, the most noticeable being the lack of fuel to provide hot water. In a monument to

Soviet inefficiency, all hot water, which also warmed the radiators of the apartment buildings, came from one hot water "factory" and was piped through the frozen ground to all quarters of the city. Even in the early fall, the nights were already quite cold and it was not uncommon to wake up in the morning and be able to see your breath. Also, with no hot water most of the time, the only way to take a "shower" was to heat up a pot of water and pour it over my head while standing in the bathtub. Plus, there was the telephone system— or should I say the lack of it. The apartment where I was staying had no phone, and even those lucky Estonians that did could not direct-dial out of the country. The only way for me to make an international call was to go downtown to the main telephone office.

I avoided this guaranteed source of unpleasantness like the plague, but one evening after a day of studying how to make telephone calls, I resolved to phone my parents back in Nebraska. I had been "in country"—as those in the Peace Corps say—a few months already and I longed to hear a friendly voice from back home. It was dark and drizzling as I made my way through the blocks of apartment buildings down to the bus stop. The buses ran quite infrequently in the evening, so I had to wait a good half an hour for the old #17. When the bus finally did come, I took it to the city center and then walked down to the telephone exchange. There I had to stand in line, then give the number I wanted to call to a clerk behind the window and pay in advance for the amount of time I wanted. Afterwards I was directed to wait on a bench next to an entire wall of phone booths. From time to time, a scratchy speaker made unintelligible sounds that I assumed was the way of notifying people when their call was ready. I couldn't understand a thing, so after a while I went back to the window and asked if my call was ready. The woman looked at her book and informed me that they had placed the call but I hadn't picked up. Slowly and politely, I tried to explain that I was a foreigner and didn't understand the system, but the clerk just pointed back to the bench. Meekly, I returned to my seat. Probably an hour went by before the woman rapped on the glass and pointed to the row of phones.

I stood up and pointed in the general direction she had indicated. The woman nodded her head and motioned for me to hurry. But which phone? I saw one that had the Estonian word for "Long Distance" so I ran in and picked up the receiver. Nothing. I pushed buttons and banged the phone on the cradle, but the only result was more silence. I gave up and stood meekly in line again. Once at the window, I tried to explain that there was no one on the line, but the woman would have none of it. With a burst of angry, high-speed Estonian that went right over my head, she counted out the money and threw it on the counter. I pleaded with her as best I could to try again, but she just shut the window and turned her back. I finally collected my money and headed back out into the rain.

As luck would have it, I had missed the last bus back to Annelinn, so I had to make the entire trip on foot. To add to my misery, every time a car whizzed by it splashed water on me. As I trudged along, I felt overwhelmed by hopelessness. I couldn't even speak enough Estonian to make a simple phone call. For the first time in my life, I felt that I could never really belong. Cold, depressed and lonely, I slowly made my way back to my transitory home.

Throughout the years I spent in Estonia, that was about the closest I came to abandoning my mission and catching a plane back to the States.

3—THE MEETING OF
THE MINDS

Ten weeks of training passed quickly and soon it was almost time for us to separate to our different corners of Estonia. The Peace Corps had given us a very thorough program of lectures, field trips and language studies, not to mention a few scary lectures on the evils of the local food and water—oh yes, and lots of shots from our faithful medical officer. I think everyone was getting a little stir-crazy and we were dying to get out and do some real work. Training had given us lots of valuable insight about the way Estonians worked and lived. It also gave us a good share of humorous and sometimes bizarre encounters during the various field trips we went on. The incident I remember best was the trip to see the Estonian psychologists from Tartu University. They were supposed to give us a lecture on how Estonians and Americans interact, but we got a little more than we bargained for.

Braving an early October snowstorm, our group walked from our training center over to a large classroom in one of the campus buildings. There were two in our group from Arkansas, and they complained bitterly about the quick change in the weather. Carol and Pam, two ladies from the East Coast were a little tight-lipped but more tolerant. The rest of us, all Midwesterners, stoically pressed on without comment. When we reached our destination, we found a room completely empty except for a wooden desk, a circle of chairs and a video camera mounted on a tripod. A huge blackboard took up most of one wall. We sat in the chairs and waited patiently for our lecturers to arrive. Finally, they showed up and introduced themselves as Heino and Heikki. Both were middle-aged, scholarly-looking, and dressed quite formally, but there the physical similarities ended. With Heino's short fat stature next to Heikki's tall skinny one, I was immediately reminded of Laurel and Hardy. Their ill-fitting suits made them comical enough, but Heikki, who appeared to be in charge, had not one but two pairs of glasses on his face. He used one pair for reading his notes then, when he looked up to talk to us, he put the other, thicker pair on top of the smaller and peered at us with eyes that looked three times larger than normal. We somehow managed to suppress our laughter.

"Good morning, everyone," Heikki said in thickly accented English. "Today we are going to talk about how Estonians interact with Americans. Then you are going to help us do a little research."

"Research?" asked Carol, eyeing the video camera nervously.

"Yes, of course," Heikki said. "But first, a little class instruction!"

He walked over to the board, grabbed a piece of chalk, and drew the outlines of three large heads on the board. He then labeled one head "American," the second "Russian," and the third "Estonian." He then drew two concentric circles inside each head, one thick and one thin. He turned back towards us, put on his glasses and began his lesson.

"What I have here on the board is the American brain, the Russian brain and the Estonian brain. What you need to understand, if you are going to live in Estonia, are the differences between the people who live here and also their brains. Each group has its own definition of personal space, its own thought processes, and rules about what constitutes the inner self, and when they will let you into it. Americans, for example, have this very thin outer layer that you can penetrate very easily. But then, it is a very long time until you get inside the small inner-self barrier." He emphasized this by drawing inside the American head a cluster of fluffy clouds surrounding a golf ball-size solid circle of heavily drawn chalk. "Now, with the Russian head you can get right through the outer barrier, into the inner area, and out the other side with almost no effort at all." He illustrated this by quickly drawing a line entering the Russian brain at about the forehead and exiting at the base of the neck. "Finally, you have the Estonian brain. Estonians have a very, very tough outer layer, which makes some people think we are cold and unemotional, but inside we have a vast sea of both emotional and scholarly thoughts. You must navigate this sea, which leads into the inner layer with almost no barrier." Here, he carefully drew various shapes and diagrams all through the Estonian brain. "Any questions?"

We sat in silence, trying to digest all this brain talk and what it might mean for us, but before anybody could come up with anything intelligent to say, Heino walked over to the video camera and began attaching cords.

"Now," Heikki said, and peered at us through his double glasses. "Let's begin."

Pam, one of the bolder volunteers asked the question on all our minds. "Begin what?"

"The experiment," said Heikki impatiently. "That's why you are here!"

Not all of us were as keen on this idea as our Estonian hosts were. "That's *not* why we are here, and you aren't going to video-tape me!" said Pam with finality.

Heikki seemed bewildered by our apprehension. "Oh, come now! It is just a little video for us to watch and evaluate for discussion."

"What are you going to do with it afterwards?" said Dave, one of the Arkansans.

"Why, destroy it of course. It is confidential scientific material." Unfazed by our questioning, he blinked at us from behind his glasses.

"Can we see you destroy it?" Dave pressed.

"Well, no. We will take it back to the lab and destroy it there."

"Why can't you destroy it here? How will we know you won't make copies?"

Heikki remained firm in his position but was obviously caught off guard by Dave's persistence. "Ah…it's just not the way we want to do it. I promise we won't keep it."

"If we can't see you destroy it, then I'm not going to let you tape me."

"Me neither!" said Carol, and soon the whole group was shaking their heads.

Heino and Heikki looked helplessly at one another and I could see that things were going downhill fast. Kairi and Linda were giving each other nervous looks and Mark, our Peace Corps trainer and an ex-volunteer himself, was rubbing the back of his neck and rolling his eyes like he always did when things weren't going well. For my part, I didn't see what the big problem was about being taped. After we sat in silence for a few uneasy minutes I stood up, ignoring the irritated looks from my colleagues:

"Look," I said, "you can tape me if you want to. What do I have to do?"

"Excellent!" said an obviously relieved Heikki. "We are going to do a little role playing."

"Role playing?"

"Yes. We are going to pretend that Heino is your counterpart with whom you will be working at post. You are coming to his office to meet him for the first time and to discuss your plans for working together." He began arranging the furniture at the front of the room where we were to perform.

"All right, that sounds simple."

"Yes, and I want you to remember the things we talked about when you begin your interaction with this Estonian. Now go out into the hall and pretend that you have just arrived. Give us a minute to get the video camera rolling."

I did as I was told and left the room. Out in the hall, I waited a few minutes, then knocked politely on the door. There was no response except for the muffled giggles and whispers from my colleagues. I waited for a polite period of time and knocked again. Still, no answer. After another wait, I took a deep breath, put a cheerful smile on my face, and slowly open the door a little bit. I stuck my head inside and grinned at Heino sitting silently behind the desk. Without waiting for further cues, I started out in a bright cheerful voice.

"Hi, my name is Douglas Wells and I am a Peace Corps Volunteer. Are you the gentleman with whom I am going to be working?"

Heino regarded me silently, then slowly nodded his head.

"Well great!" I said enthusiastically. "Uh, may I come in?"

Heino motioned me in with a wave of his hand.

"Boy, am I glad to finally meet you," I said as I strode over to where Heino was sitting and stuck my hand out to him across the desk. "This is going to be really great! You and me, Estonian and American, doing really cool stuff."

Heino shrank back visibly, but managed to weakly shake my hand.

"Hey, mind if I sit down?" I said and, without waiting for an answer, plopped down in the chair across from Heino's desk. I scooted my chair up to the edge of the desk, put both elbows up and, with my chin in my hands, regarded my new colleague with interest.

"Hmmm, nice place you have here. I just can't wait to get started. Why don't you tell me a little bit about yourself."

"STOP!" Heikki suddenly yelled out. "That's enough, that's enough!"

Visibly shaken, he came out from behind the video camera and huddled with Heino in the corner. They began muttering to each other in Estonian. I strained to hear what they were saying but could only pick out isolated phrases like "Oh, my God," "Unbelievable," and "It's worse than I thought." I gathered that I had done something wrong. Finally, the two psychologists came back and stood before us. Heikki put on his double glasses and took a deep breath while Heino stayed sheltered behind him.

"Mr. Wells," he said. "I am afraid you are going to have a very difficult time in Estonia."

"Huh?" I looked over at my colleagues for support.

"Yes, a very difficult time." Heikki repeated and solemnly turned to address Mark.

"I'm afraid this one probably won't make it."

"What do you mean?" I protested. "What did I do wrong?"

"What did you do wrong?" Heikki repeated incredulously. "You really don't know?"

"Well, I have some idea, but maybe you can tell me. After all, I'm here to learn."

Heikki scratched his chin before huddling with Heino in the corner again. When he came back, he had a look of grim determination on his face.

"All right, Mr. Wells. I want you to listen carefully. After all, your failure may be beneficial to the rest of the group. We will go through your actions step by step and analyze what went wrong. Now pay attention! First of all, when you knock on an Estonian's door you never, NEVER come in unless you are invited."

"But I tried and…." I was interrupted by a wave of Heikki's hand.

"Please, Mr. Wells. Just listen," Heikki said wearily. "We are trying to help you. Now when you entered the room, you approached the desk, then did what?"

"Well, I tried to shake Heino's hand."

"No," Heikki said with a sigh. He walked over to the desk where he made a broad circular motion with his arms. "You violated his personal space! This desk, this area belongs to the Estonian. It is his zone, his area, and you never, NEVER enter an Estonian's personal space uninvited. To do so will cause him to immediately withdraw, and you will have almost no chance of establishing useful communication. You must wait for the Estonian to voluntarily come out of his space and invite you in."

"But how long should I wait for him to come out of his hole, uh, I mean his zone?" Pam and Carol giggled and Heikki looked pained, but he continued patiently.

"As long as it takes, Mr. Wells. And while we are on the subject of humor, I must tell you that you smile too much. Yes, way too much. If you go around smiling all the time, the Estonians will think you are either drunk or a Russian or both!"

"Sorry," I said. With great effort, I reduced my smile to a smirk. "Please continue."

"Thank you. Now perhaps the most grievous violation was that you put your elbows on his desk and began to chatter away like a child. Just because an Estonian doesn't jump into a conversation doesn't mean he's not interested. Just be patient and let the Estonian set the pace of the conversation. You will see the benefits of waiting. Now, go out in the hall and try again. I'll set up the video camera once more."

I went out there in the hall and stood there with my head spinning. Who are these people? How am I going to survive? Will I really not be able to cut it? I couldn't help feeling that this was a little ridiculous, so I resolved to show the good doctor what his teaching methods would produce. I knocked on the door and waited. And waited. And waited. Finally, after what seemed like an eternity, a faint voice called out, "Come in!"

I opened the door all the way and stood silently in the doorway with my head bowed. The members of our group started to snicker, but a stern look from Heikki quieted them down. After a few moments I quietly introduced myself, only allowing myself brief glances up towards Heino and keeping my gaze mostly towards the floor. Finally Heino invited me in. I shuffled over and stood before his desk, shifting my feet, looking uneasily from side to side.

"Pleased to meet you," I said, and glanced briefly up before once again focusing on the ground. After a few more moments of silence, Heino offered me a cup of coffee, which I took, offering humble thanks and affording myself a faint smile.

Another long moment of silence passed before Heino offered me a seat, which I gratefully took. I sat down, hands folded in my lap, and said flatly, "I am very happy to have the opportunity to work with you." That provoked another outburst of laugher from the other volunteers, but that was quickly cut off by a wave of Mark's hand. Our Estonian language teachers just stared in amazement.

The next long moment of silence was finally broken by Heino, who took a deep breath, cleared his throat, and prepared to speak. But before he could get out that desperately awaited first sentence, a beaming Heikki interrupted him. As I looked up in disbelief, the double-bespectacled psychologist left the camera, came over and laid his hand on my shoulder.

"Now class, that's the way to communicate with Estonians. Mr. Wells, that was excellent! There may be hope for you after all!"

4—ON THE ROAD TO
HIIUMAA ISLAND

It was hard to believe, but our three months of training had finally reached its conclusion. During the last week, we were given a list of ten places where Peace Corps Volunteers from our group were going to be stationed. They asked where we would like to go, but the decision might as well have been made at random because, of course, we knew almost nothing about any of these posts. Thus, our decisions were mostly based on the size of town and the location. Some of us wanted to be in Tartu, where there was some familiarity and established contacts, while others wanted to be near the capital city of Tallinn. The rest, like me, wanted to get way out into the rural areas, where foreign aid programs rarely had any impact and most hired consultants feared to tread. I wanted to experience some genuine Estonian culture and help out where I felt I would be needed the most. To me, living someplace in a farmhouse with a cooking fire in the hearth and a couple of cows out in the barn sounded great, plus it was reasonably close to the "real Peace Corps experience". When we talked about the rural areas, it conjured up visions of thatch-roofed log houses with smoke curling out of the chimney. I could picture myself coming home from work, and walking down the main gravel road, scattering chickens ahead of me. I might even grab one and wring its neck for dinner. Then, after a family dinner with our wooden bowls and spoons, I could hang around with the guys in the village down by the pasture, where we would trade stories and talk about plans for the harvest. Yes, that is where I would find my Peace Corps Moment!

Best of all, we now knew more about what our mission would be. In exchange for a monthly living allowance of 100 dollars, we were going to help set up agricultural extension centers in each of the Estonian counties. The idea was, that with our small business experience plus the on-the-ground savvy of the local farmers, we would be able to put together a business plan that would boost the sagging agricultural sector. With the large collective farms being broken up and individual farmers getting the land back that had been taken from them, there was a great need for practical free-market business skills including accounting, marketing and finance. That was our part of the deal, the Estonians would provide the hands-on agricultural experience with the crops and livestock. Supposedly, the Estonian Ministry of Agriculture was our government partner on the national level and would give us support along with the National Farmers Union that had chapters in each of the counties. On the charts and graphs presented in numerous seminars during our training, everything looked great. I only hoped that someone had informed those at our posts about our grand plans.

Now, when Peace Corps gave us a list to choose from and asked where we wanted to go, they also made it clear that we were going to have to go wherever the Peace Corps powers-that-be decided that we should go. And so the decisions were made. Through some mysterious process we were assigned to our various posts. During one of our morning meetings we were given our assignments and that was that. My piece of paper said Hiiumaa Island (pronounced HEE-yew-ma), and I ran over to the map to find it. Indeed, I was bound for an island, and not a very big one at that. Still a little rattled from the experience with the psychologists, I looked forward to the opportunity for some peace and quiet in a nice, unpretentious rural environment. Surely it would be easier to get along with island folk than complicated urban Estonians. It seemed like a good deal all around. However, when I showed my assignment paper to our language teachers, they looked very concerned.

They looked at each other and shook their heads. Finally, Kairi spoke up.

"You know Douglas, it won't be so easy for you out there. I've heard that the Hiiumaa people, the *Hiidlased*, are a very closed group. It is hard even for mainland people to get along out there, so I can't imagine how they will react to a foreigner."

"Really?" I said, apprehension creeping into my voice. "Have you been there?"

"Well, when I was a little girl, I used to visit my grandmother on her farm. The island people always looked strangely at my mother and me. I also remember that the neighbors would come over all the time and tell strange jokes."

"Strange jokes?"

"Yes, I can't explain exactly. They just have a different sense of humor."

"Can you give me an example?"

"Hmm, let's see. Okay, there was a farmer whose neighbor had a prize pig. The farmer, who had no pig of his own, would spend many hours gazing wistfully over the fence at the pig and admiring it. One day, the man's guardian angel came down and said to the man, 'Josef, you have been a good man and I see that you admire your neighbor's pig so much that I am going to make your dreams come true.' The farmer was very happy and thanked the angel profusely. 'Don't mention it,' said the angel, 'but don't you think you had better get to work building a pen for your new pig?' 'What the hell do you mean?' said the farmer angrily, 'I thought you were going to kill his pig!'"

"That's the joke?" I asked after a long pause.

"I told you they were a little strange. I remember also that when the neighbors came over for dinner, they would say that the food was great, but that an Estonian's favorite food was really another Estonian. No matter how many times they said that, everyone still laughed. Then there was this joke about the fisherman and the talking seal...."

"Okay, let's forget about humor," I said hastily. "What do you remember about the island itself?"

"Oh, lots of farms and cows and mostly old people, like my grandmother. In the summer I remember there were a lot of tourists coming from other parts of the Soviet Union. They would ride around in big buses and the locals didn't like them because they would buy up everything in the shops. It was especially bad when a storm came and no one could get off the island for days at a time. People would eventually go hungry when the food ran out."

"Really?" I asked incredulously.

"Oh sure. The only way to get there is by ferry, you know. Hiiumaa is about 25 kilometers off the coast. However, I have heard that when the sea freezes in winter, people actually drive their cars over the ice to get supplies on the mainland."

"No way!" I said in disbelief.

"Oh sure. And some of them fall through every year. They miss the island on the return trip and fall off the edge of the ice on the way to Sweden, poor souls. That's why the population of the island keeps dropping. Soon, it will just be old people and cows. Very sad. Oh, and with the Russian soldiers and the guard towers everywhere, we couldn't even go to the beach in some places. Spotlights shining from guard towers at night—terrible, terrible."

Shaking their heads, the two language teachers walked off, leaving me with my hopes dashed and much to ponder. I thought I had gotten a choice post, and now it looked like I was being sent off into a dangerous wilderness full of old people, cows and enemy soldiers. What if something happened to me out there? What if the people resent my being there? How could I ever accomplish anything if no one accepts me? As the others drank and celebrated, I sat alone with my beer, wondering about my future and looking over the Hiiumaa postcards that I had received as a gift from someone in our group. Grainy pictures of cows, thatched-roofed farmhouses and boulder-strewn beaches did little to reduce my apprehension, but one card in particular caught my eye. It was a picture of the Hiiumaa ferry, which looked more like a troop ship, complete with a red hammer and sickle on the smokestack. Seeing this sea-going vessel restored my sense of adventure. After all, the Soviet Union had just collapsed and now Hiiumaa was open to the world. I would be like an explorer from the West, visiting a previously forbidden land and bringing the light of freedom! A symbol of the end of the Cold War! Or, maybe I just had too much to drink. At any rate, I started to feel better.

Armed with the knowledge of where we were going to spend the next two years, we all looked forward to our first site visits and the opportunity to meet our Estonian co-workers. We waited outside the training center as one by one the cars, driven by various Estonian co-workers, came and whisked away volunteers to their posts. The members of our group shook hands and nervously wished each other well. It would be the first time we would be separated for any length of time since we arrived in the Baltics and we all felt a little apprehensive. After a short visit, we would come back to Tartu one last time and be officially sworn in as bona fide Peace Corps Volunteers. Then we were off to post for good. No longer would we be trainees but full-fledged volunteers with a mission to accomplish. We had done pretty well so far and our training supervisor was obviously pleased that, up to then, no one had cut and run. Our group of ten was still intact for the time being. In the other two Baltic countries, a few volunteers had already bailed out and been sent back to the States. Peace Corps was pretty pragmatic about this and actually planned for an attrition rate of up to thirty percent. When someone said they wanted to throw in the towel, they were quietly taken to Peace Corps headquarters and were sent out of the country within 48 hours, no questions asked.

Gradually, the group standing in front of the training center grew increasingly smaller until finally I was alone, standing there in the bright fall sunshine. I sat on the concrete steps and idly tossed rocks across the parking lot. This was doing nothing do dispel my fears of being accepted on the island. Heck, they might have changed their minds and weren't even coming to get me. A feeling of despair welled up inside of me as I wondered what Peace

Corps would do with an unwanted volunteer. I was just getting up to go inside and hit the bar when a small blue pickup careened into the parking lot and screeched to a halt in front of the steps. A man in well-worn coveralls jumped down from the cab and called out to me in English.

"Hey, are you Douglas Wells?"

"That's me!" I said, grabbing my bag and walking around towards the driver's side of the pickup. I wanted to shake hands and make introductions, but the man just grabbed my bag and threw it in the back.

"Get in, we must go!"

"What's the big hurry?" I started to ask, but the man was already revving the engine. I jumped in as the tires spun flinging gravel and dust everywhere. I groped for a seatbelt and tried to keep my balance as we barreled out of the parking lot. The back of the pickup skipped around as we turned and skidded onto the main road. While I gripped the dashboard and sat in terrified silence, we sped out of Tartu and onto a rural two-lane asphalt highway. The little pickup's engine seemed ready to explode any second as my new companion mercilessly redlined it through all five gears. Eventually, we topped out at a healthy cruising speed and, as we settled in for the journey, I finally took the opportunity to size up my traveling partner and new co-worker. I knew only that his name was Tarmo and that he looked to be about my age. Like most Estonian men, he was tall, with a slender but muscular build, jet-black hair, and a bushy handlebar moustache. I noticed he seemed really concerned about the time because he kept looking for his watch on the dashboard, which was covered with all kinds of booklets and papers. The whole cab reeked of gasoline and motor oil, and there were so many tools on the seat and floor of the cab that I had to clear a place for myself to sit comfortably. For the first several minutes we rode in tense silence but finally, after about 10 kilometers had whizzed by, Tarmo seemed to relax a little. He sighed, sat back in his seat and looked over at me with a smile.

"I am Tarmo," he said in English and stuck out his hand.

"I'm Douglas," I said in Estonian and shook hands with my new partner.

"Oh," Tarmo said with a surprised look on his face. He too switched to Estonian. "Then the rumors are true. You Americans have studied our language."

"Just a little," I said modestly.

"Well," said Tarmo, who then uttered the phrase I was to hear thousands of times over the course of the next few years. "That's pretty good. Some Russians have lived here for twenty years and don't speak a word!"

"I know," I said wryly. "I ran into a few of them."

Gradually, the more populated areas at the city's edge gave way to continuous pine forest. I marveled at how Estonia was almost the polar opposite of my home state. In Nebraska it was all open land with only a few trees growing around the farms, towns and riverbeds. You got the feeling that if the people all left the place would gradually revert to only grassland. In Estonia, everything was low hills and forest. The only open spaces were where roads and rivers cut through, or where people had hacked out spaces for farmland. If the Estonians ever left, the forest would surely swallow up everything, like the lost Mayan temples in the jungles of Central America.

As we sped down the two-lane asphalt highway, things gradually fell into a rhythm. First, we would be speeding through a forested corridor, then come into an area with open fields and a few farmhouses. Then we would slow down for a small town and then the process would reverse itself until we were again rolling down a tree-lined road through the thick forest of birch and pines. It was as if you were going from one isolated little kingdom to another, and each time you came out of the forest it was like discovering a new land. The only things that seemed out of place were these ugly complexes of concrete block buildings that would pop up once in a while. These oases of industrial blight clashed strongly with the surrounding countryside. They would invariably be surrounded by torn chain link fencing and have various pieces of rusted farm equipment standing outside on oil-soaked patches of ground. Occasionally, black smoke would be billowing from a sheet-metal chimney attached to one of the low-slung structures, and huge aboveground pipes with insulation loosely tied around them would run from building to building. Nearby would always be a few of the ubiquitous concrete-slab apartment buildings that were the scourge of the former Soviet bloc. Tarmo explained that these were the collective farms I had heard so much about. In the late '40s, farmers who didn't want to participate in Stalin's grand plan were shipped off to Siberia and their farms melded together into huge, unwieldy agricultural enterprises. Now, with Estonia having regained its independence, these inefficient dinosaurs were on their last legs. I thanked my lucky stars that I was headed to a remote island that was certainly spared the worst of Stalin's forced collectivization.

So, onward we went through town after little town. The distance didn't seem that far on the map, but as the hours went by I realized that going from one side of little Estonia to the other still involved some serious traveling. I also finally found out the reason for Tarmo's breakneck speed and, at the same time, learned about another aspect of Hiiumaa life with which I would soon become familiar: racing to catch the last ferry. If we missed it, tough luck! Be it king or pauper, the Hiiumaa ferry waited for no man. Our arrival would then have to be delayed until the next day and we would have to find a place to stay in the small coastal town of Haapsalu. I fervently hoped we wouldn't miss the boat.

It was nice to finally be out of the city and on my way to post. It was there that I hoped to have the real Peace Corps experience among the rural residents of the island. Forests, farmland, quiet sandy beaches and friendly country folk awaited me! The warnings the teachers and psychologists had given me were now almost for-gotten. As we sped on towards the coast, I dozed off while think-ing happy thoughts about my arrival, and dreamed how the is-landers would be waiting to welcome the American at the harbor with cheering crowds and colorful flags flying in the sunshine.

Probably there would even be speeches by local dignitaries. It would be a fitting and beautiful beginning to two years of productive cooperation.

Tarmo nudging me and, pointing out the window, jolted me out of my pleasant reverie. I sat up and looked over to the left at what appeared to be some innocent-looking mounds of earth. Then I noticed the huge blast doors on the front and the double barbed-wire fencing surrounding them.

"This was a MIG base until a few months ago," Tarmo said matter-of-factly.

As I stared at this relic of the all-to-recent Cold War, the only response I could manage was a weak "Wow."

"They used to run low-level training missions over the island. We even had some dishes broken one time at the house when they came right over our village at low altitude. Another favorite game of theirs was dive-bombing the ferry. You would just be standing there looking out over the sea when all of a sudden this jet would blast over at about a hundred feet."

"Not very considerate," I said, and continued staring at the rows of abandoned hangars.

"Well, that's all over now. The base is closed and things are much quieter."

"That's good," I said with relief. "I'm not interested in being dive-bombed. As a matter of fact, the less I see of Russian soldiers the better. By the way, you said that the fighter planes took off from this base to make runs over Hiiumaa. Does that mean we're pretty close to the ferry harbor?"

"That's right!" Tarmo said, and made one last turn, which brought us out of the forest.

Suddenly, the vast expanse of the Baltic Sea opened up before us. The suddenness of our arrival and the limitless expanse of the sea took my breath away. After the claustrophobic trip through the miles of forest, the seacoast was truly a beautiful sight. Hiiumaa was hidden seventeen miles over the horizon, but I knew it was out there somewhere. A few fishing boats bobbed in the water near the shore as the fisherman checked their nets and pulled in their catch. It was a pastoral scene worthy of any impressionist painter. Then, like a vision, I saw the Hiiumaa ferry chugging into the harbor. It was just like on the postcard, painted a gleaming white but minus the hammer and sickle, which had apparently been painted over. The whole thing was like something out of a film and I felt an enormous sense of well being. I had made it through training, escaped the city, and was now headed off to my post where I, together with the Hiiumaa people, would rebuild what the Evil Empire had taken away.

I was rudely jerked out of my daydreaming and back to the present as we passed through the harbor gates and were suddenly surrounded by what seemed like half the Russian Army. Trucks and trailers with searchlights on the back and the infamous red stars painted on the side where parked all around the small harbor office. Soldiers lounged around smoking, with Kalashnikov automatic rifles hanging about their necks. A few officers were running around barking orders but no one seemed to be interested in moving anywhere. My first reaction was to wonder if the Peace Corps had sent me to a Soviet base. Here they had given us all these lectures about staying clear of the military and they were sending me into Red Army Central. Or maybe they didn't know that this was some sort of secret base. Heart racing, I slumped down in my seat, trying to hide as we pulled to a stop in the middle of the crowd. Tarmo set the emergency brake and started to open the door of the pickup. A few soldiers gave us some bored looks but made no move towards the car. Tarmo must have noticed that I had turned white as a sheet because he stopped getting out and looked at me curiously.

"What's the matter with you?" he said with concern. "Are you sick?"

"No!" I whispered. "Just act normal and don't attract their attention."

"What are you talking about?"

"Them, the soldiers, the officers! Don't let them know who I am!"

Tarmo stared at me incredulously. "You're kidding, right?"

"No, I'm not kidding!" I hissed. "I'm an American, remember? These are Russian soldiers. What do you think they're going to do if they find out who I am?"

"They don't care!" said Tarmo, who then began to smile. "You really are scared, aren't you?"

"Just get the tickets and let's go park somewhere else."

"Oh, the American is scared of the big, bad Russians!" Tarmo teased.

I scowled and hunched further down in the seat.

"Maybe you want to say hi to them, eh?" he said mischievously.

"No, no, that's okay," I stammered. "I'll just wait here."

"Come on, I'll ask that officer over there to come and welcome the American."

Before I could stop him, Tarmo got out and walked towards a group of soldiers. I felt a sense of panic taking hold of me, but at the last minute Tarmo veered off and headed towards the ticket office. As he went in the door, he turned and gave me a big grin. So this was the Hiiumaa sense of humor I was going to have to deal with? I focused my attention back on the Communist hordes and watched with suspicion as the Hiiumaa ferry dropped its stern like a drawbridge and disgorged another load of trucks and men. I wondered why so many soldiers were moving back and forth to such a little island.

After what seemed like an eternity, Tarmo returned with the ferry tickets (ten cents per person, fifty cents for the car) and we pulled away from the groups of trucks and soldiers, taking our place in the line for the ferry. The ship looked a lot bigger than it did on the postcard. It would be by far the largest I had ever ridden on, but of course Nebraska didn't have a lot to offer in the way of sea-going vessels. As the last of the army vehicles rolled off, a man in blue coveralls motioned for the cars to begin coming on board.

When it was our turn, we bounced up the ramp and down onto the mostly open lower deck, which was like driving into a hundred-foot long cast iron bathtub. There was a narrow steel superstructure that had been built crossways across the car deck, but only covered about half of it, so many cars including ours were out in the open air. The expert deckhands guided each car, shouting at each other in Russian and gesturing emphatically until it looked like no more cars would fit. Still, one lone vehicle remained on the ramp. We had a good thirty cars on board and the crew seemed pretty expert at fitting the maximum load onto the boat, placing the little Russian cars so close together that people could barely open their doors. Finally, they squeezed everyone aboard but only after taking the last car and literally picking it up and turning it sideways so it would fit. No one was left behind. With a groaning, clanking sound, the drawbridge rose and blocked out the view of the mainland. Now the only thing visible was the open sea out the front end of the ferry.

"Do you want to go upstairs to the bar?" asked Tarmo.

"Bar?" I replied in disbelief. Where on this cast iron bucket could there be a bar?

"Yeah, let's go upstairs. The view is better anyway."

I followed Tarmo over to a thick steel hatch in the wall along the side of the open car deck. With a heave, he pulled it open and I followed him up a set of narrow steel steps, then down an even narrower corridor filled with the hum of machinery and the smell of diesel oil. We actually had to turn sideways to squeeze through a few of the really tight spots. Up another set of steps and we found ourselves in a living room-sized area with metal walls, metal floor and a few plain wooden benches to reinforce the troop-ship decor. On one side of the room was a small cashier's window, which was bolted shut. The only lighting was provided by several bare bulbs inside small shatterproof cages that would have looked perfect on a submarine. We took a seat on one of the hard benches and I took the opportunity to observe my surroundings and fellow travelers. The only decorations on the light green steel walls were a series of Russian posters showing how to use the life rafts and what to do in an emergency. I looked these over intently but the rest of the passengers paid them little attention. Most were obviously veterans as they had staked out a full bench to lie on and were already snoring. So there I was on board the Hiiumaa ferry and this was the bar. But where could a guy get a beer? I think Tarmo read my thoughts, because he pointed at the window and spoke up.

"They open up after we start sailing. Do you want to go out on deck and see our departure?"

"Sure!" I said enthusiastically. After all, it was this farm boy's first sea voyage.

We went back down the first flight of stairs and out onto one of the narrow walkways that ran along each side of the ferry above the car deck. I was filled with excitement as the crew yelled to one another and unhooked the huge ropes holding the ship to the jetty. We began to drift away from shore as the captain kicked in the huge diesel engines that made a slow "thup-thup-thup" sound and belched gray and black smoke out of the ship's stack. With the powerful engines swirling the water and the gulls wheeling and diving to feed on the disoriented fish cast up in the wake, we made a slow turn and headed out to sea. I leaned out over the rail into the chilly wind and watched the mainland slowly fade from view. I felt a mixture of sadness and exhilaration as one chapter of my life in Estonia drew to a close. The coastline faded and eventually disappeared altogether. Tarmo and I finally got our beer, then sat up near the front of the boat. We didn't talk much, just gazed over the bow towards the still-invisible Hiiumaa. I think we were both wondering what lay ahead.

5—THE FIRST VOYAGE

The farther we got out to sea, the harsher the conditions became. The gentle waves that at first let us effortlessly plow through them soon offered up a good deal of resistance. The bow of the ferry heaved up when we hit some of the larger waves, sending plumes of spray over the bow and drenching the vehicles parked below. The wind picked up, bringing in clouds from the west. At first, I wasn't very concerned. My attention was drawn to an identical ferry, also overloaded with troops and trucks, coming from the opposite direction. It seemed strange that there could be this kind of military traffic going back and forth on a regular basis unless something really important was going on. I turned to Tarmo, who was looking towards some small islands off the starboard side.

"Are there always this many soldiers on the ferries?" I asked.

"No," said Tarmo, glancing towards the oncoming ferry. "Do you know what's happening?"

"I have no idea."

"Well, the Red Army is leaving Hiiumaa today. Troops, tanks, trucks, everything."

"Really?"

"After fifty years they are finally pulling out. Well, most of them anyway."

"You've got to be kidding. The same day that I'm coming, they leave?"

"Yes," Tarmo said laughing. "Maybe they knew that the fearsome Yankee was coming!"

I ignored Tarmo's teasing and focused on the ferry, which was now almost alongside. There I was, the fearless Peace Corps Volunteer, heading out to my post and the Russians were fleeing like rats before my arrival. It almost seemed as if my job was to reclaim the island in the name of democracy and a free Estonia! Think of the party that must be taking place on the island to celebrate the departure of the foreign troops, and I was going to land right in the middle of it! I stood up a little straighter as the ferry passed us, staring with contempt at the retreating occupiers who, for their part, merely returned bored glances between pulls on their cigarettes. After the ferry was safely passed us and I was sure no one was looking, I flipped them off. Tarmo laughed and shook his head at my show of "bravado."

As I turned back towards the front of the boat, light rain began to fall and the sun disappeared behind the onrushing clouds. The sea was getting even rougher, the waves sharper. More briny water sprayed onto the car deck. The strengthening October wind drove Tarmo and me back up to the passenger lounge, where we sat near one of the larger portholes. I watched nervously while more and more water cascaded over the bow and sloshed around the tires of our truck. The heaving of the ferry was becoming more noticeable but, to my relief, I wasn't feeling any signs of seasickness on this, my first open-sea voyage. The last thing I wanted to do was to show weakness by puking my guts out in front of my new partner. Still, I was starting to feel a little nervous about the seaworthiness of the old ferry. Tarmo seemed to read my mind.

"These boats are tough." he said without looking over at me.

"Has one ever sunk?" I asked, looking for reassurance.

"No, they can't sink."

"That's what they said about the Titanic!"

"You don't understand. They *can't* sink. The water here is only four meters deep. Where we are standing now is about ten meters above the water. You do the math, and stop worrying so much!"

"Oh." My unjustified apprehension now seemed ludicrous, so I hurriedly changed the subject. "Have the ferries been around a long time?"

"Oh, yeah. They were made in Latvia and built to carry tanks back and forth to the island."

"Tanks? You mean army tanks? What for?"

"You know, to practice. There's a torn-up place in the forest where they did maneuvers."

"Let me understand this, they brought tanks all the way out here just to drive around?"

"Sure," Tarmo said and laughed. "You never know when and where NATO will strike."

"Does that have something to do with why the ferry's bow is all banged up?"

"No, these ships are icebreakers. They can break through ice thirty centimeters thick or more."

"Do they run all year round?"

"Well, most of the time. Unless they get stuck or the wind is too strong."

My temporary blanket of security was whisked away at his words. "What do you mean, stuck?" I asked, but Tarmo ignored me.

"Look! There's Hiiumaa!"

Sure enough, the low, dark green silhouette of an island was now in view a few miles ahead. As if on cue, the clouds parted and beams of the setting sun shone through and danced across the forested shore. Soon the rain let up and the seas became calmer as we approached the island's rocky coast. For me, our arrival was not a moment too soon, as darkness was starting to fall. I wanted there to be plenty of light so I could see the big reception that awaited me. I pictured the flags flying on the harbor buildings and the gleaming white pleasure boats lined up at the town's docks. I began to practice in Estonian what I would say after disembarking and being led to the podium by Hiiumaa's governor. I gripped the rail in anticipation and strained my eyes to catch a glimpse of the crowds that would certainly be gathered at the harbor. As the sleeping passengers began to stir and gather their belongings, I could finally see the ferry port clearly.

Problem was, there were no crowd, not a single human soul—only a big yellow dog who limped through the line of waiting cars, barking his way out onto the quay where a few dockhands waited to catch the mooring lines. No lines of yachts and pleasure boats awaited us either, just a few small wooden fishing boats pulled up onto the beach with nets hanging out to dry. Instead of a big terminal with flags flying, the harbor consisted mostly of a few low-slung, gray cinderblock buildings, a couple of rusting shipping containers, and a lonely loading crane. Worst of all, it seemed there was no town—nothing but the small harbor at the edge of a seemingly impenetrable forest. The picture was much more like the backside of a warehouse complex than how I'd imagined the main ferry port of an entire island. This was the big Baltic tourist destination? There were supposed to be 12,000 people living here!

As I stared in disbelief at the empty shore, the ferry captain cut the engines and we bumped gently against the quay. Like a curtain, silence descended on my wonderful fantasy. I stood there dumbfounded, like an actor looking out over a theater hall that has emptied during his performance. Finally, Tarmo grabbed my arm and woke me from my daydream. "C'mon, let's go!" he said, leading me away from the window and down the stairs. Numbly, I followed him down to the pickup truck. After the deckhands lowered the bow, we pulled the truck off the ship and over to the side near the harbor fence. Tarmo started to get out and, when I didn't follow, he bent down and peered into the cab.

"Hey you! Welcome to Hiiumaa!"

"Uh, yeah," I replied weakly.

"C'mon, get out. We have to go through passport control."

"Passport control? But we haven't left Estonia, have we?"

"Doesn't matter. All people coming onto the island have to get their documents checked. It's been that way since the Soviet times. They still check for some reason, but at least now they don't check the trunk for rubber boats you might use for an escape attempt to the West."

I grabbed my passport from my bag and followed Tarmo across the gravelly asphalt tarmac. We approached the low-slung buildings and lined up behind the other passengers. The line moved fairly quickly, with a couple of dour-faced policemen in crisp blue uniforms giving only cursory glances at the passengers' documents. When our turn came, Tarmo showed his passport and started to explain something about me to the policeman. I, however, wanted to show off my newly learned Estonian skills, so I pushed ahead of Tarmo and boldly faced the two officers. I thrust out my passport and introduced myself. They looked at one another with raised eyebrows, then turned back to face me with not-too-amused expressions. One of them grabbed my passport and started going through it. I figured they were probably tired at the end of a long day, so I smiled brightly and held out my hand for the return of my identification. The policeman turned the passport over and over in his hands, flipping through the pages. Then he handed it to his partner, who also spent quite a bit of time looking it over. Finally, he looked up and regarded me curiously.

"Can we help you?" he said in a suspicious voice.

"No, I'm fine. Just a little tired from the voyage."

"What is your business here?"　.

I paused for a moment, uncertain how to proceed. This line of questioning wasn't quite going as I'd expected. "Weren't you expecting me? I'm the new Peace Corps Volunteer."

"The what?"

"Peace Corps. You know: John F. Kennedy, goodwill, 'toughest job you'll ever love'?"

"Look, just tell me what you are doing here," the officer said with growing irritation.

I answered with a tone of the utmost certainty. "I'm coming to live here for two years."

"I'm serious." His tone told me he thought I was joking, a behavior he apparently wasn't quite fond of. "How long will you be here?"

"Like I said: two years."

"Now look," said the officer as he dropped the passport on the table. "Do you see that ferry over there? In ten minutes it's heading back to the mainland. Either you start giving me some straight answers or you're going to be on it!"

"I'm sure there's someone who knows I'm coming," I said hopefully, but to no avail. My bright smile was fast disappearing. "There must be someone in authority you can call."

"You can't stay here anyway," the other policeman said with finality. "You have no visa."

"Visa? But this is still Estonia!"

"Yes, but you don't have a Hiiumaa visa and your living permit was issued in Tartu. You can't just come in here and think you are going to stay for two years."

Just when I thought I was going to be bodily carried out and thrown onto the ferry, Tarmo stepped in. He pulled one of the officers off to the side and spoke to him in a low voice. I couldn't hear what they were saying, but after some initial protest the policeman finally went in the back office, grabbed the phone and made a call. The conversation went on for quite a while, punctuated by lots of exasperated gestures and head scratching. At last, he came back out, looked at his partner, and sighed. Without a word, he handed over my passport and waved us out the door.

I was too embarrassed to tell Tarmo about my now-shattered grand expectations so I sat silently while he fired up the motor and sped out through the harbor gates. My last hopes of seeing any kind of civilization related to the harbor vanished as we found ourselves once again in a familiar and impenetrable corridor of trees. It was as if the sea voyage had never even taken place and, as if to emphasize this, when I looked back the coastline had already vanished behind a curve. If that was the main ferry port, I thought, I couldn't imagine what the less-inhabited parts of the island looked like. Not for the first time, I started to wonder what I had gotten myself into. Nobody from Peace Corps had said anything about getting a new living permit, and because of that I had almost gotten tossed off the island on my first day. Most importantly, nobody had even come meet me. I could get over the absence of a welcoming committee, but it seemed that no one even knew I was

coming, a point that didn't bode well for hopes of future cooperation. I decided the first order of business would be to go to the
Maavalitsus (County Government) officials and find out what was
up with this Hiiumaa "visa." But right then, all I wanted to do was
drop into a warm bed and get some sleep after our daylong journey through Estonia.

After the forest, we drove a few kilometers through open fields
until we came upon one of the collective farm complexes just like
those I had seen all the way through my drive on the mainland. It
was an unpleasant surprise to see the same run-down buildings
and rusting farm machinery sitting idly on oil-soaked earth. They
even had the same dreaded slab apartments, only smaller—three
stories high. Tarmo slowed down and pulled off the road into a
parking lot. He skidded to a stop, set the parking brake and turned
to me with a relieved sigh.

"Well, here we are. This is home!"

"Here?" I said and looked around. "This is Putkaste Village?"

"That's right! Seventy-five people, eight dogs and now one
American. See that big rundown house over there? That was Putkaste
Manor in the 18th and 19th centuries, but for the last fifty years it's
been Putkaste State Farm headquarters. That is where I worked
until the farm went out of business after Estonia regained independence. What do you think?"

"Well, I…. I mean…. it looks good." I tried to hide my disappointment.

So, no thatched roofs, no chickens running around, no village
well—just another cold gray apartment building like all the others I'd already experienced. I followed Tarmo through the now-
familiar old wooden door that squeaked when you opened it and
slammed shut when you let it go. We went up the same old concrete stairwell that echoed with the sounds of our steps, passed the
same old doors with the same old door handles. It never ceased to
amaze me how every light fixture, wall outlet, bathtub and toilet
seemed to come from the same factory in the Soviet Union. It was

so depressing to see all this again. I wondered if we would even have hot water.

Finally, we reached the third floor. I remember very clearly it was at this moment, standing there in that darkened stairwell and convinced that things were going to be just the same as on the mainland, that all similarities to my previous Estonian experiences stopped cold, never to return. This first departure from mainland reality was when Tarmo reached down, grabbed a boot that was sitting on the landing and, after some fishing around, pulled out his keys and started to open the door.

"You keep your keys in your boot by the door?" I asked in amazement.

"Yeah, my wife left them there. She's not home."

"Don't you worry about someone breaking in?"

"This isn't the mainland," Tarmo laughed. "Everyone knows each other and let's just say we don't have a lot of strangers coming through!" With that, he pushed open the door.

I stepped inside to a different world. The contrast to the drab outside of the building was astounding. Plus, it was *warm* inside! After being starved so long for color and originality, the apartment was truly a feast for the eyes. I looked into the living room and saw a stereo, which was hooked up to huge speakers hanging from the ceiling. A full-sized color TV took up one whole corner of the room with a plush armchair facing it. Tarmo took off his coat, walked over to the TV and patted it proudly.

"Satellite TV," he said, then pulled the cover off a VCR.

"Do you have hot water?" I asked, more concerned with basic things.

"Of course! Three times a week."

"That's great, but how cold does it get in here when the hot water isn't working?"

"We have an electric boiler for heat, so it's warm all the time."

I felt my face melt into a smile of relief and content. I was already starting to like my new home.

Tarmo led me into the kitchen where I found a gleaming stainless steel sink, a modern gas stove and—wonder of wonders!—a dishwasher, the first I had seen in Estonia. Tarmo smiled as I carefully opened it up and peered inside with awe.

We went down the corridor where he next showed me the washroom. I was pleased to see that there was a full-sized tub, but my attention was drawn to a large white metal box covered with T-shirts and pants. It couldn't possibly be, but as I drew closer and moved some of the clothes I saw that it was true: Tarmo had a washing machine! And not some Soviet job either. This beautiful appliance was from Finland and sported several dials set into a bright stainless steel face. I knew it wasn't polite to ask, but I had to find out how this supposedly unemployed collective farm worker had amassed all these treasures. I thought awhile how to tactfully broach the subject, but in the end I settled for the direct approach.

"Where did you get all this stuff?"

"I go to Finland," Tarmo said simply.

"You mean you buy this stuff over there and bring it back?"

"I go there and do some construction work. Then I pick up some broken appliances for cheap. I bring them back in my truck, fix them up, and sell the ones I don't keep."

"You can really fix all this stuff yourself?"

"Sure, sometimes I even bring cars. I have four of them outside," Tarmo said nonchalantly.

"You have *four* cars?" All the preconceived notions I had arrived with seemed to be flying right out the window.

"Yeah, sometimes more. Tomorrow I'll show you around the village. But for now, let's get some sleep. It's been a long day. Your bedroom is down the hall and on the right."

So, after a steaming hot bath, the first I had enjoyed in months, I slipped between the sheets in my own bed, in my own room, and drifted peacefully off to sleep. Riga, Tartu and the sea journey already seemed like distant memories.

6—FIRST DAY ON THE JOB

On my first morning in Hiiumaa I woke up to the sound of scream-ing gulls. I had slept the soundest I had in weeks and it felt rejuve-nating to finally start my first day at post. I stepped out onto the porch and took a deep breath of the fresh sea air. Down below, an old woman pushed her bicycle towards the barn behind the manor house. The empty milk pail that swung from the handlebars be-lied her purpose. Now that it was daylight, I noticed that in addi-tion to the apartment buildings there were several wood-frame houses in the charming little village.

Soon Tarmo came into the kitchen and started up the auto-matic coffee machine. He stretched and took a look out the win-dow.

"Looks like a nice day," he said sleepily. "What do you want to do?"

I answered without hesitation. "I want to go to Kärdla."

"Are you sure you want to visit the capital already?" Tarmo asked. "You just got here."

"I'd like to meet the folks in the *Maavalitsus* and our co-worker in the Farmers Union. Can you take me there, or should I take the bus?"

"Well, the bus is long gone. I need to buy some things anyway so I can take you. Let's go after we eat some breakfast."

Tarmo pulled out some sausage and cheese, and we had the traditional Estonian open-faced sandwiches, washed down with fresh whole milk from a mason jar. I could tell it was unpasteur-ized farm milk because the cream had risen to the top overnight. The old woman I had seen probably sold her milk straight from the cow to the others in the village. Though we had been warned of the dangers, by now I just drank it without a second thought. After a cup of coffee, we headed downstairs and Tarmo pointed out the other vehicles that belonged to him: a small Russian Lada, a large flatbed truck, and another pickup like the one we had drove from the mainland. I was impressed with his fleet of vehicles, especially considering that he worked on them all himself. Between fixing appliances and the cars, he seemed quite the handyman.

Kärdla, population 4000, was straight across the island on the north side, a distance of about twenty kilometers. We left the village and almost immediately entered into a nearly uninterrupted corridor through the forest that stretched until the outskirts of town. This seemed to be the way to travel in Estonia, into the trees and out again. As we drove, I noticed that the asphalt road was completely devoid of lane or shoulder markings. Tarmo took a leisurely course straight down the middle, the oncoming cars heading straight for us. My companion seemed completely unperturbed by this driving arrangement. We would play something similar to a game of chicken until one driver would decide to make way. Sometime it was us, sometime it was them—I couldn't figure out the system. I also noticed with concern that there was also an almost complete lack of road signs.

The landscape was so similar to that of the mainland, at least in that region, that it was easy to forget that miles of water separated us. The island was so flat and forested that we only saw the sea when we were practically right on the beach. In about thirty minutes, we arrived on the outskirts of Kärdla. A few quick turns brought us right up to the *Maavalitsus* building, an imposing two-story structure that looked suspiciously like a military headquarters. (I later found out that it was indeed the former headquarters of the island's army commandant.)

We walked up to the large wooden door and pulled it open. Of course it creaked loudly, and when we went inside it slammed behind us with a bang that echoed throughout the spacious foyer. The place looked empty—no telephones ringing, no people bustling about. Just eerie silence. Tarmo led me across the concrete slab floor and down one of the corridors until we came to an office door that had "Farmers Union" written on it in Estonian. We went in without knocking. Inside, the office looked a lot like something you would find in a U.S. government building during the '50s. The telephones, the desks, the windows—everything had that look about it. There was even one of those pull-open windows above the door like I remembered from grade school. Two women and a young man, who I took to be the director, occupied the three office desks. By now, I had gotten used to the idea of seeing twentysomethings in charge of organizations. Sure enough, the young man stood up and came out from behind the desk to shake my hand. (So much for the psychologists' advice in Tartu!)

"Hi, I'm Mart, Farmers Union Director," he said with a smile. "Welcome to Hiiumaa! We heard you arrived and have been looking forward to meeting our American agricultural advisor."

"Yes, well, I am more of a businessperson but—"

"No problem! It just so happens there is a meeting going on today in the auditorium. Everyone will get a chance to meet you."

Mart's enthusiasm made up for my anticlimactic arrival the day before, but his agricultural advisor remark worried me a little bit. Though I was to be working with the Farmers Union, my official sponsor was the *Maavalitsus*, an extension of the national government and they hadn't exactly rolled out the red carpet. I fervently hoped that at least some of the folks in Hiiumaa had been briefed on my background. The last thing I needed was some kind of misunderstanding on my first workday, especially after yesterday's fiasco in the harbor.

As it turned out, my worst fears were realized as I was led into the auditorium filled with about a hundred stern-faced Hiiumaa farmers. The room was dead quiet as Mart led me in and up to the podium. The room went silent as he introduced me as "the American Agricultural Advisor from Peace *Corpse* who has come to reform Hiiumaa's agricultural system for the new market economy." I cringed at his words.

Mart then turned over the microphone while the farmers applauded politely and looked at one another in expectation. After they had quieted down, I nervously introduced myself in Estonian. The effect was dramatic, as I had hoped. The farmers' jaws practically dropped into their laps and they whispered among themselves. I relaxed a little, gaining confidence from the impact of using the local language. However, my self-assurance was short-lived. No sooner had I finished than the questions poured in from the audience.

"Mr. Wells, how many acres of land do you have in America?" asked one elderly farmer.

"I, uh, actually lived in an apartment. But I like the outdoors!"

"So, someone else takes care of your farm?" offered another younger union member.

"Well, I don't . . . have . . . my own farm." The words came out slowly as a cold sweat broke out on my brow.

"Ah, of course, you are from the American West and you have a ranch with animals."

"Well, not exactly, but we did have some pets–including two cats—when I was growing up."

"Well then, what agricultural degree do you have?" asked a third farmer.

"You see, my degree is in business, but I'm sure Mart explained to you our plans...."

My voice trailed off as I realized the destruction was complete. You could have heard a pin drop in the hall. I looked helplessly at Mart and Tarmo, but they looked as surprised as the others. Realizing that explaining the complexities of our project required language skills way beyond my capabilities, I decided to cut and run. I smiled brightly at the crowd, handed the microphone to Mart, and exited the stage with as much as grace as I could muster.

Out in the foyer, I sat on a bench with my head in my hands, listening to the mutter of conversation going on in the hall. I could only imagine what they were saying. My thoughts were interrupted by a middle-aged Estonian woman in thick glasses, who stood in front of me and cleared her throat.

"Excuse me, are you Mr. Wells?" she said with an old-school British accent.

"Yes, that's me." I felt a momentary sense of relief that somebody at least knew my name.

"My name is Helgi. I am the County Tourism Advisor and translator for the governor."

"Great! You know we have a lot to talk about. First of all, this visa thing…"

"The governor would like to see you," Helgi said simply and motioned for me to follow.

We went up a set of concrete steps and across a corridor into the outer office of the governor. A secretary hurried around preparing coffee as Helgi stood nervously by my side. After a time, the phone on the secretary's desk rang and we were ushered through two doors with thick leather upholstery, one right after the other, and into the governor's office. Three men in dark suits sat stone-faced and silent in a semi-circle around a large upholstered chair in the middle of the room. After leading me to the hot seat, Helgi nervously took a position in the corner. I sat down and the three regarded me suspiciously for some time. Just when I could hardly stand the silence any more, the large middle-aged bald man in the center spoke up. As the governor began speaking, I understood the need for a translator. He spoke in low quick tones, directing his comments toward the translator but never taking his eyes off me. The other two men sat unsmiling and silent on either side like bodyguards.

"Governor Mänd welcomes you to the island," Helgi translated.

"Thank you. I'm glad to be here," I said, noting that the governor's name translated as "pine tree."

"You are working with the farmers, right?"

"Yes, we will be cooperating on some projects. Do you know about the extension office?"

"No."

"I'm sorry to hear that. Maybe the Farmers Union hasn't told you."

"What do you think you can do to save Hiiumaa agriculture? Times are very hard."

"Well, uh, it is a little bit early to tell. I must learn about things here first."

"But why are you here exactly?"

Here we go again, I thought to myself. I opted for the simple yet direct approach. "I am here to help people."

"How?"

"However they want me to. I need to find out their needs."

"But what specifically can you do for us, Mr. Wells from America?"

"We do many different things besides our assigned task. It doesn't have to be all agriculture. For example, I know that you have some abandoned army bases here that may be posing a risk to the environment. I can help clean those up, for example."

As soon as the words left my mouth I realized my mistake. As Helgi nervously translated my words into Estonian, the two silent men raised their eyebrows and leaned over to whisper to the governor. This consultation went on for some time as I fidgeted in my seat and Helgi shifted nervously from one foot to another. When the three men had finished whispering among themselves, the governor stood and gave me a forced smile.

' "Thank you for your offer, Mr. Wells, but we have people to take care of things like that. I am sure that your skills can benefit our farmers. I wish you luck with your endeavors. We will be watching your progress and hoping that the American Peace Corps can be successful in reforming Hiiumaa's agriculture. Good day."

Without further ceremony I was ushered out and the double doors closed behind me.

Helgi led me downstairs and left me outside the Farmers Union office without more than a polite farewell. I knocked and then entered to find Tarmo sitting with Mart. Despite the seemingly disastrous meeting with the farmers, they seemed to be in pretty good spirits.

"Hey, how did it go with the governor?" Tarmo asked cheerfully.

"Don't ask. Have you got any vodka at home?"

"Well, well, that good, huh?" Tarmo slapped me heartily on the back. "You know, I don't drink much myself, but I think we can find something just for you at the Putkaste village store. Let's go home."

We left the *Maavalitsus* building and the rest of Kärdla behind, hopefully for some time. I had enjoyed meeting Mart, but this "savior of Hiiumaa agriculture" thing was a little too much to handle. In one day I had blown the expectations of a hundred or so farmers and managed to alienate the governor of the whole island. Not bad, and I still had two years to go.

7—HAMMERFISHING

I have to admit that after only a few weeks on Hiiumaa Island I was worshipping the ground Tarmo walked on. I was pleased that my companion was the head of the household where I was to spend my first year on Hiiumaa. He was about my age but was already married and had started a family. My chauffeur from the mainland was also the one who patiently dealt with the strange neuroses of a displaced American living in his house. Perhaps most importantly, Tarmo was my guide who showed me around and gave invaluable lessons in how to have a good time on a rocky island in the Baltic Sea where it's dark and frigid half of the year.

Tarmo had answered a local newspaper ad, placed by Peace Corps, about housing an American volunteer for a year. There was a certain amount of rent money offered, but it wasn't such a big amount that a young man in a two-bedroom apartment with a wife and young child should quickly jump at the opportunity. But when Tarmo read the ad, he not only saw a chance to learn English and have contact with somebody from the West, he realized that someone would have to house the poor Peace Corps Volunteer who had come to aid the ailing agricultural sector on his home island.

The most intriguing and attractive quality about Tarmo was that he could do *anything* and fix *everything*: electronics, cars, plumbing, construction—you name it, this man could do it all. And he did it with an unperturbed calm, never displaying even the slightest shred of fear or doubt. He could fieldstrip an entire Volga automobile with a bandana wrapped around his eyes. When the heat went out in the apartment building, he would disappear down the basement stairs and, after some horrendous banging, the radiators would start to grow warm again. He even fixed the neck of my guitar, which had cracked during the flight from the U.S. to Estonia.

Most of these skills Tarmo had learned during his mandatory two-year stint in the Russian Army. Hunting and fishing were second nature to him, which was fortunate as his job at the *sovhoos* (state farm) had been eliminated and he had a wife and young child to feed. He approached the taking of an animal or fish as a matter of grim necessity. He lived by the motto "success by any means necessary." He was John Wayne, Davey Crockett, and Rambo all rolled into one. The more I learned about Tarmo, the more I realized I couldn't have asked for a better host.

Tarmo saw right away that I liked the outdoors. I had brought my fishing pole from Nebraska, which is a true sign of its importance considering we were only allowed a hundred pounds of luggage for two years' service. Tarmo was impressed with my rod and reel and said that we would have to go out fishing sometime. Little did I know that even though I would go fishing many times that first winter, my fancy gear would only collect dust in Tarmo's closet.

One cold and clear Saturday I came back from a walk to find Tarmo puttering around in his garage. He motioned for me to come over and I, relishing a chance to see Tarmo's inner sanctum, rushed to comply. He didn't even look up as he rooted around in one of his mysterious toolboxes. "We're going fishing," he said simply. I started towards the apartment building to retrieve my pole, but he called me back. Puzzled, I watched as he dug out an ax, a length of rope, a big screwdriver and what looked like a huge croquet mallet. It had a handle about six feet long and a thick fireplace log stuck on the end. I was completely baffled, but a quick check of my language skills confirmed that fishing was indeed the activity in which we were going to engage.

Tarmo threw everything in the back of the truck. We bounced over the potholed parking lot toward the main road, but stopped just before turning onto the highway. Tarmo whistled and motioned for me to open the passenger door of the pickup. I complied and in jumped a medium-sized fox-colored dog who promptly planted himself in my lap and panted happily. This was Bella, Tarmo's partner-in-crime, and he went everywhere with us.

We drove for a while and then cut off onto a forest road that brought us to the edge of the sea. We were in a sheltered cove and the shoreline was typically rocky and covered with pines and junipers. The first thing I noticed was that the sea had a thin coating of ice that seemed to preclude fishing, at least in the traditional sense. Tarmo hopped out of the truck, grabbed his huge hammer and walked down to the water's edge. Full of expectation, I grabbed the rest of the gear and followed. To my surprise, Tarmo didn't stop at the shoreline, but gingerly stepped out onto the thin, clear ice. The frozen sheet groaned and made cracking sounds but didn't give way, so Tarmo moved farther out. Seemingly satisfied, he motioned for me to follow. My fear was overcome by my desire to not be perceived as a wimp, so I hesitantly ventured onto the glass-like surface. More creaking and groaning followed and I braced myself for a plunge into the water. Fortunately the ice held and, as I looked down, I noticed that the water was less than a foot deep. With my confidence restored and curiosity piqued, I looked forward to Tarmo's next move. My host didn't like to talk much, and I had learned not to bother him with unnecessary questions.

Tarmo put his huge hammer over his shoulder and moved even farther out, making sliding side steps. He peered intently down through the clear ice. I followed cautiously over the creaking surface, completely baffled about what our game plan was to catch fish. The only thing that seemed certain was that we were going to get wet, which was not a happy prospect in the sub-freezing weather.

The answer to my question came quick enough, as I saw a blur of movement under Tarmo's feet. Tarmo quickly shifted the huge hammer off his shoulder and with great effort brought it down on the ice with a boom that resounded throughout the whole cove. He slid quickly forward a few yards and slammed the hammer down again in a huge arc, sending cracks shooting all the way to the shoreline. All the while, the dog danced around him, barking excitedly. I watched with amazement, expecting us both to get an ice-water bath at any moment. However, the ice held and after a few more swings Tarmo motioned for me to bring the ax.

As I approached, I looked closely through the ice and was surprised to see four or five good-sized fish belly-up and quivering just under the frozen surface. Finally, I realized what was going on: Tarmo was stunning the fish with the shock waves from his mammoth hammer blows. This was his method of fishing for this particular time of year, after ice made it impossible to use the boat but before it was thick enough to do proper ice fishing.

As I stood there, mouth open, Tarmo took the ax from my grasp and quickly chopped open a hole in the ice. He then reached into the freezing water, pulled the fish out one by one, and tossed them onto the surface of the ice where the dog happily batted them around with his front paws. Once again I was filled with admiration and amazement for this man who could do seemingly anything.

We moved around in the bay as he nabbed several more fish. I took over hole-chopping duties and gamely thrust my bare hands into the frozen sea, grasping the slippery fish and bringing them out. Tarmo eventually decided it was time for me to give it a try and handed me the huge mallet. Looking like a drunken midget off to a croquet game, I staggered under the weight and slid around on the ice with my head down. I saw a few fish but they shot away long before I could bring the hammer down on the ice. I could barely even swing it and the weak impacts I made were a far cry from Tarmo's massive strikes. I finally gave up and, with an embarrassed shrug, handed the hammer back to Tarmo. We gathered up the fish we had and headed back toward the truck.

Suddenly, a big pike shot out from under our feet, stirring up a cloud of silt. Tarmo took off with the hammer and, after tracking the fish a few yards, brought it down with a resounding boom. He slid a few more yards and struck again, but the monster pike wasn't giving up that easily. Back and forth they went across the bay with the barking dog in hot pursuit. I was amazed at Tarmo's stamina in continuously swinging that huge hammer. When the chase was over Tarmo, breathing heavily, leaned on the hammer and motioned for me to come over with the ax. I dutifully chopped a hole for my hero and went after the defeated fish.

By now my hands were completely numb from the freezing seawater and I groped around unsuccessfully in the silty murk. Suddenly I felt my hand catch on something that resisted my efforts to pull away. I struggled to pull my arm out of the hole. When I finally pulled free and stood up, I was horrified to find the toothy pike firmly fastened onto my hand. In a near panic, I tried to shake him off, but this only increased his determination as he gnawed away and blood began dripping onto the ice. Luckily my hands were so numb I couldn't feel anything. I looked helplessly at Tarmo who, always ready for anything, calmly reached into my coat pocket and pulled out the giant screwdriver, which he used to pry the stubborn fish's jaws apart. The defeated pike released his grip and dropped to the ice. I nursed my wounded hand as we made our way back to the truck, throwing our catch in the back.

I sat on the passenger side with the dog trying to lick my bleeding hand. The wound seemed pretty serious and I was trying to think what the Peace Corps Medical Officer would have me do in this particular situation. As always, Tarmo took charge. He glanced over at me sitting with a helpless look on my face, then sighed and shook his head. Between gearshifts, he grabbed an oily rag from under his seat and quickly wrapped it around my hand before I could protest. Problem solved. In silence, we headed back to the house for a well-earned fish dinner.

8—UNSPORTSMANLIKE CONDUCT?

Tarmo was the one who showed me how to hammerfish but the real title "God of Fishing" had to go to his downstairs neighbor Erik, who was also about our age. Erik had also been through two years of Soviet military training, during which he acquired an amazing array of survival skills. He too had lost his job at the *sovhoos* and had a family to feed, so he pursued fish mostly out of necessity. But make no mistake—this man enjoyed what he was doing. He was another one of these Rambo-like characters in the village, and I was immediately drawn to him. He, like Tarmo, also felt a certain obligation to show me the ropes, me being a soft Westerner and all. He was a tall man, slender but muscular like Tarmo, with very little fat on him. He had dark hair and a mustache that he would pull on whenever he was deciding his next course of action. His favorite garb was a worn Soviet army jacket and a T-shirt.

Erik would search me out for an adventure, either after work before it got dark or on the weekend. He'd come to the door of the apartment where I lived with Tarmo's family, knock politely, and invite me out into the dimly lit concrete stairwell. He didn't go into great detail about what our mission would be, but instead would say, "We have something to do," and jerk his head towards the outside. I always went along because I knew that with Erik there was never a dull moment.

We had already gone fishing with poles, traps and nets, but little did I know there was still much to learn in the ways of Estonian fishing. You see, Erik was trained by the Soviets in underwater demolition and he possessed an air tank, regulator and spear gun left over from his glory days. Now that there was no need to defend the glorious motherland, he still wanted to put his cool gear to use. So it was that on a sunny Saturday, I followed Erik to one of Hiiumaa Island's "rivers" where he immersed himself as far as he could in the chilly waters of the ten-foot wide stream. I followed along the bank as he moved downstream, the water not even covering his aqualung, and poked around in the reeds with his spear gun. From reed bed to reed bed he propelled himself, aided by his black regulation frogman's flippers. The way I describe it may sound comical but I can't argue with success. Every time we went on one of these missions he landed (speared) as least one sizable fish while providing hours of entertainment, both for me and the old men we encountered fishing with the more traditional cane poles. These exploits earned him my first nomination for the title God of Fishing.

The second nomination was earned one day when I came home and found Erik in his workroom, located in the musty-smelling basement of the apartment building. His layout was even better than Tarmo's garage. He had an amazing variety of tools, electrical equipment and cables hanging on the walls, plus shelves lined with jars containing mysterious liquids and powders. His work-bench was covered with cans containing various screws, nails and drill bits. Like Tarmo, he believed in being ready to fix anything and everything that even had a chance of breaking.

When I poked my head through the doorway, Erik was hold-ing an empty champagne bottle up to the light of a single 75-watt bulb and carefully pouring some liquid inside. "We're going fish-ing," he said simply. I, not understanding the relationship be-tween the bottle and the statement, asked if I should grab my pole. Without looking at me, he shook his head and grabbed a can of white powder. He carefully added some powder to the bottle, then motioned for us to go outside. To my surprise, all we carried to the truck was the bottle and a landing net—no poles, traps, hammers or any other now-familiar gear. I desperately wanted to ask what was going on, but I knew from experience that Erik, like most Estonian men, was a man of few words, so I kept silent and got in the truck. We drove for a few kilometers until we came to a small stone bridge over a deep stream. Erik brought the bottle with us down to the bank where we stood in silence for a moment while he looked upstream and down. Apparently satisfied, he shoved the cork into the bottle, turned it upside down and tossed it into the water.

Nothing seemed to happen. We stood staring at the spot where the bottle had vanished, the ripples it had created long since carried away by the current. My curiosity finally got the better of me. "What do we do now?" Erik pulled a cigarette out of his pocket and intently studied the water's surface. "Do we-" I started to inquire, but was interrupted by a horrendous explosion. I ducked for cover as a six-foot geyser of water rose out of the stream. As I cowered on the ground it finally dawned on me that Erik had made a fishing bomb. A simple champagne bottle and the right combination of powders and liquids had, in the trained hands of this Estonian, turned into a lethal fishing tool. As the water settled and the sound of the blast faded away, a few unfortunate residents of the stream floated to the surface. Erik calmly pulled the landing net out of the back of the truck, and soon dinner was in the bag.

I had experienced fishing with nets, traps, spear guns and now homemade bombs, but I still wasn't ready to award Erik his title. The crowning achievement came the next week when I visited him after he had returned from a fishing trip. I found Erik in the kitchen of his apartment, cleaning some fish. I couldn't help but notice that they had some strange looking gashes on their backs. My curiosity was piqued, but knowing better than to ask too direct a question, I decided to ask how things went. The conversation was vintage Estonian, with me asking ten questions just to get a simple piece of information from my reticent companion.

"How did it go today?"

"Pretty bad. It was a windy day and hard to cast for anything."

"Well, what about these fish? They look pretty nice."

"They weren't after my lures. I got them in another way," was Erik's cryptic response

"What do you mean?"

"I was out there casting all afternoon and was getting nothing. Windy, rainy, and not a bite to be had for hours! Then I saw a school of fish swimming near the surface about thirty yards away."

"What did you do then? Did you change lures and cast into the middle of them?"

"No, by that time I was really fed up. I just turned the boat toward them, revved up the outboard motor and ran through the middle of the school."

So it was that Erik earned his title by scoring a huge catch by way of the prop of his outboard motor combined with a little Estonian grit and determination.

* * *

Not surprisingly, fishing wasn't the only sporting field in which Erik exhibited expertise. I guess his family eventually tired of fish because one day, Erik suddenly showed an interest in hunting. The problem was, he didn't have a gun and he didn't belong to any of the semi-elite Hiiumaa hunters' clubs. Supposedly, you had to have a license to own a gun and you had to have a hunting club membership before you could go out into the island's forests and hunt animals. Erik solved the first problem fairly quickly. Somehow he got hold of a Makarov pistol, which was the standard issue sidearm for officers in the Soviet Army. He then went through the required training program with the Estonian police and acquired a license to carry the gun. That wasn't the same as getting a hunting license or joining one of the hunters' clubs, but Erik seemed to feel that the right to carry gave him the right to use his weapon should some edible animal present itself within range. In Erik's opinion, what he did wasn't really hunting. It was simply wandering about with a gun, and if some animal got in your way, then you had the right to bring it home for dinner.

I was a more traditional hunter and probably would have joined one of the clubs but, according to Peace Corps rules, I wasn't supposed to own or carry a gun so I had to settle for being a spectator. I relished the chance to go around with Erik, though I must admit hunting with a Russian automatic pistol seemed a bit odd. Also, I found some of his tactics questionable. Like the time we were driving down a back road in his pickup and he pointed out some snow geese that had landed in the nearby field. I was admiring them when suddenly Erik braked the truck to a screeching halt. In one movement he pushed my head down into my lap and reached for the pistol under his seat. I tried to raise my head but abandoned that idea when the Makarov roared to life. It would be difficult to describe the noise that even one pistol shot made inside the cab of a pickup, and Erik emptied an entire clip over my head and out the window at the resting flock. After the gun fell silent, all I heard above the ringing in my ears was Erik cursing and the sound of a hundred geese flying off to safety.

On a cold drizzly night the following week, I found myself crawling through the brush in order to reach one of Hiiumaa's shallow bays. We made it to the shore and in the narrow open space between the forest and the water's edge, Erik had me scan the surface of the water with a huge flashlight. He dropped into a half-crouch with a two-handed grip (I guess he had been watching American cop show reruns) and swept the surface of the water, following my light. The only thing that showed up in the flashlight beam was a pair of swans and I was relieved to see that even Erik wasn't about to open up on such beautiful and graceful animals. We retreated back to the workroom and plotted our next move. At that time of year, there was an abundance of waterfowl resting on Hiiumaa's fields and in the waters surrounding the island. The island lay right in the path of a major migratory flyway running from the Arctic to the Mediterranean and Africa. It was only a matter of being in the right place at the right time. We decided to try for a duck dinner the next night after I came from Kärdla.

Erik already had the truck out and running when I arrived on the bus outside the village. I hopped in and we drove down the main road for a few kilometers, then turned off at one of the many trails that ran through Hiiumaa's forest. I could never figure out exactly where I was in the densely packed trees, so I just sat back and let Erik drive. After several minutes and two or three turns onto other unmarked roads, we pulled into a small clearing and stopped.

I followed Erik into the wet undergrowth and we pushed our way through the branches and leaves for probably a hundred yards before I caught a glimpse of the water. We moved stealthily along the coastline and Erik turned back to me every ten yards or so to put his fingers to his lips as a signal to be quiet. Suddenly, he stomped down a bush that was between him and the water and opened fire. "Pop, pop, pop!" the Makarov barked, and then there was silence. I moved closer to get a better look, heard some quacking, then fell back as the pistol barked a few more times. When it was all over, there were two ducks floating lifeless on the water, illuminated in the light of the full moon that had just broke through the clouds hovering on the horizon. Erik waded into the water and put the ducks into a bag. I had hunted myself since I was about twelve years old but just for pheasants and quail. I felt a little guilty about engaging in this exciting, but still semi-legal hunting activity. As we rode silently back in the truck, I think Erik sensed my ambiguity about the event. He held up the bag to me and said with unabashed pride, "Tonight, my little girl will eat!"

9—THE SAUNA

When giving us lessons about Estonian culture, our language teachers back in Tartu had often talked about the sauna. Not just "a" sauna but "the" sauna, an event of near-religious proportions that took place once a week, either in a household, a farm or an entire village. I listened to their talk about how sweating in a sauna would leach out the "poisons" in the body, and that going from the intense heat of the sauna to the intense cold of, say, a hole in the ice of a frozen lake would somehow improve your health. For me, that seemed like the best recipe for a heart attack. Stranger still was the fact that my Estonian teachers Linda and Kairi had referred several times to "beating," a practice that involved bundles of birch branches (real men, according to them, used the spiny juniper).

I figured all this was just some sort of miscommunication caused by the differences between our languages. My only experience with saunas had been at either a health club or hotel, and those certainly weren't warm enough to encourage me to jump in ice water. In addition, those saunas always had all kinds of warning stickers on them saying that pregnant women, children and old people should stay away, and that if even healthy young men stayed in for more than fifteen minutes their hearts would explode. I couldn't imagine a family spending a whole evening in the sauna. However, Peace Corps training emphasized cultural sensitivity, so one of the first weekends I spent on Hiiumaa Island, I asked Tarmo to take me to the village sauna, which took place every Saturday. I figured it would be a good chance to meet some of the local men, as well as show that I wanted to become involved in the community. Maybe then they would stop staring at me and whispering to each other whenever I crossed their paths. I counted the days until Saturday finally arrived.

That morning, Tarmo informed me that there was a village "sauna man" who would make the preparations, and that the women would occupy the sauna from 4-7 in the evening. Then the men would take over and go as late as they wanted. After breakfast, I went for a walk around the village and decided to check out what the sauna looked like. Tarmo had told me it was located in the 200-year-old Baltic-German manor house that dominated the village, so I went to see if I could find it. I walked around the manor house a few times and peered through several of the windows, but for the life of me I couldn't figure out where the sauna was located and how it could even be incorporated into this old wooden building. The structure was a little worse for wear after being turned into offices for the *sovhoos*, but it still had much of its architectural grandeur. The morning light shining through the giant oak trees in the manor park made it easy to imagine what the place must have looked like a century ago.

I was jerked out of my reverie by a little old man who almost ran me over as he pushed a huge wheelbarrow towards the manor house. I quickly jumped out of the way and the old man passed me without a word, dwarfed by this huge wheelbarrow filled with what looked like giant fireplace logs—sections of tree trunk easily three or four times the size of anything we would consider stuffing into a wood burning stove. I deduced that this must be the sauna man.

I retreated across the street and watched intently as the man pushed the wheelbarrow up to the side of the manor house and opened a large iron door near the ground. He then proceeded to wrestle the logs out of the wheelbarrow one by one and toss them through door. Some kind of chute evidently lay behind the door because there was a moment of silence after he chucked in each log, followed by a horrendous boom as it hit bottom. He repeated this process until the cart was empty, and then rolled the wheelbarrow around the corner of the building out of sight. I crept a little closer to look down the chute, but had to jump out of the way when the little old man returned with another load of wood. By the time he chucked in his third load, I figured he had enough wood to heat the whole manor house for a week, not to mention a little sauna. Then he closed the iron door with a bang, pulled a ring of huge keys out of his pocket, and opened another door next to the chute. He disappeared inside and when I came up a little closer, I could see that he had gone down a flight of stairs into the inky blackness under the manor house.

I stood there looking down the stairs, when all of a sudden a series of loud bangs, grinding noises and clanging made me step back in alarm. I was starting to think that I should go down and make sure the poor man hadn't hurt himself when the noises ceased. My curiosity was piqued and I waited to see what would come next. I stood there for several minutes, but nothing happened. I was just about to go back to the apartment when I was distracted by a strange shadow that blocked out the sun in front of the manor house. I looked up and was startled to see a huge pall of black smoke billowing out of one of the four chimneys that poked through the steeply peaked roof. The smoke stopped briefly, but after some more banging and clanging from the cellar it started again. The manor house took on the look of an old steamboat gliding through the park as it continued to belch black clouds out of its stack.

The volume of smoke that was coming out amazed and even frightened me a little. It appeared as if the fires of hell had been kindled under the mansion. A few tendrils even escaped out of the side doorway as the old man came up the stairs, wiping his hands. He watched as I stared upwards, and shook his head. He then coughed a few times and disappeared around the corner before I could ask him any questions about what was in store for that evening. It felt good to have seen the "sauna man," but I was now even more curious about what the sauna looked like. I stayed for a few moments just to make sure the whole manor house wasn't on fire and then went back to our apartment building.

The day dragged on forever as I waited impatiently for my first Estonian sauna experience. When I saw Tarmo's wife getting ready to go with their young daughter, I knew the time would soon arrive. I sat with Tarmo, watching TV and nervously glancing at the clock. When seven o'clock came, I sprang from my seat, went to my bedroom and returned with a towel, some soap and shampoo. I stood impatiently by Tarmo's chair until he finally sighed and clicked off the television with the remote. He grabbed his toiletries and I eagerly followed him down the echoing concrete steps of our stairwell and across to the manor house. We stopped and grabbed a few Estonian beers from the village store and proceeded on. From different points of the village, men were slowly walking towards the sauna, reminding me of a Sunday at a country church. Even a few cars pulled up from other villages and men got out with their plastic soap containers and towels. To my surprise, the sauna customers didn't enter through the majestic front entrance but instead filed down the same stairs that the little old man had used. Beer bottles in one hand and my towel in the other, I followed Tarmo down into the darkness.

I couldn't really see anything at first in the dim light, but I was almost overcome by the smell of mildew, wet concrete and sweaty bodies. This obviously was not going to be one of these tile-floored squeaky-clean health club saunas! We had entered what I can only describe as a medieval dungeon, complete with chains hanging on the walls like in a torture chamber. Ionic stone pillars reached from the ceiling to the cracked concrete floor. Tarmo dropped a couple of coins in a can by the door then led me through a dark corridor into the brick-walled changing room, where I was relieved to see that at least one small bare bulb burned. The men were undressing and tossing their clothes on the few wooden benches to be found, or simply left them on the floor. I had never felt so weak and scrawny as the tanned and muscular former collective farm workers stripped down naked. These were real men— big, hairy, strong brutes who tilled the land and fixed the tractors. They laughed and yelled at each other as they started to undress.

Occasionally, one of them would nudge Tarmo and point at me. I supposed he explained who I was, but I couldn't understand much and only smiled and nodded my head in greeting.

I felt excited, as if I was about to become part of a long-standing fraternal tradition. I hesitantly undid the top few buttons of my shirt, feeling rather self-conscious next to the brawny men surrounding me. I am blond with fair, almost pink skin, and the years I spent as a bookkeeper didn't exactly turn me into a raging hardbody, so I felt quite out of place among these swarthy field hands and construction workers. I finished undressing and held my breath as the smell of stale sweat filled the room. These guys smelled bad enough when they were fully dressed, and the effect was only magnified when they removed their clothes. Our teachers in Tartu had told us the sauna was only once a week, but I hadn't realized that meant this was the only time these folks bathed.

Everyone filed out and into another room. Following Tarmo, I brought up the rear. We slipped across a mildewed, cracked tile floor, past a row of dripping, rusty showerheads, and came to a huge wooden door. One of the men dragged it open and I was almost bowled over by the wave of heat that came rolling out. Holding my head down in the cooler air, I followed the men into the sauna chamber. It was a room about twenty feet long and eight feet wide, with a three-tier wooden bench along the length of the back wall. Like the other room, it was lit by a single bulb, which hung over the door. I also saw what the "sauna man" had to deal with every week. On one end of the room was a gigantic iron cylinder resting on legs whose ends glowed a dull red. The enormous contraption resembled the boiler of a steam engine and radiated a tremendous amount of heat as the wood inside crackled and popped.

Tarmo pulled the sauna door shut and most of the men arranged themselves along the top bench. I also climbed up, but was forced back by the intense heat near the ceiling. I settled for the second row and hunched over to keep my head down as far as possible. There we were, all naked and sweaty together in the sauna. Everyone chanted nonchalantly amongst themselves, but as the heat began to build again in the closed room I started to feel like I was suffocating. I noticed a thermometer on the wall and when I looked closely I could see it measured 125 degrees Celsius. A quick math conversion to Fahrenheit told me that the sauna was nearly hot enough to cook meat! I withstood the heat as long as I could, but finally hopped down and slipped out the door. As I stood panting in the cooler shower room, I heard the men laugh and make comments to Tarmo. I scolded myself for giving up so easily. I was determined to show these Hiiumaa guys that I wasn't some wimp, so I took a few breaths of cool air and went back in the sauna. The men suddenly stopped talking and all turned to look at me. Trying to look nonchalant, I climbed up all the way up to the top row. I tried to appear unflustered as my ears began to burn off and each short breath sucked through the closed fist I held to my mouth seared my lungs.

The men continued to stare at me in silence until one of them reached for a bucket of water resting on the second bench. I watched as he took a ladle full of water and threw it on the glowing iron cylinder. The water disappeared almost immediately into a hissing cloud of steam and the men nearest the stove squinted and turned their heads away. Everyone else ducked down and watched to see what I would do. I was on the other end of the bench in what I felt was a safe zone, so at first I only held my hands over my ears and kept my head bent slightly down. I didn't feel anything, so after a few moments I stuck my head back up and grinned proudly. That was when the now-invisible cloud of steam finally made its way across the ceiling and hit me full force. It felt like somebody had just tossed a bucket of scalding water on my head. I cried out in pain and scrambled off the benches and out the door. As I stood under one of the showerheads and doused myself with cold water, I could hear the men laughing heartily in the sauna room. This was humiliating.

After a while, the rest of the men came out and went outside to have a few beers. I was hesitant to follow at first because they were standing out in the open without even so much as a towel. After a while, I came up out of the dark cellar and stood behind Tarmo as a couple of old women rode by on bicycles. I gradually became more at ease and took one of the beers offered to me. Camaraderie reigned as the men exchanged stories and drank beer, while steam rose from their bodies into the evening air. I tried to follow what they were saying, but most of the time the conversation was too fast for me. Whenever anyone would ask me a question, I would just smile and nod my head and everyone would laugh.

One particular word was liberally sprinkled throughout every sentence, and I had no problem picking it up. In Estonian, *kurat* is used roughly the same way that we use the word "damn." I had heard the word used before, but never so profusely. Even Tarmo got into the act and talked in a way I had never heard from him. As I strained to understand, I heard a sentence that, if translated into English, would have sounded something like this: "Damn, you know, I went to the damn store to get some damn eggs but damn, there weren't any so I asked the damn shopkeeper when the damn eggs were coming and damn if she didn't say she didn't have no damn idea! Damn!"

Our cursing, sweaty mob of naked men hung around a while longer and had some more beers. I practiced saying *kurat,* which earned quite a few laughs. I decided I liked sauna night, even if I was the first one out the door.

I noticed that one of the guys had nasty jagged-looking scars on his lower leg. When he noticed me staring, he came over and grabbed Tarmo to help in translation. He pointed emphatically at his leg and spoke to me in Estonian as one would speak to the village idiot.

"Me Mart," he said and thumped his chest with his finger.

"Hi, my name is Douglas. Nice to meet you," I answered, attempting to pick up the pace.

"Pig, pig!" he said and pointed at his leg.

"All right, pig." I wondered what that had to do with anything.

"No, no! Big pig!" Mart said in exasperation and looked to Tarmo for help.

"He means forest boar," Tarmo said with an air of authority, now that he was translator.

"Forest boar?" I repeated. "A boar did that? Here on the island?"

"Sure. There are many of them in the more remote parts of the forest."

This was news to me. "How big are they?"

"Oh, pretty big. They weigh two or three times as much as a man."

"And they attack people?" I asked, thinking about those late night bike rides I enjoyed.

"Well," Tarmo said and scratched his chin, "only rarely, and usually only when provoked."

I phrased my next question with caution. "How exactly do they define provoked?"

Mart could no longer stand being left out of the conversation. He pushed Tarmo aside and stepped in front of me, demanding my attention. Tired of the language barrier, he decided to try pantomime, much to the amusement of the others in the group. He began walking in place, pretending to hold a gun and look around. The guy seemed pretty intent on sharing his story, so I decided to play along.

"Okay, you were out hunting."

Mart put the pretended gun to his shoulder and made gunshot sounds.

"You took a shot at the boar."

Mart threw up his arms, ran a few steps and then looked back and grabbed his leg.

"Ah. The boar attacked you and hurt your leg."

Mart made some slashing motions with his make-believe gun and then looked to the left.

This bit of charade took a little longer. "Uh, you hit the boar with your gun and it ran off."

Mart nodded vigorously, and made several rapid, hobbling steps.

"Then you ran home."

Mart shook his head emphatically and repeated his hobbling steps, pointing to the left.

I wasn't sure if I had understood correctly. "You went after the boar?" I said in disbelief.

Mart nodded again, made a few more steps, then dove to the ground and rolled around.

"Oh my God. You caught up with the wounded boar and tackled it?"

Mart made wide slashing arcs with one arm, then stood and looked around proudly.

"You wrestled the boar down and killed it with your knife?"

Mart nodded again and I made a mental note never to make this man angry.

When the beers were gone, we filed back into the sauna room and took our places on the benches. Pretty soon, everyone was looking at me expectantly and the same guy who had thrown the water before reached slowly for the ladle. This time I steeled my-self against the onslaught of superheated steam I knew was com-ing. When the scalding blast hit me, I lasted maybe five seconds more than the last time and then fled the room, much to the delight of the rest of the group. I only stayed out for a short breather before lowering my head and going back in.

The men were waiting for me and snickered as I crawled back up to the top bench. Now they wanted to play another game with the hapless foreigner. The same guy reached for a second bucket, which I noticed contained a bundle of leafy birch branches. He pulled the branches out, shook the excess water out over the hot metal and, with a menacing look on his face, slid down the bench toward me with the bundle held high. I retreated back into the corner and looked to Tarmo for help, but none was coming as the man pressed in closer. I cringed as he held the branches out to me and shook them, motioning for me to take the leafy bundle, but I just looked at him wide-eyed and shook my head. The guy then slapped the branches on his arms a few times and then pushed them towards me again. Seeing that there was no way out, I took the offered birch branches and half-heartedly whacked my legs a few times. This evidently wasn't good enough for my tormenter, who grabbed back the bundle and, while I cowered with my hands over my head and protested loudly, proceeded to give me a thorough thrashing from the back of my neck down to the soles of my feet. Birch leaves and superheated water droplets flew everywhere as the rest of the group ducked for cover and laughed uproariously.

Suddenly the beating stopped and the men fell silent when we heard the outer door to the shower room open. The group gave worried looks to each other and listened carefully as somebody entered the shower room and stood outside the door, muttering and growling. The men talked in hushed tones amongst themselves, and I asked Tarmo what was going on. "It's Sauna Ants," he whispered, "the guy who comes in from the forest only once a month to shop and take sauna." We sat in silence as Ants banged a few buckets around and turned on the water in the shower room. We heard him crank the faucet shut and head for the sauna door, which flung open abruptly. The entryway was completely filled with a huge red-haired beast of a man standing at least six-foot-five. The barrel-chested behemoth sported a scraggly beard and carried a full bucket of water in one hand and a massive, thorny juniper branch in the other. As he mounted the first bench, the guys on the top row immediately made room and we all hastily fled the sauna, leaving Ants alone with his bucket of water.

I stayed behind in the shower room just to see what would happen. I heard Ants muttering, then the sound of a huge splash and the hiss of steam as he threw the entire bucket onto the red-hot metal. He let out an earth-shattering bellow and pounded on the benches. Next I heard a series of whacking sounds and yelling as steam leaked around the frame of the door. I couldn't blame the others for not sticking around to witness such a spectacle.

Although I continued to attend the village sauna, every week I was the first one to bail out when the water was thrown. I came to realize that extreme heat didn't necessarily make your heart explode, and I came to find it somewhat invigorating to beat myself with birch branches (I later found out they had to be picked on the night of the full moon) before showering off in ice-cold water. When winter came, I followed the men outside and even tried their practice of rolling naked in the snow, but I drew the line at entering the hole some of the guys had cut through the ice covering the manor house pond. They seemed so obsessed in having me experience every facet of the village sauna culture that I felt fortunate they didn't try to drag me to the pond and throw me in.

I kept up my sauna "training" and gradually built up a tolerance to the pain of being parboiled alive. It got to the point where this one fat sheepherder in our group would bail out of the sauna only a few minutes after I did. I made it my goal—no, my *obsession*—to eventually not be the first guy to cut and run. Every week the gap grew shorter between the time I fled and the time the fat guy was forced to come out. I could see that he was getting worried because it would bring unspeakable shame on him, and probably his whole family, to be outlasted in the sauna by a mere American. Even so, I relentlessly kept up the pressure until one week I was sure I was going to be victorious. I felt that this Saturday, I would prove I had the mettle to last in the sauna longer than at least one of the Hiiumaa regulars. Unfortunately, Mother Nature chose that same time to display her notorious cruelty and snatch the moment of triumph from my grasp. That fateful week, a brutal cold snap swept over the island and temperatures dipped way below zero. Somebody left a window open in the manor house cellar and the harsh cold air got into the shower room and froze the pipes so hard they burst. With the state collective farm defunct, there was no one to organize and pay for repairs, so the era of the Putkaste Village sauna had come to an end.

Years later, Tarmo told me that the men got together and did some repairs to put the medieval torture chamber/sauna back in operation–meaning there's still the possibility for me to one-up my fat sheepherder friend.

10—THE GREAT SHEEP RIOT

As I mentioned earlier, I was initially brought to Estonia by the Peace Corps and sent to Hiiumaa Island as an Agricultural Advisor, regardless of the fact that I had never lived on a farm or studied agriculture. My chief qualification for this position seemed to be that I was from Nebraska, albeit the largest city in Nebraska, and that I could explain the difference between hay and straw, which really seemed to impress the recruiter in Kansas City.

Absurd as the situation was, I figured that if I was supposed to help farmers, I should know what farmers do. After the initial disastrous meeting with the farmers union, I decided to spend every Wednesday working on a family farm, learning the basics. I found a farmer named Karl who was friends with Tarmo and asked if I could come and help out. After a lot of questions and skeptical looks, Farmer Karl finally threw me a pair of dirty overalls and told me to report to work the next week. Soon enough, I found myself enjoying some genuine manual labor—real romantic, back-to-nature stuff. I cleaned the barn, fed the pigs and shoveled cow manure, much to the delight of my young farmer friend, who by now had warmed up to the whole idea. He even boasted to his farmer buddies about having the only American migrant worker in Estonia—and a college grad at that!

One Wednesday, I rode my bike to the farm as usual and found the farmer out in the tractor shed. Imagine my delight when he informed me that today was the day to round up the sheep, a particularly surprising announcement considering I had yet to see any sheep on his farm. Fall was in full swing, and with winter approaching it was time to bring them into the barn with the rest of the animals. Sheep roundup! Visions of horses and ropes and

other manly stuff flashed through my head. Now was my chance
to show what Peace Corps Volunteers were made of!

Events took a strange turn when Karl's wife came out, gave me
a pair of high rubber boots and motioned for me to put them on.
They seemed a little inappropriate for the job at hand, but I became even more puzzled when Karl asked me to help him load his
rowboat, a small outboard motor and some nets onto the back of
the tractor. A quick check of my Estonian language skills showed
that he had indeed said "sheep." I wanted to pursue the matter
further, but after being in so many confusing situations already, I
had learned to just sit back and go with the flow.

As Karl fired up the old blue Belarus tractor, I jumped up on
one side and his dog jumped on the other. With a grinding sound
and a sharp jerk, we were off in a cloud of smoke, headed out of the
farmyard. Instead of heading for the pastures, we went across the
road and through the forest towards the sea. It was a chilly, cloudy
day and a wind laced with mist blew off the water. I buttoned the
top button of my jacket and held on tightly to the bouncing vehicle.

We stopped at the shoreline and Karl hopped down and motioned for me to help him with the boat and motor. The dog was
jumping around and barking wildly, as he usually did when a trip
was imminent. I could no longer contain myself. As we lowered
the small boat to the ground I cleared my throat and started in
with my halting Estonian.

"Uh, what exactly are we doing?"

Karl stopped and rubbed his scruffy beard. "We get the sheep
today, I told you."

I tried to phrase my questions carefully. In these situations, I
already knew that I must have seemed a little ignorant.
"But...um...why do we need the boat?"

"For the sheep. How else will we carry them?"

"And the nets?"

"You'll see."

"Oh sure. Uh, just one last question. Where *are* the sheep?"

It finally dawned on Karl that I had not the slightest idea what the hell was going on. A strange smile came over his face. It was one of the few times he had ever smiled and this smile was unique, full of anticipation, something I had rarely seen from these stoic islanders. Karl straightened up, turned, and pointed dramatically seaward. I looked out to sea and, eyes squinted against the wind-blown mist, I could just make out the low silhouette of a small island about a mile off shore. "Out there," he said, and waited for my reaction.

I was silent for a moment, then slowly nodded my head. Inside my mind was racing. I had heard about this: the farmers take the sheep out to the islands in spring to eat the grass and bring them back in the fall. The surrounding sea keeps the sheep in and predators out. In theory, it seemed like a great idea, but now that it was November and it looked like a storm was rolling in, the thought that I was actually about to take part in this practice seemed absurd. We were going to sea in a twelve-foot rowboat with a dog and a bunch of nets. This was definitely not in my Peace Corps training manual and certainly way beyond what I had expected to do while learning the farming trade.

I almost called it quits right there, but something stopped me. Up until that point, the Estonians had been treating me like a wimp—lifting heavy things for me, asking me all the time if I could eat this or that, worrying about my health. I had to prove that we Americans could handle tough assignments. I wanted to show that I wasn't just some soft city boy. If Farmer Karl wanted to get his sheep, then I was going to help him get the *kurat* sheep! So with a nonchalant shrug, conscious that Karl was watching me closely, I stooped down and grabbed my side of the boat. The dog jumped in for the ride as we dragged the small craft down across the gravel into the water.

I climbed into the front of the boat as the farmer pushed us out a little before hopping in. Karl hooked up the gas can to the beat-up Russian outboard, wrapped some rope around the flywheel, and gave it a pull. The motor didn't even think about starting, so he tried again. Nothing. By this time, we had drifted back against the rocky shore and I grabbed an oar to push us out against the stiffening wind. A third try brought a cough and some sparks flying out of the exhaust. After more tinkering, muttering and swearing, the motor finally burst to life in a cloud of blue smoke. We turned and accelerated out to sea and I sat in the front with the dog, leaning into the wind. What an adventure! What a story to tell my friends! This was the making of a real Peace Corps moment.

Reality abruptly returned, heralded by a blast of cold seawater in the face, as we hit the first of the waves offshore. I cursed and turned my back to the wind as the cold seawater dripped off my nose and ran down into my collar. I glanced back at Karl, who just shrugged and motioned for me to move to the center of the boat. I sat facing astern and cringing as wave after wave burst against the bow and sent spray like handfuls of wet sand against my back. My legs started to get wet as I hunched miserably against the assault. I noticed the light had started to fade even though it was early afternoon. A storm was moving in. Oblivious to my discomfort, the dog stayed in the front with his tongue hanging out, snapping at the spray and obviously enjoying the whole affair. We rode in silence for nearly half an hour with only the buzzing sound of the little outboard motor and the whap-whap-whap of the bow bouncing on the waves.

By the time we arrived at the island, I was already thoroughly soaked and shivering, but I wasn't about to let on that I felt any discomfort. As we approached the shore, I jumped out to pull the boat up. With the dog happily romping around us, we unloaded the nets. I looked over at Karl, who was intently surveying the round islet, which was probably only a few hundred yards in diameter. There were no sheep to be seen.

"What do we do now?"

Karl motioned with his hand towards the large clusters of reeds, which in places were taller than me. "We start walking through the grass and reeds. When we flush the sheep, we chase them until they get tired. Then we corner them and take them back."

Before I could ask any more questions, he threw a bunch of netting over his shoulder and headed off at a brisk pace. I followed in my squishy wet boots, happy that at least I could stretch out my legs that had become stiff and cramped during the long boat ride. As I walked, pushing the tall reeds out of my face, I was reminded of pheasant hunting back home in Nebraska. We would be out around this time of year, tromping through the fields, making as much noise as possible and waiting for the whir of wings. The only difference was that in my current situation, I would be waiting for the thundering of sheep hooves.

My reverie was interrupted and I jumped about a foot in the air as the sheep finally broke from cover. I counted about ten of them as they sped away across the island, muddy balls of gray wool on little black spindly legs. I could see terror in their eyes as they looked over their shoulders as they fled. "C'mon!" Karl yelled as he headed after them on the run. I tried to keep up with him, but my big floppy boots and soggy wet clothing made it a lost cause. He kept looking back over his shoulder and motioning for me to catch up. As we chased the sheep futilely around the island, I started sucking wind. Between gasps, I realized there were two serious flaws in the farmer's strategy: 1. It was very likely that we would be worn out before the sheep. 2. Cornering sheep on a round island sounded like one of those tacky Polish jokes we used to tell in junior high.

Farmer Karl kept encouraging me. "Come on, Douglas!" he called back to me repeatedly. "They are almost worn out!" I didn't want to let on that I was the one who was worn out, so I stumbled after him through the tall wet grass for another lap around the island. The dog had long since disappeared, happily chasing after seabirds on the shore. Finally, the sheep stopped. Backs to the sea and panting hard, they stood their ground. As I stumbled up beside Karl, the sheep stared at us, wide-eyed in fear, but with a certain taunting look that seemed to say, "Okay, smart guys. What now?" The farmer dropped his nets, put his hand on my shoulder, and spoke to me in conspiratorial tones. "You see the big one?

That's Yeltsin, he's the leader. We take him out and the others will be easy to catch!" I sized up Yeltsin the sheep. I couldn't tell if he was actually bigger than the rest, or if he was just muddier and had more things stuck in his wool, making him resemble a medieval Scottish chieftain. Yeltsin kept a steady gaze on his would-be captors, steam rising from his coat as he panted and waited for us to make the next move.

Karl motioned for me to pick up one end of the net. "Okay, easy now," he whispered to me, as if the sheep might listen in on our plans. "We stretch out the net, then back them up to the water's edge. When we get close enough, we throw the net over them!" Seemed like a reasonable plan, something straight out of *Wild Kingdom* as we prepared to take on the untamed sheep of Hiiumaa Island.

However, the sheep had their own agenda. As we crept up towards them, spreading out the net as we went, Yeltsin suddenly reared his head and led his flock on a headlong dash into the sea. The flock splashed out into the water about twenty yards until the water was up to their bellies. Then they turned and faced us with a defiant "All right, your move" look on their black faces.

"Game over," I said in English, more to myself than to Karl. "I ain't going into the water after them. No way, no how." By this time, the temperature had dropped down to just above freezing and the wind had increased even more. The farmer stood for a while, thoughtfully scratching his beard before calling a huddle. With our backs to the sheep, he laid out the plans by drawing with a finger on his palm. This time it was going to be an amphibious assault. I would keep their attention while he went back and got into the boat. He would come quietly around behind them and approach from the sea. When he got close enough, he would grab the trapped sheep one by one and throw them into the boat, hopefully Yeltsin first. He gave me a slap on the back and headed across the little island towards the boat.

I turned and looked at the sheep, who were now shivering and shifting uncomfortably from hoof to hoof in the cold water. I was feeling pretty good. So far I had held up my end of the job and I was finally going to prove to the farmer that I wasn't some pansy from America. "All right, sheep," I taunted, "end of the line! It's all over but the cryin'. You're going *down!*" I emphasized this by shaking my finger towards the ground and doing a little victory dance. The absurdity of the situation—an American standing on a lonely Baltic islet, taunting Estonian sheep in English—didn't really hit me until later.

I faced Yeltsin and his band for what seemed like an hour until I finally noticed Karl rowing out from behind some reeds on the left. I waved at him, but he scowled and motioned for me to look straight ahead. I guess he was afraid I would give him away.

He moved silently out to sea, then turned and came in behind the sheep. He drew closer as I paced back and forth on the shore, trying to draw the sheep's attention. He finally got near enough to the one sheep farthest from the shore (not Yeltsin) and lunged at it, burying his hands in the wet wool and pulling the sheep into the boat on top of himself. This was no small feat as sheep are quite heavy, and a water-soaked sheep would weigh much more since their wool acts like a giant sponge. All I saw for the next few minutes was flailing arms and legs, spraying water, and flying wool. A hand holding a length of twine appeared briefly above the gunwale, and then disappeared. The sheep bleated a few more times and then all went silent. I stared, the rest of the sheep stared, and we all waited as the seemingly empty boat rocked gently back and forth on the waves.

After a few moments, Karl stood up, triumphantly raising the four legs of the sheep bound together by twine. One sheep was bagged, hog-tied and lying upside-down in the bottom of the boat with his feet in the air. The farmer raised an oar and began to pole in toward the rest of Yeltsin's flock. The element of surprise was now lost, however, and the sheep looked anxiously at the boat, then back at me, then back at the boat. They did this a few times, but I noticed Yeltsin had stopped looking at the boat and was focusing only on me. Now I don't want to go overboard with giving human attributes to animals, but I swear I could see what he was thinking: "We can take this guy."

Suddenly, on some signal indiscernible to me, the sheep burst from the deeper water and began running through the shallows toward the shore. Facing nine wet sheep, and knowing I was the only thing standing between going home or doing several more laps around the island, I made a stand. I lowered my head with grim determination and faked back and forth like a good Cornhusker football player. They kept coming. I yelled and waved my arms. They still kept coming. Remembering what the farmer said about getting the leader, I concentrated on Yeltsin as the wet mass of panic-stricken mutton hit the beach. I planted myself squarely in front of him, went down to a three-point stance and looked as threatening as I could. It was man against sheep, one on one.

Yeltsin didn't stop. I don't think the idea of stopping ever crossed his mind. He didn't even slow down. He put what seemed like a hundred pounds of wet wool straight into my chest and sent me flying backward. I landed on my back with a thud and looked up at the clouds with a strange sense of peace. That all ended pretty quickly as a hoof was planted in my crotch, mud sprayed in my mouth and a wet smelly woolen belly dragged up my chest and across my face. As Yeltsin finished humiliating me and tried to continue on his way, I at least had the presence of mind to grab a back leg. As the rest of the flock thundered by, I held on for dear life and screamed obscenities at the top of my lungs. "You goddamn sheep! I got you now, you S.O.B.! You ain't gettin' away, you're *mine*!" Yeltsin responded by dragging me on my back a few yards, while kicking me repeatedly in the head with his free hind leg. After submitting to this abuse for a while, I finally managed to roll over and grab his other back leg. By grabbing handfuls of wool, I worked my way up his back until I was able to get an arm around his neck. When I locked my legs around the thrashing sheep's belly, he finally stopped struggling. It was over and I had Yeltsin. I couldn't resist rubbing it in, so I put my face close to his and told him in a low even voice what I thought about him and his kind.

"How do you like them apples, you mangy lamb chop! That'll teach you to mess with me."

I looked proudly toward the boat, expecting a thumbs-up from Karl, but I think the poor guy was in shock. He just stared, mouth open, at the spectacle before him. The flock had vanished into the reeds. An American, the first one he had ever met, had just been assaulted by his prize sheep. They had fought it out on the gravelly beach with the American screaming unintelligibly at the top of his lungs, and now they were locked together in a death grip, the American muttering something into the sheep's ear.

Karl snapped out of his shock and brought the boat to shore, extricating the sheep from my grasp leg by leg and binding him with twine. We carried the now helpless Yeltsin to the boat and chucked him in with his comrade. Two down, eight to go. The farmer again scratched his beard and took stock of the situation, looking first at the small island, then back at the distant Hiiumaa shore. A storm was definitely imminent and the light was fading fast. In the end, he just looked at me, shrugged, and started walking after the remaining sheep. We both were muddy, wet and cold, but there was nothing to do but head back into the tall grass after more of the leaderless flock. We captured two sheep over the next hour through a combination of strength, guile, and a little help from the dog, who had finally reappeared. As darkness closed in, we loaded up the boat with our hog-tied victims and pushed off into the windblown sea. With the farmer, the dog, four sheep, and me, the sides of the boat were only a few inches above the waterline. I wanted to say something, but kept my mouth shut this time.

The motor started fairly easily and we headed back towards the shore. We cruised for only about ten minutes before I was once again drenched to the bone. This time, I had no place to retreat to as the sheep were occupying the center of the boat. As each wave struck the bow, the wind brought the spray up against me. To make things worse, the storm that had been threatening us all afternoon finally let down on us. I hunched down and gritted my teeth to keep them from chattering, then closed my eyes and listened to the buzzing of the motor. At least we were headed home and could look forward to a nice warm fire and some cognac.

Without even a warning sputter, the motor stopped. Immediately the boat started pitching in the waves and the wind, now parallel to the shore, started taking us off course. The sheep began to struggle in the bottom of the boat, which didn't help matters. I knew the temperature was dropping, but I wasn't prepared for what I saw when I looked back towards the motor. Karl was hunched over blowing into the carburetor that was covered in ice. The carb had actually frozen up and now we were drifting with water coming over the sides. Through the rain and darkness, I saw that we were headed towards some big boulders in the sea and I began to wonder if we were to become shipwrecked, if I would be the first Peace Corps Volunteer to be lost at sea.

I heard the motor sputter to life and soon we were back on course. But after only a few minutes it died again. Our situation grew bleaker still. Karl pulled and pulled, but the motor just wouldn't fire. He blew into the carb and tried to warm it with his hands. Nothing. We were getting blown closer and closer to the rocks and the white surf. Numb from the cold, I just sat there helplessly watching as we drifted towards disaster. I started wondering if there would be a memorial stone placed on the shore. Would my story become part of a Peace Corps training session about what *not* to do at your post? When I thought our situation couldn't get any worse, it happened. I don't know whether to call it a mutiny, an uprising or a full-blown sheep riot, but all at once, like some scene out of *Animal Farm*, the sheep started breaking lose and bouncing around in our cramped fishing boat.

I want to say here that sheep are really stupid. I'm not just talking a little slow in the gray matter. I mean stupid in the sense that they could make a doorknob seem intelligent. I couldn't understand where they thought they were going when we were all stuck in a twelve-foot boat at sea. As they thrashed about and jumped from side to side, water started coming into the boat in such amounts that we were in danger of sinking.

I looked helplessly at Karl back by the motor. "Hold 'em down!" he yelled. "We're going to go under!"

Hold 'em down? This seemed about as practical a task as gift wrapping a flaming log. My mind was racing as I looked at the seething mass of wool that was just a few moments ago a group of docile, hog-tied farm animals. Not knowing what else to do, I stood up, spread my arms and legs apart and swan-dived into the melee. With my legs over two of them, I held the other two under my arms as close as I could—close enough that I was breathing their wheezing, stinking, sheep's breath and was almost overcome by the smell of wet wool, coated in manure. We were eye to eye and I told them what I thought were probably going to be my last words: "You worthless sheep, you stupid, pathetic sheep!"

As darkness closed in and Karl pulled furiously on the starter rope, we continued to drift towards the wave-swept rocks, which were now only a few yards from us. In this situation, I suppose most people would have their life flash before their eyes. All I could do was curse myself for being such an idiot. Just a few months ago, I was in a nice warm office in Omaha. In only a few days, my former co-workers would receive word that I had drowned off the coast of Estonia in a dinghy with a farmer, a dog and four sheep. I wouldn't blame them if upon hearing the news they didn't know whether to laugh or cry. Had I known that the water we were in wasn't even waist-deep, I could have foregone the melodramatics and simply laughed at yet another ludicrous situation I had put myself in.

Just when I had made peace with my maker, by some miracle the motor gave a cough and kicked in. Karl gave it the gas and we steered away, gaining precious distance from the rocks. We had dodged a bullet and I said a silent prayer of thanks as I lay spread-eagled over the mutinous sheep. But we weren't out of the woods yet. The problem now was that it was totally dark, the wind and rain were lashing us, the boat was half full of water, and I had no idea where the shore was. One wrong turn, I thought, and our next stop would be Sweden. Fortunately the farmer's wife had realized something was amiss when we didn't return before dark. She didn't panic or call the border guards, but instead calmly asked her daughter to bring her an oil lantern, which she brought down to the shore and hung on the tractor parked there. Back at sea, it was that glow that Karl saw and aimed for.

When we hit the shore I wanted to jump out and kiss the ground, but Karl ordered me to stay in the boat as he pried the sheep one by one from my grasp and loaded them on the trailer behind the tractor. It was only then that I could step onto land and breathe a sigh of relief. After my harrowing experience, I thought we might hug each other or cry or something. I thought maybe I'd at least get an encouraging slap on the back, but Karl didn't say a word. He didn't even look at me as he calmly climbed on board the tractor and fired it up. I only just managed to hop up on the running board as he took off.

Back at the farm, there was no welcoming committee, no anxious group of relatives gathered around—only the farmer's wife, who poured me some warm milk before placing a shot of vodka on the table. When she asked matter-of-factly how it went and what took so long, the farmer just shrugged. I did the shot and stood up to take my leave. The next day was a workday in town and I had a six-mile bike ride ahead of me yet that night. The farmer walked me to the door, shook my hand and said, "See you next week."

I hopped on my bike and rode out of the farmyard, shaking my head. These Estonians, I thought, what an emotionally impaired bunch. Nothing gets them riled up. Then, as I turned on to the dirt road through the forest, I heard a sound and stopped. I listened closely. It seemed to be coming from the farmhouse. It went away for a moment, but then I heard it again—high, clear and this time unmistakable: wild peals of laughter.

11—THE BAND

Whenever I felt lonely or homesick, I would take out the twelve-string acoustic guitar I had brought with me to the island. Playing it reminded me of the good ol' days back in Nebraska when I performed in bars and at parties with various bands, playing drums or keyboard. I never performed in public as a guitar player, though. It was just something I played around with when I was writing songs for whatever band I was in, or when I wanted to quickly duplicate something I had heard on the radio. My first musical stint was back in high school as a drummer in a Top 40 band. In college, I got into hard rock, as well as the partying lifestyle that went along with it. In both of the bands, I also sang backup vocals and even did lead on a song or two. I always thought that our college band, Hard Left, would eventually hit it big, but despite our best efforts, we all ended up graduating from the University of Nebraska without so much as a produced single. The band broke up and we drifted apart to start the nine-to-five jobs we had always scoffed at. A few years later, I hooked up with a country-rock band and played keyboards with them until I joined the Peace Corps. Altogether, I played in different groups for about ten years, writing songs and searching for the big break that never came.

My decision to bring a guitar over any other instrument was purely practical: bringing a piano or a drum set was out of the question as we were allowed only two suitcases and one carry-on bag totaling 100 pounds for the entire two-year trip. In addition, the Peace Corps literature regarding packing specifically stated that bikes, skis and guitars were not permitted. So, with a heavy heart, I sold my old twelve-string acoustic guitar before I left for three days of "staging" in Washington, D.C. At the hotel, the logistics person there instructed us to put our suitcases in one pile and "anything else, like a guitar" in another. My ears perked up, and on further investigation I discovered that we were indeed allowed to bring musical instruments of a reasonable size. Music had always been very important to me and I had read that it was also very important to Estonians, so on my last night in the States, I slipped out in search of a music store. I found a place that was open late and hastily picked out a decent used twelve-string, right before the shop closed. The next day we took off for the Baltics with my new baby stowed safely in the cargo hold.

I had no plans to do any performing in the Baltics and so mainly used my new instrument to write songs and to play a few three-chord '60s folk tunes. The guitar was more of a security blanket than anything else, a piece of my "former life" that brought comfort even though it was also a sad reminder of my failed dream. I wrote one song during training in Riga as a sort of theme for our group called "Hundred Pounds of Home", in reference to our limited allotment of baggage. I played it dozens of times for the Peace Corps staff and the other volunteers, but when we split up and went to our posts, the song was unofficially retired. In Estonia, I played only at home. That's probably all I would have ever done if it hadn't been for a little bit of Christmas Spirit.

I arrived in Hiiumaa during October, and before I knew it the Christmas season was upon us. Compared to holiday time in America, it was pretty hard to tell that it was the holiday season at all. The signs of the season with which I was familiar were nowhere to be seen: no Christmas lights, flashy store displays or annoying commercials. In some ways, it was refreshing not to have all the commercialism, but on the other hand, it was a little weird. You couldn't even buy a string of Christmas lights anywhere, not for any price. If it weren't for the occasional song on the radio, you wouldn't even have known the holiday was on the way.

For me, Christmas had always been the high point of my year, the season to watch as many versions of *A Christmas Carol* as possible and light advent candles every Sunday while reading parts of the story of Jesus' birth. I would spend hours driving around Omaha with my friends, looking at Christmas lights and searching out the best-decorated houses. I loved Christmas with all my heart and I just couldn't figure out why Estonians seemed so casual about it. So when I asked a few people why this was, I was shocked to hear the answer: people weren't used to celebrating the holiday season because up until just a year before I arrived Christmas had officially been illegal.

Despite my knowledge of history and the Soviets' intolerance of religion, I found this injustice difficult to believe. Even Ebenezer Scrooge grudgingly gave his employee the day off, but during the Soviet Union's domination of Estonia, December 25 had been a regular workday. The Communist government made it illegal to have parties at work or even to put up Christmas decorations in your own home. Christmas trees were absolutely out of the question if you wanted to keep your job and your freedom, although some brave souls kept small trees hidden behind tightly closed curtains. The churches were allowed to have subdued services on Christmas Eve, but the government invariably monitored these, causing even the most devout to steer clear. Back then, Christians were considered by the Soviets to be crazy cultists who at the minimum had to be closely watched as they were susceptible to "outside influences"; in extreme cases, they were considered a threat to the government. Now all that had changed, at least officially. But with no traditions, no memories of Christmases gone by (except for the few citizens who had lived in a very different, pre-war Estonia), the Estonian people held a kind of uncertainty about the holiday. In short, people just weren't sure what to make of Christmas.

For my part, I was simply flabbergasted at the idea that a real-life Grinch situation had existed up until a year before. My anger was offset only by my happiness and relief that the Soviet system had finally collapsed. I felt a strong urge to do something, to help welcome Christmas back to Estonia in some way, but I couldn't figure out what I could do. Then one evening, as I played some old

Christmas carols and lit one of my own little advent candles, it came to me: I would put on a Christmas program.

Tarmo helped with a few contacts and with no trouble at all, the performance was arranged. I wasn't sure if anyone would even show up but on that night, people came from all over the village to pack the small hall in the majestic old manor house. As I played some classic Christmas carols, to my surprise people began to sing along in Estonian. Then it occurred to me that Estonia was actually much closer to the birthplace of these long-standing European melodies than my home state of Nebraska. I will always remember the candlelit room with the parquet floor, the snow falling outside the huge windows and the beautiful sound of Estonian voices softly singing.

When we finished with the Christmas carols, I opened an Estonian bible and, in the native language of the audience, read the famous verses from the book of Luke. To be honest, I couldn't understand everything I was reading but I knew the story well enough that it didn't matter. My voice rose and fell as I talked about the journey of Mary and Joseph, the coming of the baby Jesus, and how the angels appeared before the shepherds in the fields. Some people glanced around nervously, obviously uncomfortable about what was taking place, but most watched with rapt attention, smiling slightly as I wrapped my tongue around some of the more difficult Estonian words. When I was finished, there was no applause, no outburst of emotion, just a comforting silence. The group stood up and quietly filed out into the snow. A few came by to stop and pat me on the back. "That was nice," they whispered, and I knew that in the reserved, understated vernacular of the island folk that the evening had been a success.

Christmas came and went without much ado, but word about the concert spread. A few weeks later, a young man named Andres from a nearby village approached me and asked if I wanted to practice with his rock band, which he explained played a mixture of pop and traditional songs. At first I wasn't sure how much of a contribution my joining would make. After all, they had a keyboard player and a drummer already and had been together for ten years. They had their own repertoire, in their own language, and I was simply a novice guitar player and backup singer. But Andres persisted, and I finally agreed to show up for a practice.

I walked through the snowy village streets to a building that used to be a repair and transport facility for the local Friendship Collective Farm. The band's name, HEPT, was an acronym that came from the official title of this facility, *Hiiumaa Eesti Põllumajandus Tehnikum,* the Estonian Agricultural Technological College in Hiiumaa.

I opened the creaking wooden door which, as was usually the case in government buildings, slammed behind me as I entered. I went up the stairs and down a hall, following the sound of drums and scattered guitar riffs. I thought the facility was a rather odd setting for a rock band until I opened the doors to the practice room. It was as if I had stepped back in time. Half-filled ashtrays sat scattered about on top of the amps and beer bottles lay behind the drum set while five guys crowded around a small tape recorder trying to reproduce the riffs from the latest radio hit. It reminded me of countless practices back home. The guys in the band looked to be between thirty and forty and fairly clean-cut. Andres had told me earlier that most of them were married and some, including Andres, had kids at home. But even though their heyday seemed to be over, they still wanted to rock, so they met once or twice a week to practice for the gigs they continued to book in abundance, mostly private summer parties and various holiday celebrations. There were only one or two other bands on the island so though the market was small they had as much work as they wanted.

Everybody looked up and smiled when I came in. We shook hands, but there were no awkward introductions, no long explanations about the band's history, their philosophy or what they wanted to accomplish. I just pulled out my guitar, sat down next to a microphone and started following along. I couldn't communicate with them very well, but it really didn't matter. We just clicked.

The old cliché about music being the universal language proved true. I was happy to find they did mostly Estonian versions of the same Top 40 songs Americans enjoyed, plus some oldies that were easy to pick up. The Estonian folk songs were pretty easy to follow and fun to play. Before I knew it, we had practiced four hours and I had learned a couple sets of their music. As we broke down the equipment, nobody said much of anything, not even to have a discussion about whether or not I had been officially accepted. It was just understood.

I practiced with HEPT over the next few months. When they had gigs, mostly small parties, I stood at the back of the stage and played along. I really enjoyed it, but it was a little awkward after-wards when we were paid and the guys in the band (plus the female singer that sometimes accompanied us) wanted to divide the money. Of course, they wanted to give me a share, but I couldn't accept. They thought I was just being polite and it took me a long time to make them understand why I didn't want the money. As a Peace Corps Volunteer, I wasn't allowed to accept money for any activity, the logic being that since U.S. taxpayers were paying for us to be there, we shouldn't profit from our situation. I really don't think they understood completely, but they eventually relented and took me to a restaurant for a pleasant meal and many drinks. This became a tradition for future gigs.

I enjoyed the small gatherings we played during the colder months, but I was really looking forward to playing some summer gigs during tourist season. I had heard that around Midsummer Night's Eve, the season of "White Nights" when the sun never fully set even at night, hundreds of people would come for endless partying. Anticipating this, I wrote a couple of songs and played them for the group at the next practice. I had written one called "The Hiiumaa Blues" and another half-Estonian, half-English song about how I had gotten the brush-off when trying to impress a local girl with my fractured Estonian. I called the latter "*Kas Sa Räägid Inglise Keelt?*" ("Do You Speak English?"), which my fellow band mates enjoyed and picked up very quickly. Throughout the summer we played it several times to rave reviews. It became so popular that Andres got the idea to record it, along with some of our other more popular tunes.

One summer day, we dragged our equipment over to an abandoned building, formerly the collective farm headquarters. It was definitely a low-tech operation, but we did the best we could to create a makeshift recording studio. We put the mixing board in what had been the director's office, the lead guitarist in a broom closet, and the drums where the secretary used to sit. I think we did lead vocals in the bathroom but I don't remember exactly. We had cables running everywhere and, with the help of the mixer board and some mysterious homemade black boxes, we managed to do a simple two-track recording: instruments first and then the vocals. We recorded the entire tape of six songs over about ten hours, with lots of food, beer and cigarettes to keep us going. For my part, I put down an entire bottle of the dreaded "Vana Tallinn" liqueur, mainly because no one else in the band would touch the stuff. Finally, around midnight, we had the finished product and everyone took a copy home.

I expected the typical basement tape sound, but the quality was actually rather good. I had kept the master tape so I made copies for my friends and family. One of the guys in the band gave a copy to the engineer at Hiiumaa's ten-watt radio station and they started playing it on occasion. The tape became pretty popular on Hiiumaa Radio, especially the song that I wrote about being shot down by the local girl. The newness eventually wore off and the tape was relegated to the radio station's archives.

A month or so later, I was standing in line at the grocery store, half-listening to the Estonian National Radio news coming over the store's intercom. When the broadcast ended, I heard the disk jockey announce the next song: "Now, here's a song by an American named Douglas Wells, playing with a band from Hiiumaa."

I about dropped all my groceries when the strains of *"Kas Sa Räägid Inglise Keelt?"* came over the speaker. How had Estonian National Radio gotten a copy of the tape? I looked around and saw that several people were looking at me and smiling. The woman behind me must have noticed my startled look because she nudged me and said, "Didn't you know your song is on the charts?"

"Charts?" I stood dumbly, trying to digest what I had just heard. Finally, at the prodding of a couple of customers, I jumped out of line, ran over to the newspaper rack and hastily flipped through the pages of one of the national newspapers. I traced my finger down the page listing Estonia's Top 10. There we were: Douglas Wells and HEPT with the hit song "*Kas Sa Räägid Inglise Keelt?*" That week we were just barely on the list at #10, but the song crawled its way up the charts for ten weeks until finally, it hit number one.

Of course, the irony was not lost on me that I had struggled for ten years in different bands back home and that I had to come to Estonia to finally get a hit. The fact that my first recording success was an American singing in heavily accented Estonian about getting the brush-off from a local girl made it all the more unbelievable. The requests poured in and KUKU Radio on the mainland even called me at the info center to ask for an interview. They told me that they heard the song was going to be declared a gold record for Estonia, but nothing ever came of that or the anticipated year-end "Music Awards" banquet. The Sunday program *Morning TV* had me on to banter with the host in Estonian, just to show that it was indeed possible for foreigners to learn the language. Then, in something straight out of *American Bandstand*, they played the song while I lip-synched and danced around with a microphone. The whole event was a little embarrassing, but I must have made a big impression because, even years later, I would run into people who would identify me as "that guy who sang on TV." In the end, I didn't make a cent off the record, but that was fine with me. I didn't want to draw the ire of the Peace Corps should there be any talk of forbidden gifts or money.

One thing I did want to do, however, was make a decent copy of the songs at a genuine recording studio on the mainland. I got together with the band and excitedly told them of my plans.

Unfortunately they weren't as enamored with the idea as I was. Their initial reaction was lukewarm at best. In typical Hiiumaa fashion, they dug in their heels as soon as they felt somebody was rushing them into something. Instead of wanting to strike while the iron was hot and sell some CD's, they wanted time to think. After that came the monetary excuses. When I offered to pick up the entire tab, they grudgingly agreed to go along. But every time I tried to arrange the trip, somebody had to work or watch the kids, etc., etc. When the keyboard player left to do construction work in Moscow for several months, the matter was over. I was left with only the master tape and some great memories of my short time in the limelight.

12—A CAREER CHANGE

One morning, after I had been on the island for several months, the phone rang in Tarmo's apartment. It was pretty early so I was still half-asleep in my room at the end of the hall when I heard Tarmo's wife, Merike, pick up the phone. Her English wasn't very good, but she understood that the call was for me.

It was our Assistant Peace Corps Director, who was stationed in Latvia. She cut straight to the point.

"Doug, you are no longer an agricultural volunteer," she said simply.

"What do you mean?" I asked, the last remnants of sleep falling away.

"The funding for the project didn't make it through the Estonian Parliament."

"You mean this wasn't all set up beforehand?" I had already had a few experiences that had made me question Peace Corps' organizational abilities, most notably the problem with my lack of a visa upon arriving in Hiiumaa, but this seemed out of character even for them.

"We were under pressure to get you here as quick as possible. Mistakes were made."

"So, now what?"

The director cut to the chase. "Well, it's up to you. You can stay if you want, but you don't have to."

"Of course I want to stay. But what will I do?"

"If you decide to stay, you will be a small business advisor."

"Just like that?"

"Just like that."

So it happened that I was re-designated as a small business advisor volunteer, which was fine with me, considering I had not done much of anything as an agricultural volunteer. After I had broken the news to my farmer friends, I started commuting to Kärdla. I spent each workday there, futilely searching for some way to make myself useful. I felt very uncertain about my future on the island, especially with the reactions I was getting. The poor locals couldn't quite figure out what to make of this American going door to door and asking storekeepers how he could help them. Tarmo later told me that population was about evenly split on three different explanations for my presence on Hiiumaa. One theory was that I was working for the CIA. The second, which I found quite amusing, was that I was running from some kind of criminal charges in the U.S. The third theory was a little more complicated and involved something about me escaping from an insane asylum and bluffing my way onto an international flight. This seemed the most logical explanation to the Estonians. Who else but an insane man would give up their job, apartment, friends and family to come all the way to Estonia? The true version—that I was sane, there of my own free will and simply desired to help independent Estonia make a go of it—didn't have many takers.

Since I now had to commute, I decided to go to the charming little wood-frame bus station for a schedule of the buses that went from Kärdla to Käina. Although this may seem like a simple enough task, gathering information on Hiiumaa was never quite that straightforward. First of all, the woman at the window informed me that there were no printed schedules and pointed me towards a list of departures and arrivals hanging on the wall. Normally, this would have been sufficient, but all the routes seemed to have different villages as their end points and I couldn't make heads or tails of what roads they would actually follow. There was no map either, so I went back to the window to sort things out. An older woman sat behind the window shuffling papers and flipping the beads on an abacus back and forth. Knowing better than to wait for acknowledgement, I took the lead.

"*Tere,*" I said politely.

No response.

"Uh, I would like to know when I can go from Kärdla to Käina on the bus."

The woman responded without looking up. "When do you want to go?"

"Well, I commute back and forth to work everyday so I need all the times."

"We don't have a printed schedule," said the woman firmly and flipped more abacus beads.

"I know that. Maybe you could just tell me the times and I could write them down."

"All the times?" said the woman, finally looking up over the tops of her glasses.

I hesitated, uncertain of what her reaction might be. "Ah…yes. All the times, please."

"Well, okay. Let's do it this way." She gave a small exasperated sigh and grabbed a huge sheaf of papers.

"What way is that?"

"Well, you tell me when you want to go and I'll tell you if a bus goes." I started to protest but buckled under a withering look from my adversary. "Now, let's proceed," she said firmly, and adjusted her glasses.

"How about three o'clock?" I asked hopefully.

She shuffled some of the papers. "Nope."

"Okay, how about four o'clock?"

"Sorry."

"Four-fifteen?"

"Ah, yes. A bus leaves at four-fifteen."

"Great," I said, feeling a boost of confidence. "How about five-fifteen?"

"Nope." I thought I detected a hint of satisfaction.

After a good half-hour of guesses I finally had my prize: a handwritten list of all the times that buses left Kärdla for the south side of the island. As I left, I clutched the paper triumphantly to my chest as if it were some priceless relic. I also made a mental note to myself to suggest that they print schedules before tourist season.

I headed back to my office at the *Maavalitsus*, on foot as usual. I noticed that when I walked around Kärdla, people would always stare at me out of the back window of their cars as they drove by. Little kids with their mothers would point and ask questions until their mother shushed and hurried them away. I realized that everyone knew who I was but that I hardly knew anyone. In this small town of 4000, I felt a little like the village idiot.

Fortunately, it was a very beautiful town in which to be an idiot. A green, lush garden spot in the summer, it held its beauty even in the grayer times of fall. Small, neat houses with well-kept yards lined narrow asphalt streets. According to the literature I had received from the *Maavalitsus* building, the town lay at the bottom of an enormous ancient meteor crater. Because of this unique geological situation, there were many artesian wells scattered throughout the neighborhoods where water spurted up through fractures in the earth's crust. People took advantage of these natural fountains and made decorative pools and gardens. The pure water was also used for drinking, cooking and clothes washing. I always enjoyed walking down one of the quiet back streets and listening to the sound of the splashing water.

During those first months, I was alone in Kärdla most of the time. However, I did make a few friends among those who spoke English very well and wanted to keep in practice. One guy named Aivar was a scientist at what he called the "Hiiumaa Biosphere Office." I immediately equated this to the plastic dome in Arizona and excitedly asked Dr. Aivar when I could see it. His surprised answer was "You're in it!" It seems that some years before, the United Nations had designated the West Estonian Islands as an International Biosphere Reserve, sort of like an international nature park only with fewer restrictions. I learned a lot of interesting facts about the flora and fauna of Hiiumaa from Dr. Aivar. I also found a good friend who actually seemed to understand my real motives for being on the island–although he didn't hide the fact that he still thought I was a little crazy.

I also made friends with two local English teachers, Maris and Tiina. I ended up hiring Maris to give me some tutoring in Estonian and Tiina gave me some inside tips on the "Who's Who" aspect of the island. For my part, I helped them put together English materials for their classes and assisted them in their translating work. It kept me busy, but I was far from working at full capacity. Most days I just didn't have much to do at all and so explored the streets of Kärdla, which sometimes led me to the seashore. I would sit on the big boulders and ponder my fate. Would my stay amount to two years of killing time?

My aimless wanderings went on for several weeks until finally Helgi, the tourism advisor from the *Maavalitsus,* approached me and, with some hesitation, asked for help with a translation project. Peering up at me through her thick glasses, she explained her predicament in her clipped British English. Two years prior, a Canadian-Estonian had written a few pages in English about Hiiumaa. The *Maavalitsus* had been giving copies of this work to visitors ever since, but Helgi had suspected that there were some errors. Unfortunately, there was no money to hire a translator so she hoped I could give the text a once over. I had the sneaking suspicion that her hesitation was due to the fact that, although I was a native English speaker, it was American and not the Queen's English that I knew. However, I was overjoyed to be doing something useful and so readily agreed. I took the text home with me that evening, eager to get to work and possibly learn more about my new home

When I started reading the text, I was astounded. There weren't just a few grammatical errors, there were whole sentences mangled almost beyond recognition. I couldn't believe they had been passing this text out to visitors for two years. It was all I could do to try to piece together what the original author had to say. In some places I just had to take a guess at what was intended. After three hours, I was ready with my polished version of the corrected document.

When I brought it back to Helgi the next day, I told her about the disastrous state of the text and that she should certainly throw any remaining copies away. I couldn't believe that a Canadian would create such a monstrous assault on the English language, so I pressed Helgi for details about the document's origin. After some questioning, I found out the real reason for the sad state of the printed text about Hiiumaa Island. The author had written the original, unsolicited text by hand as he traveled around the island. The wonderful descriptions of places and retellings of intriguing legends seemed perfect for those first becoming acquainted with Hiiumaa. When Helgi told the governor about it, he agreed that the text was worth using. Helgi then gave it to the secretary to type up. The problem was that the secretary didn't speak English and just tapped out what she thought she saw in the author's handwriting. The results were what I saw and the original was long gone. That single, tortured document was the extent of the English-language information available about Hiiumaa. That day, a light went on in my head. After more than three months, I finally saw how I could be useful.

I told Tarmo about my idea and he was very supportive. He took it upon himself to take me to all sorts of places around the island. Thanks to him, I really began to see the hidden beauty of my adopted home. Unlike the U.S., where every point of interest was staked out with blinking signs and colorful brochures boasting of the oldest this or the tallest that, Hiiumaa simply had great places to visit. Every weekend, when we weren't hunting or fishing, Tarmo had a new place to show me—sometimes it was just a beautiful natural spot, sometimes it was a place that held some importance because of a local legend. With my weak Estonian and Tarmo's broken English, it was sometimes hard for me to discern the exact history of a certain place or the details of the legend connected to it, but it didn't matter. It actually helped that I was forced to use my imagination to fill in the details. As I learned more about my surroundings, I started to feel more at home.

A few months after the fateful phone call, I received word that some project money for Peace Corps Volunteers in Estonia had become available. We were to be given the chance to write proposals for small economic development projects costing a few thousand dollars and submit them to the main office in Riga for consideration. The selection process was to be competitive, as there wasn't much money to go around. To me this represented the perfect opportunity to finally do something concrete. I could establish myself as a useful island resource and show the local populace what Peace Corps was all about. I had visions of working hand in hand with smiling locals on some building project. Pulling in unison, we would raise the last beam in front of a cheering crowd, slap each other on the back, and head off to the bar. I would raise a glass with the now-smiling governor and drink a toast to Peace Corps and Hiiumaa Island. It would be the elusive Peace Corps Moment! During my long bus rides to work, my mind started formulating plans.

13—ASSAULT ON KÕPU
RADAR BASE

Of the many novel facets about being in Estonia in the early 90's, perhaps the most exotic was the fact that I was behind the former Iron Curtain. This was always a source of excitement, especially in the early days. Sometimes though, it could be quite unnerving, especially when the Soviet military was still there. (Although Estonia was again independent, the Soviets didn't completely pull out until 1994.)

As a Cold War baby, I had been born and bred just miles from the Strategic Air Command (SAC) headquarters, the nerve center for the Cold War. The "Looking Glass," a Boeing 747 equipped with all kinds of space age electronic gadgetry, was in the skies over Omaha twenty-four hours a day, the theory being that if Omaha took a hit, the Big Red Button could be pushed from 35,000 feet—a little late for us, but I suppose a good idea nonetheless. Our elementary school teachers used to delight in telling us that we were Target Number Three on the Soviets' nuclear hit list: Washington, New York and then...Omaha. I am not sure that it was such a good idea to tell this to elementary school kids, but evidence of the Cold War was all around anyway. After all the James Bond movies, information on fallout shelters and Bullwinkle, I knew full well that anybody with a Russian accent had something up his sleeve.

I had seen missiles in their silos out in western Nebraska, all pointed east, so I was dying to see what was on the other side, pointing west. Unfortunately, Hiiumaa Island didn't have any big underground silos, although it did have some old WWII bunkers and Soviet radar bases with anti-aircraft rockets. Strangely enough, the island was also ringed with guard towers and barbed wire, making it look like a kind of floating prison camp. Just like a scene out of *The Great Escape*, the tower searchlights would blink on to sweep the water and the coastline. The soldiers even hand-raked the sand near the beaches into neat rows so they could see if someone had been walking there. Rumor had it there were mines in some places. Ostensibly, they were "protecting" Hiiumaa from NATO or some Finns or Swedes bent on invading Estonia or something to that effect. I always used to joke that the Soviet border guards had to work twice as hard: not only did they have to keep people out, but they had to keep people in as well. Sadly, this forced isolation almost destroyed the boat building and fishing traditions on Hiiumaa, which are only now starting to recover.

The point is, I was simply dying to see an "enemy" base. Of course, for a Peace Corps Volunteer, it was considered very bad form to go sneaking around military establishments of any sort. It was probably #2 on the list of things "not to do" in the training manual, right after attempting to assassinate a government official. I don't think they've come up with a measurement of time small enough to gauge how long it would take to get sent home if you were caught doing something like trespassing on a military facility—not to mention the jail time you would probably have to do in Estonia first. But for me, it was a mission I had to accept. I was behind the lines and had to see what all the fuss was about, why I had to hide under my desk in school during air raid drills, what we were up against for all those years. So after I heard that most of the Russian soldiers had left Hiiumaa, I mercilessly pestered my friend Tarmo to take me out to see some of the abandoned bases.

Tarmo was somewhat bemused with my wide-eyed wonderment and suspicion of anything Russian. He, like most Estonian males, had had to serve two years in the Soviet military and had seen so much waste, corruption and inefficiency that he didn't take this Cold War thing that seriously. He smiled patiently as I ooh'ed and ah'ed over his old Soviet military ID and tried on his army boots. This was all ancient history for him, so at first he waved off my requests to check out the bases. To keep me quiet, we visited some old WWII sights. These were pretty interesting for a WWII history buff such as myself, and I even went so far as to order a metal detector from the States so I could hunt for war souvenirs.

The metal detector kept me occupied for a while, but soon I was again pestering Tarmo to take me to a Soviet Army base. Finally he agreed to take me to one of the old radar installations. We picked one, which was supposedly abandoned, out on the sparsely populated west side of the island. As I jumped into his blue Nissan pickup, I could barely contain myself. With the tape recorder I had brought along I immediately started to make a narrative, "Assault on the Commie Base," for the folks back in Nebraska. When I told Tarmo what I was doing, he just sighed, shook his head, and jammed the truck into gear.

After almost an hour of bouncy dirt roads, we arrived at the gate to the radar base, high on Kõpu peninsula, its revolving dish now still. We were at the extreme northwest edge of the former Soviet Union. To the west over the Baltic Sea lay Sweden. The coast of Finland was only about sixty miles to the north. Shadowy ocean-going freighters plied the waters out on the horizon. It was easy to see why a radar installation was built here. The metal gate, its red star intact, was wide open and I felt a rush of excitement and nervousness as we passed through. I clicked on the tape recorder and continued my running commentary for my friends and family back in Omaha. Once inside the gate, I started to see signs in Russian, which to me were totally illegible. I turned to Tarmo, who was calmly focused on the road ahead.

"Tarmo, what does that sign say?"

He paused as if deciding whether or not to acknowledge my question. "'Do not enter.'"

"Are you sure this base is abandoned?"

"Well, that's what the folks in the village said. I wouldn't worry about it."

"If you say so. Hey, what does that say?" I pointed to another sign as we passed.

Tarmo read it aloud. "'You are on a military base. Use of deadly force authorized.'"

The word "deadly" hit me like a punch in the stomach. "You're sure nobody's here, right?"

"Right. That's what I just said. Now take it easy."

We passed another ominous sign. "And what does that one say?"

"Let me see. 'Trespassers will be…'"–he paused, uncertain how much to tell me–"shot on sight.'"

My lower limbs went numb. "Maybe we should go."

Tarmo was used to my nervousness, so he just smiled and ignored me. I hunched down a little in the seat and continued talking into the recorder, documenting the arrival of me, the first American in this far-flung Soviet outpost. When Tarmo stopped the pickup in the middle of a clearing, I jumped out with my camera, heart pounding. Here I was on a Soviet military installation, with a camera around my neck and a tape recorder in my pocket. This was either a victory for democracy or a disaster waiting to happen!

There was nobody around and things seemed pretty quiet, so I took a few pictures of the radar mast, spoke into the tape recorder and took a few more pictures of some of the outbuildings with red stars on them. The base was in a forested area on a hill above the sea. The pine trees stood straight and tall in the sandy soil, almost obscuring the radar mast. As I poked around the base, I was amazed at how slipshod the construction was—nothing like the spotless U.S. military installations I was used to. Behind the garage was a big pile of garbage consisting mainly of empty sardine cans and broken vodka bottles. I picked up what seemed to be a manual of some kind and showed it to Tarmo, hoping I had found some kind of top secret military document. Tarmo shook his head at my enthusiasm and declared my find as a simple instruction manual of some sort. Despite his nonchalance, I felt a great deal of excitement. To me, this was real James Bond stuff!

I was just starting to enjoy myself when I looked over towards the main building. What I saw caused a sharp stab of fear in my stomach. There, at the window of the main building, was a man looking out at us. I tugged at the back of Tarmo's jacket and whispered hoarsely to him, never once taking my eyes off the man at the window.

"Tarmo, Tarmo! There's a guy over there! Let's get the hell out of here!"

My host didn't seem to hear the urgency in my voice. "Huh? Where? What are you talking about?"

"Over there! At the window! Hurry, let's get in the truck!"

By now, Tarmo was used to my overreacting. "What's the matter with you? Stop pulling on my jacket!"

"Look! See? At the window! C'mon, c'mon!"

"That guy? So what? He's probably just some Estonian guarding the place."

"I don't care! Please, get in the truck! I want to go home!"

"Stop panicking and let go of my arm!" Tarmo had not only become used to my overreacting, he had become bored with it. "What's the matter with you? You need to get over being such a nervous wreck about these kinds of things. This time I'm going to show you that there is nothing to be scared of. Let's go see who it is."

"But we'll be killed!" I pleaded. "Please Tarmo, get in the truck and let's go before it's too late!"

But Tarmo had already started walking toward the low-slung cinder block building, which looked like a jail with the bars on its windows. With nowhere to run and Tarmo holding the keys to the truck, there was little I could do. Resigned to my fate and weak in the knees, I meekly followed him up to the door. As he knocked, I tried to calm myself. Maybe he was right, I thought. Maybe it is just some Estonian. Maybe we wouldn't be beaten and killed.

Maybe I wouldn't be thrown out of the Peace Corps for causing a diplomatic incident. Just in case, I tucked the camera inside my jacket and held the tape recorder behind my back. I stood behind Tarmo and peered over his shoulder as the door opened. There, framed in the doorway, was a living and breathing, fully armed Russian soldier. My life was over. I whispered a farewell to my mother into the tape recorder before dropping it into my pocket in the hopes that someone would find it on my bullet-ridden body and send it home.

The Russian guard didn't kill us right away as I had expected he would. As a matter of fact, he didn't even seem that upset as he spoke to Tarmo in unintelligible, rapid-fire Russian (even slow Russian would have been unintelligible to me). Tarmo didn't seem bothered at all as he responded in a matter-of-fact tone of voice. But of course, Tarmo never seemed bothered by anything. From the sound of it, the two could have been talking about the weather or a weekend football game. I finally summoned up the courage to peek out from behind Tarmo's back and take in the rumpled brown uniform, the black boots and the thick, black leather belt with the five-pointed star on the buckle. The soldier was quite young, probably under twenty, and somewhat slight in build. He wasn't one of those bear-like, gruff-voiced characters like I was used to seeing in the movies. Maybe they would just let us off with a warning. But then cold reality came crashing in again when the soldier motioned for us to come inside. I was certain they would torture us for information. Who sent us? What were we doing on the base? I followed Tarmo uneasily over the threshold.

We walked through the entryway into a room with a wooden floor and a wood-burning stove crackling in the corner. There sat two of the soldier's comrades, young guys also, sitting in a dimly lit room on a ratty old couch with their AK-47s next to them. They looked up when we walked in, but didn't seem unduly upset. I thought they where cleaning their weapons, but as we drew closer I saw that they were . . . darning socks? The conversation continued among the four of them as I silently looked on. I couldn't understand a word and my mind was racing. What were they saying? What if they talked to me? They would realize I was a foreigner and then it would all be over. Occasionally, one of the soldiers would look at me, at which point I would simply give him an idiotic toothy smile and nod my head. What was I supposed to do? Now they seemed to be talking about me. One of the soldiers gestured in my direction and I stiffened in fear. Tarmo said something and the soldier laughed. So they were toying with us, playing with us before beating us to a pulp! The heartless swine! I would never forgive Tarmo for this if I got out alive!

Tarmo waved me toward the door and made as if to leave. I stood dumbfounded as he brushed passed and motioned for me to follow. How could this be? Were we just going to walk out? At the door, Tarmo turned back to look at me. He motioned again for me to follow, this time more insistently. I glanced back at the soldiers and started easing my way slowly towards the door, expecting them to tackle me at any second. I had almost made it when one of the soldiers stepped in front of me and blocked my way. He made a gesture with his hand and started speaking to me in Russian. All I could do was stare at him. He gave me a funny look and said something else, holding out his hand. I looked helplessly over the soldier's shoulder at Tarmo who just winked, looked down and patted his shirt pocket. I looked down at my shirt pocket and saw my pack of cigarettes. So that was it! The guy was asking for a smoke! I quickly yanked the pack from my pocket and almost threw it at the soldier, who just barely managed to catch it. He gave me a puzzled look as he pulled out a cigarette and lit it. He tried to give me the pack back but I just gave him that same idiotic toothy smile again and motioned for him to keep it. The soldier looked at me curiously for a moment, then just shrugged his shoulders and went back to the couch. He said something to his comrades and the three of them laughed. I took the opportunity to slip quickly past Tarmo and rush out the door back to the truck. Tarmo calmly waved goodbye and got in on the driver's side.

As we pulled out of the base I kept looking back over my shoulder. I couldn't believe my luck. Then slowly my relief switched over to anger and I turned on Tarmo, who was driving along like nothing had happened. I was so outraged I was almost apoplectic. I couldn't even speak Estonian without sputtering in anger. After a couple of false starts, I gave up and switched to English.

"Are you crazy? Are you out of your friggin' mind?"

As always, Tarmo was a master of calm. "What do you mean?"

"What do I *mean*?! You almost got us killed!"

Tarmo dismissed my accusation with a wave of his hand. "That was nothing. They were just kids from someplace in Central Asia."

"Kids, yes. But how many kids do you know who carry such big guns? They were just looking for a reason to kill a foreigner!"

"You have too much of an imagination." Tarmo shook his head and shifted into fourth gear. The experience had hardly fazed him.

"We barely escaped with our lives!" I reminded him. "Did you see how they looked at me?"

"They were just curious. We were never in danger. Relax."

"Never in danger? Relax? Have you forgotten that I don't speak Russian? What in the hell were you talking about with them?" I hardly needed to ask such a question. I could have guessed the answer.

"Oh you know, just stuff."

"Yeah, right! Just another day at the radar base! What if they had started asking me questions? Everybody around here speaks at least a little Russian."

"I took care of that." Tarmo's response raised more questions than it answered.

"Took care of what? How? Why were they looking at me so funny?"

"Well, I took the logical approach. I told them that you were my cousin, and when you were four years old, a tree fell and hit you on the head. You survived the accident but could never learn Russian. They actually felt sorry for you."

I started to protest, but realized that I was a beaten man. Had I known what Tarmo had been saying to the Russians, I most certainly would have protested, but in retrospect my host's reply was better than anything I could have come up with. With a defeated sigh, I slumped down in my seat, resigned to the fact that a dozen Russian soldiers would forever feel pity for Tarmo's retarded cousin.

14—THE ENERGY TRIANGLE

I thought it was a pretty harmless thing, getting a metal detector, but as soon as word spread that I had it, rumors started flying that "the foreigner" was up to no good, maybe even going places where he shouldn't go and digging up things he shouldn't dig up. This drew the attention of the local representative of the oddly named Office of Antiquities, who also happened to be second in command in the local National Guard. He came to my office at the *Maavalitsus* one day and read me the riot act about "looting and pillaging" and warned me of the "local backlash" that could result if I misused the device. I took what he said very seriously, knowing that people were always a little nervous about new technology. But what could I do? I had already paid 600 dollars for the detector, plus shipping. My only hope was that after people saw that I was just out to dig up a few WWII souvenirs in the forest then things would quiet down. So, I resolved to keep a low profile and use the detector sparingly at first.

My friend Tarmo had other plans. He saw the device as opening up a whole realm of possibilities for both legal and semi-legal activities. Mainly, he believed that we could find some kind of treasure on the many abandoned farmsteads scattered around the island and mostly reclaimed by the forest. According to Tarmo, when people were deported during Stalin's drive to collectivize agriculture, many farmers buried heirlooms, money, and even weapons on their land to save them from being confiscated. Sadly, most never made it back to reclaim their possessions, and now these items were just lying there, waiting for the person with the right equipment to find them and dig them up.

I was absolutely against using the metal detector on private property without permission, even if the owners of the land were either off in some faraway place or dead. So Tarmo and I went on a few excursions deep in the forests on the north side of the island where there were no people or farmsteads. The first time out, we found some old grenades and a few rusty bullets near what looked like a line of abandoned trenches. Tarmo looked them over, pronounced them Soviet Army issue, and put them into a canvas bag. We had evidently stumbled onto the site where the battle for Hiiumaa had taken place in 1941. It didn't really occur to me that what we were doing could be dangerous, despite the fact that every month or so there was a story in the media about somebody in Estonia getting blown up by leftover WWII ordinance. Tarmo was pretty much game for anything and I was too excited with my new toy to really care, but the next item we found finally brought home the reality of the risk we were taking. The metal detector indicated that there was a pretty good-sized metal object near the base of a tree. I handed Tarmo the metal detector and dug a shovel into the ground. It hit hard on a solid metal object just under the surface and, to get an idea of how big the thing was, I made a few more jabs into the ground nearby and was rewarded with a loud "Clang!" each time. Tarmo knelt and scooped the dirt away until gradually the object came into view. The excitement over possibly finding something valuable was replaced by a cold feeling in the pit of my stomach as I realized I had been blissfully banging with the shovel on an unexploded artillery shell. We decided that we had done enough digging for the day and, marking the spot where we had found the shell, headed for home with the bullets and grenades in the back of Tarmo's pickup.

My real goal was to find something from the German Army, so I kept searching and Tarmo kept trying to get me to go look around one of the old farmsteads. One day he talked me into going to a neutral place of his choosing just to "test" the detector's ability to find small objects. We arrived at a pasture on the south side of the island and, after making sure we weren't near any farmhouses,

I pulled out the detector and followed Tarmo over the gate. We walked for quite a while until Tarmo pointed towards a large boulder and asked me to make a few sweeps over the ground. Finding nothing, we went to another boulder on the other side of the pasture. This one had a handwritten sign nearby on a wooden stick that had been stuck into the ground. I tried to read the handwriting, but even though the sheet of paper was covered in plastic the writing had faded so much it was illegible. I asked Tarmo about it, but all he said was that people came here a lot, and he thought that maybe somebody had dropped something. After a few hours without finding anything, we went home and I thought that was the end of it. I couldn't have been more wrong.

A few days later, I was at the store when an elderly woman came up to me. She didn't say anything at first, just stood and glared at me. Finally, she spat, "We know what you did!" then stalked off before I could ask what she was talking about. That same afternoon, a man came up to me on the street and started ranting about something. I couldn't understand him at all and so just stood there until he was finished with his tirade. He then shook his finger at me emphatically and walked away.

I had just decided that maybe it would be a good idea to go home when the Office of Antiquities guy drove by. Upon seeing me, he screeched to a halt and jumped out of his car. His face red with anger, he strode quickly towards where I was standing, and for a moment I thought he was going to attack me. He stopped about a foot away, stuck his finger in my face and angrily began lecturing me about the evil I had perpetrated by violating local customs and traditions. I tried to explain that I didn't know what he was talking about, but that only made him angrier.

"I will make sure you are taken away from this island," he threatened. "I will call your Peace Corps!"

"What are you talking about?" I finally managed to ask.

"Ah, you pretend you don't know!" he sputtered. "You think we Hiiumaa people are just superstitious and stupid."

I was dumbfounded by his accusations. "About what? Really, I really don't know what this is about."

"You must respect our beliefs," he continued. "What were you looking for anyway?"

"Looking for? Where?" I asked.

"You just stay out of the Energy Triangle or things will go very bad for you."

With that, he jumped back in his car and drove off, spinning the tires so that gravel spit at my feet and legs. I watched his car recede into the distance, the inexplicable words "Energy Triangle" still echoing in my head. I had a strange feeling that this had something to do with the empty pasture where we had been using the metal detector. Only one person could explain this to me, and I had a sneaking suspicion he knew a lot more about that place than he had let on that day.

Tarmo was working on his car when I arrived. He stood up and wiped the grease off his hands when I walked over.

"Tarmo," I asked accusingly, "what do you know about this 'Energy Triangle' thing?"

"Oh, it's nothing," he said and shrugged his shoulders. "Just a few crazy people believe in it."

"Is that so?" I said. "Well, two of those crazy people accosted me on the street today."

"Really?" Tarmo said innocently.

"Yes, really." Then I went in for the kicker. "And that National Guard guy threatened to get me kicked off the island!"

That piece of information hit home. "Uh-oh."

"So maybe you had better tell me more about this place where we went."

"Well, okay," he said, sounding a little guilty, "but I really didn't think you would get in trouble."

As it turned out, the place we had searched wasn't just an empty pasture with a few boulders in it. It was indeed the locally famous Hiiumaa "Energy Triangle," which took its name from the fact that the large boulders I had seen were arranged roughly in a triangle that supposedly concentrated the energy from an underground "line of force" that came very near the surface under Hiiumaa Island. According to the locals, if you went there and held your arms out at just the right angle, you could focus this Earth energy through your body and improve your life force. Also, and by no means the least important purpose of this place, the "Energy Triangle" also functioned as a–no joke–giant UFO antenna. Evidently, the energy was focused and beamed out into space by the perfectly arranged boulders, and thus acted as a giant navigational beacon used by extraterrestrials. And I was just out there tramping around, looking for stray coins and stuff. No wonder people were ticked off!

The last thing I wanted to do was besmirch the name of Peace Corps, so after this latest fiasco I vowed to use the power of the detector in the name of good. Maybe this would allay people's suspicions when they saw the helpful things my little toy could do. When the local museum excavated the site of a 17th century chapel, I helped find some small metal artifacts that otherwise might have gone unnoticed. For my troubles, I was rewarded with a coin dated 1666. I provided my services at a lumberyard where I checked their logs for WWII shrapnel before they were run through the sawmill (the metal pieces tore up the giant saw blades if they weren't taken out). I also helped the Highway Department find some underground utility lines during road construction and even offered my services to the Department of Public Safety, should there ever be a need to check an area for mines or other ordnance. They graciously declined my offer of assistance, explaining that they didn't want to be the one responsible for getting Hiiumaa's only American blown into tiny bits.

I sincerely hoped the whole Energy Triangle affair would blow over after my numerous good deeds, but it was not to be. One of the officers in the National Guard, the same guy who had hassled me before, actually went so far as to demand that I keep the metal detector in their armory. At first I protested, but when he threatened to lodge a formal complaint with Peace Corps I gave in. They were still so worried that I was going to pillage ancient religious sites or find some guns or something and not tell them. So, there it sat, under armed guard. When I wanted to use it, I had to go to the armory and tell the duty officer why I wanted it and exactly where I was going to search. Only then would he give me my "weapon". I had to sign for it and then sign again when I brought it back.

The National Guard still was suspicious of my intentions, even when I followed their requirements to the letter, but pretty soon the change of seasons put an end to my forays anyway. Eventually the metal detector scandal was forgotten and the fearsome device sat collecting dust in the gun locker. I happily played with my collection of shrapnel, grenades and bullets and dreamed of finding a perfectly preserved German submachine gun the next spring. For his part, Tarmo felt a little guilty about getting me in so much trouble, so he didn't bring up the subject of the abandoned farmsteads anymore. However, I could tell that he still held out hope that when winter was over, we would go out hunting for real loot.

15—THE LIGHTHOUSE TOUR

To be honest, the first official Peace Corps project I finally decided to submit for a piece of the newly available funding was for my benefit just as much as it was for the benefit of the fledgling Hiiumaa tourism industry. The idea was born out of both frustration with the local bureaucracy and my complete inability to find my way around the island, which was mostly due to the lack of any road signs. I figured if I couldn't find my way back to the interesting and historical places Tarmo showed me, tourists on their own would hardly fare any better.

I brought up the issue one time at a Hiiumaa "development meeting" after I had been on the island about six months. The meeting was attended by members of a workgroup–consisting of government representatives, entrepreneurs, educators, scientists and common townsfolk–who would put together, under the guidance of a high-paid consultant from Tallinn, a "development concept" for the island that would steer it into the new millennium. I sat in the corner and couldn't understand much of what was being said but one thing was clear: they all seemed to agree that tourism was going to be Hiiumaa's future. This in itself was very heartening, and I hoped the discussion would naturally lead to how to bring tourists to Hiiumaa as well as how to feed and accommodate them.

To my dismay, the meeting quickly dissolved into arguing, most of which went right over my head. This much I could discern: those in attendance were split into roughly two ideological groups. The first group, whom I'll call the pessimists, felt that there was no chance in hell that a tourist from abroad would ever find his or her way to a little rock like Hiiumaa Island. Therefore, they argued, now that the artificial economy of the Soviet Union had evaporated, Hiiumaa was doomed to economic ruin and there was nothing anybody could do about it. The second group, who were little more than optimistic pessimists, immediately began suggesting ways to keep out the ravenous hordes of tourists that were sure to invade now that Hiiumaa was "open." The island would shortly be overrun with vacationing foreigners, which would result in the complete destruction of both the local culture and natural environment. Ideas from this group involved increasing shore patrols and implementing additional "visa" requirements or limits. As the meeting progressed into a debate, the mediator threw up his hands and jokingly suggested that perhaps he could organize tourist flights from Tallinn that could fly very low and slow over the island while the tourists just tossed out bundles of money. Dr. Aivar, following along this line and using his best dry humor, got in the best shot when he told the optimistic pessimists that they could organize "off-shore tourism." This official-sounding name drew the group's interest, and when asked to explain Dr Aivar deadpanned that the tourists could anchor outside the three-mile limit and simply send in their money by longboat. This pleased the group and they all nodded thoughtfully, until the laughs of others made them realize the good doctor was pulling their leg. After that, the meeting deteriorated rapidly.

After enduring more muttering and gesturing from the meeting's attendees, I decided I had to put my two cents in. Not sure if anybody had even noticed me in the corner, I stood up and politely interrupted the group. In my best Estonian, I introduced myself as an American Peace Corps Volunteer and asked if I could say something. The reaction I received reminded me of something out of *Planet of the Apes* when the captive and supposedly mute Charleton Heston speaks to the simians for the first time. People just stared with their mouths open while I took advantage of the stunned silence and launched into my speech.

"You know," I offered helpfully, "it would really be nice if there were some signs in English pointing out some of the more interesting places. That way people could find them and make

their visit more interesting. Or maybe just some highway markers?"

"Signs?" said one of the optimistic pessimists. "We already have
tourism signs, don't we?"

"Well, some," I conceded, "but they're in Estonian and Russian."

"But if we have signs," my dissenter continued, "that means
tourists will find their own way around the island."

Leave it to an Estonian to take all the practicality out of logic.
"Well, yeah, that's the idea."

"But what about us guides?" said another woman. "We need
work or we'll all starve!"

"We can't just let people go around and look at things!" said a
horrified older man.

"Ah, signs are expensive and no one will look at them anyway,"
grumbled a true pessimist.

And on it went. Although the meeting with the development
group wound up a complete flop, I remained determined to follow through on my idea. I enlisted the support of Helgi, the tourism advisor from the *Maavalitsus*, and began gathering information about the island. Helgi provided me with some general material written in Estonian and I began asking people about local
landmarks and the legends surrounding them. An amazing tapes-
try of folklore emerged from the dozens of stories I heard. It seemed
that every rock, tree and lighthouse had a story–or two or three–
attached to it. Sometimes there were even two or three elaborate
stories for a single location. Plus, according to the locals, little
Hiiumaa had mountains, rivers, haunted castles and even its own
Stonehenge. The real crown jewel of Hiiumaa was the 350-year-
old Kõpu Lighthouse, which, according to the people I talked to
at the museum was the third oldest continuously operating lighthouse 'in the world. Most of the material I unearthed was quite
exciting, though at times a little hard to believe. Greatly inspired,
I spent long days in front of the computer, typing out the stories
from notes I had taken while talking to different people. I felt this

seemingly nondescript, forested island was starting to show promise as a tourist destination, even if most of its locations borrowed from the notoriety of other more famous world destinations.

Tarmo seemed a little skeptical of my work. He had his doubts that tourists from abroad would find these obscure local legends very interesting. Moreover, mainland Europe was full of old buildings and natural wonders. He couldn't understand why anyone would take the trouble to visit such a remote unheard-of destination as his island home. Tarmo also shared with me a well-known saying about the *Hiidlased* (Hiiumaa people): if you believe half of what a Hiiumaa person says, you still only have a quarter of the truth.

I remained unperturbed by his lack of confidence and quickly made arrangements to drive around the island with Helgi. I pegged out a route on the map that made a rough circle around the island and set out early one morning in an official car courtesy of the governor. Our first stop was *Ristimägi*, the Hill of Crosses. I had in my mind the picture of a sweeping, sun-drenched hillside dotted with colored flowers and covered with an impressive array of gleaming white crosses. As we drove, I pulled out my notes for the place and gave them a once over. This was one of those places with more than one story and I had described the competing legends as best I could:

> *Ristimägi is a reminder of the island's long-lasting historical ties with Sweden that ended tragically in 1781. Before this fateful year there were about two thousand Swedish people living on Hiiumaa. As free people they enjoyed certain privileges that the Estonian peasants did not. The peasants were literally owned by the landlords and had to work on the manors for free, but the Swedes did not. This caused some resentment among the local landowners who wanted the Swedes to do free work for them too. This resentment, combined with a Russian desire to tighten control over the region, resulted in a government decree*

by Catherine II for the forced deportation of the last twelve hundred Swedish people from the island.

The Swedish had been guaranteed freedom in letters from their king, but these letters could not protect them from the combined forces of Catherine II of Russia, a high rank-ing officer in the Russian army and the owners of the vari-ous estates on Hiiumaa. A deal was made to deport the Swedes to be farm workers for an area in the Ukraine and their departure was scheduled for August. The pain that the Swedes must have felt by being ordered from their home was tempered somewhat by the fact that they were promised good lands, provisions and safe transport. They gathered for a farewell church service at this site and bid farewell to their Estonian friends and adopted homeland.

The journey turned out to be longer and more difficult than expected and many people died during the months of travel. When they reached their destination they found that many of the promises made to them were not going to be kept. During the 1920s, the descendants of these ill-fated settlers managed to make their way back to Sweden. This was made possible by an agreement between the Swedish and Russian governments. Most of them now live on the island of Gotland.

A farmer who lived in this area at the time the Swedes were deported placed a small wooden cross on the spot where this last church service was held. Later visitors also placed hand-made crosses on this spot. Eventually it became a tradition for first-time visitors to the island to make a cross out of sticks that they would find lying around the site. Now there are thousands of these crosses along the path leading into the forest. You too are encouraged to make a cross out of natural materials and add to this memorial.

Local legend tells a completely different story about the origin of this tradition. Long ago, a wedding party was travel-ing along the road from Kärdla and met another wedding party coming from the opposite direction. The road was too

narrow for them to pass each other and each refused to give way.
Discussion soon gave way to argument. A fight broke out among
the participants in the weddings. In the resulting chaos, the
groom of one wedding party and the bride of the other were
killed. After the fighting stopped, the people realized what a
terrible thing they had done and were overcome with remorse.
They all decided that the best way to put this sad event behind
them would be for the surviving groom and surviving bride to
be married, thus proving that love triumphs over all.

The stories had piqued my excitement in visiting the actual site of the two supposed events. We headed down the long straight and level highway through the forest in the aging Latvian van. As the driver chain-smoked, I stared out the window and Helgi thumbed nervously through the dictionary. I guess she wanted to be prepared for an entire day with a native English speaker. The Estonian driver looked back over his shoulder and said a few words to me, which I recognized as Russian. This had happened before when I met folks who saw that I couldn't speak well in Estonian. They would start right in with Russian even though they knew I was from the U.S. I shook my head and told the driver in Estonian I didn't understand. He simply laughed, ground out one cigarette in the ashtray and reached for another. It seemed that was the only foreign language they were accustomed to using. At times they would even try Finnish, which really frustrated me. Finnish sounds incredibly similar to Estonian and, not realizing it wasn't the local language, I would strain myself trying to pick out words before I finally realized what was going on.

The driver pulled off the road and skidded to a stop on the grassy shoulder. Helgi got out and motioned for me to follow. I couldn't see anything except dense trees on either side of the road and wondered what we were doing, stopping on this flat stretch of highway. I followed close behind as Helgi picked her way solemnly across the roadside ditch and into a grove of trees. After a short distance, she stopped beside a little shoulder-height berm of sand.

Upon closer inspection I saw it was covered with little crosses, the largest of which was perhaps two feet high, made of sticks tied together with bark and roots. Helgi made a dramatic gesture with her arm and it dawned on me that we had arrived at our destination, the majestic Hill of Crosses.

"Here we are," Helgi said proudly. "The most visited place on Hiiumaa Island." I stared at the crosses that spread across the forest floor like mushrooms. "All visitors must first come here and make a cross for the lost young lovers. This brings luck and guarantees that their visit on Hiiumaa will be a safe one. Also, if you are separated from your lover, making a cross means you will soon be reunited. If you have no one, then making a cross will bring you love."

I scribbled in my notes. "Great, great," I said, trying to get everything down. "Now where's the actual hill?"

"Why, this is the hill!" said Helgi in surprise.

"You're kidding, right?" I countered. "This isn't a hill, this is a mound of sand!"

"No, no," said Helgi firmly and pulled out her dictionary. "This is a *mägi*, which means hill or mountain in your language. Here, look at my dictionary."

"I don't care what the dictionary says, this isn't a hill! It's a pile of sand, a dune at most!"

"It has always been the Hill of Crosses, in English or Estonian," Helgi huffed.

"But that's false advertising!" I pleaded, but she was already heading back to the van.

We continued our journey around the island, Helgi pointing out the sites of interest as I marked down where I felt directional and informational signs should go. We saw majestic lighthouses, including the oldest one at Kõpu, quaint farming villages and stately churches. All of these treasures, so well hidden, would be a wonderful discovery for any tourist. We headed down the west side of the island towards a spot that I was dying to see, the Old River Valley, which was billed as Hiiumaa's "Grand Canyon.". I had pictured a sweeping vista, something out of an old cowboy movie with maybe some small farmhouses along a tree-lined watercourse, surrounded by grazing cattle dotting the pastures. The local legend regarding the origin of the river went this way:

> *A man was walking home after a hard day's work. He was very tired and was also in a bad mood because his boss had made his day quite difficult and now he had to walk several kilometers home carrying a heavy shovel. He decided to stop for a rest and, still thinking about his boss, angrily thrust the shovel into the sandy soil so hard that it went about halfway up the handle. After a short rest, he tried to pull the shovel out of the ground, but it would not come. He pulled on the shovel, kicked it, cursed at it and finally the shovel came out and water began to flow from the hole, washing away the soil. The man walked off towards home grumbling to himself, never realizing that he was responsible for the beginning of this beautiful gorge.*

We pulled off the main highway and bounced down a forest road before coming to a stop in a clearing. Once again dense forest surrounded us, with only a small path leading through the trees. I followed Helgi about a few hundred yards until we came upon a wooden fence guarding an area where the forest floor fell away. With Helgi looking on approvingly, I gingerly approached the edge and looked down into…a gully. There, about thirty feet down, a small gurgling stream cut through the sandy soil. Occasionally the sandy sides of the gully would collapse, temporarily blocking the flow until the water built up and washed it away. As picturesque as it was, it hardly lived up to its name.

"Well, what do you think?" said Helgi, smiling proudly.

"I think we have a problem," I said, and began crossing out some of my notes.

Helgi's smile faded as she reached for her dictionary. "What do you mean?"

"Look, this is no river valley. It's a gully, a ravine with a creek in it!"

She remained firm. "I'm sorry but I translated it myself. The name is Old River Valley."

"I don't care!" I said in frustration. "This is a middle-aged stream ditch, nothing more!"

She had outgrown her patience for me. "Well, if you are going to misrepresent our island, than we may as well go back."

"Helgi, wait!" I called out as she marched back to the van. "We can talk about this."

"There's nothing to talk about." Helgi said, clearly offended by my critical remarks.

I adopted a more conciliatory tone. "Okay, look. I'm just trying to be honest about this."

"But you can be honest. We do have hills and valleys here, just not so big as in America."

"Fair enough" I conceded wearily. "No more comments about language."

I sat quietly as we went around the island and back towards the ferry harbor. I continued to add to my notes and mark where guideposts should be placed to keep tourists on the right path. I still marveled at the apparent lack of any numbering system for the various highways. With a sincere desire to be cooperative and not to offend, I remained quiet when Helgi showed me Hiiumaa's "Mississippi River," the longest "river" on the island at an impressive two miles long and an imposing three to six feet in width. We also visited Hiiumaa's "Stonehenge," which held the record for the number of legends attached to one place. It was also a fairly controversial site as people vigorously defended their particular version of where the stones came from and why they were placed here. I had visited this enigmatic arrangement of boulders a few times before and various people had related the different stories, which I had summed up in my notes like this:

The origin and purpose of this large pile of boulders is unclear. However, one thing is certain: someone went to a lot of trouble to carry and stack these rocks. One legend cites the boulders as the grave markers of a Swedish king named Ingvar, who ruled in the late sixth century and was buried with a horde of gold. Another story alleges that sailors would bring one large rock to this place before they went to sea. They believed that by doing this they made an agreement with God to bring them good luck on their voyage and ensure a safe return. For this reason, some local residents refer to these boulders as "contract stones." A third story cites this location as serving a religious purpose for the followers of an ancient Estonian religion. Today, some people discount all of these stories and believe that the boulders were placed here much more recently by the landlord of this area, who lived nearby in the late eighteenth century. The landlord came from a wealthy German family and traveled all over the world in his younger days. He saw many things during his voyages, but what impressed him most were the pyramids in Egypt. When he finally settled down on Hiiumaa he decided to try and build a small replica of a pyramid to remind him of his travels. However, it proved extremely difficult to construct a pyramid out of round uncut boulders, so the end result was somewhat less than perfect. It is unlikely that the real truth about this place will ever be known. It will remain forever a mystery for visitors to ponder and locals to debate.

Our last stop was the little village of Suuremõisa, which had Hiiumaa's "Notre Dame Cathedral" (a thirteenth century stone church) and Hiiumaa's "Versailles," the haunted castle of Count Otto Reinhold Ludwig von Ungern Sternberg. We drove down a narrow tree-lined alley and through a huge park containing several picturesque ponds. Our driver stopped the van in front of a very impressive eighteenth century manor house. A beautiful piece of architecture, it nonetheless lacked the features that most of us would consider essential for a castle. It was more than just an matter of size: there were no stone walls, moat or even parapets with flags fluttering on them. I'd had my suspicions from the beginning about this whole castle issue, and I resolved to make a final stand. Helgi seemed to anticipate my intentions and brandished her dictionary like a shield against my protests. Luckily, we came to a compromise. It was not to be listed as a simple "manor house" (which it was) nor as a "castle" (which it certainly wasn't) but as "Suuremõisa Palace," haunted by the infamous count Ungern Sternberg. With that, we headed back north to Kärdla to complete the circular route. I think Helgi and I were both happy to finish up the tour.

Once back in my office, I immediately began sorting my notes and working on the guidebook that I would call *The Lighthouse Tour*. It would take a roughly circular course around the island, sticking to the main roads and visiting sixteen points of interest. There would be guideposts to tell people where to turn and signs to identify the sights. I was a little concerned that the signs would only be in English, in apparent contradiction with existing language law that made it mandatory to have Estonian on all outdoor advertisement, but the folks at the *Maavalitsus* assured me that there would be no problem. After all, they reasoned, there were some little blue signs in Estonian at most of the places on the tour. Satisfied with their response, I sent the complete project proposal off to Peace Corps headquarters and waited for an answer.

16—SIGNS OF THE TIMES

Several weeks passed as the volunteers from Estonia and the other two Baltic States sent in their projects for consideration by the Peace Corps office in Riga, Latvia. There a project board was to look them over and select the ones they felt were most worthy of funding. I had no idea what my competition was, so all I could do was wait, uncertain of how my project would stack up against the others. I wasn't asking for much money, about three thousand dollars (the limit was ten thousand). That would pay for printing five hundred copies of the guidebook at the local printers, plus provide the money for a local woodworking shop to produce the scores of signs needed to mark out the route and identify the points of interest. All the funds would stay on Hiiumaa and help Hiiumaa businesses. To meet the local buy-in requirement, the *Maavalitsus* had agreed to pay for the installation of the signs, so if the project was approved we were ready to move ahead.

For those long weeks I was constantly on edge, jumping at every phone call and checking the fax every few hours. My Estonian colleagues were considerably more relaxed. "If it comes, it comes," was their take on the situation. I admired their patience but sometimes felt perturbed at their apparent lack of enthusiasm. To make matters more frustrating, I could never seem to get a straight answer from anybody about my ideas for future projects to promote tourism. I am sure my tortured Estonian was sometimes hard to understand, but considering that tourism was being touted as the "future of Hiiumaa," I was surprised at the lukewarm reception my proposals received. I kept at it though, and even came up with a humorous project to help keep me amused whenever I was beginning to feel discouraged. After the experience of countless meetings with government officials and business leaders, I made a little phrase book of the sentences I most commonly heard. It had the Estonian, the English translation, and then a final take on what they were really saying minus the bureaucratic doubletalk. For example:

Estonian: Meil ei ole raha.

Literal translation: We don't have any money.

Real meaning: Your uninteresting project is not a priority for us. Go ask somebody else.

Estonian: Sa ei saa aru.

Literal translation: You don't understand.

Real meaning: Don't you think it's rather arrogant of you to tell us what we need?

Estonian: Räägime sellest.

Literal translation: Let's talk about it.

Real meaning: Come back another time and ask. As a matter of fact, come back fifty times if you want. You still won't get a definitive answer out of us.

And finally, the most lethal, the most Hiiumaa-like, seemingly innocuous phrase that was in fact an emphatic throwing down of the gauntlet. It would come to strike fear in my heart whenever I heard it uttered:

Estonian: Ootame, vaatame.

Literal translation: Let's wait and see.

Real meaning: Silly mortal, you have now brought the full fury of the Hiiumaa Islanders' stubbornness and conservatism down on your head. Just try to turn your vision into reality. We will dig our heels and all ten fingernails into the ground to resist you. We will stonewall you until the seas dry up, the stars fall from the sky and the bones of your children's children have long turned to dust!

In short, I had to learn to take the long view. Whereas Americans like to burst into a meeting with a colorful presentation, a dynamic speaking style and whip people into a frenzy of support, the character traits that seemed to serve me the best were persistence and the ability to be annoying and repetitive. I came to believe that Peace Corps really had the right idea about having volunteers stay for at least two years and also having them learn the local language. I saw many a Euro-consultant sweep onto the island with their years of development experience, a healthy supply of condescension and a lot of grand ideas. The *Hiidlased* would cart them around the island, listen patiently (though many of them didn't understand English), nod their heads and then dump the miracle worker back on the ferry, much to everyone's relief. I, on the other hand, wasn't going away and the Estonians couldn't simply play dumb when I talked to them. As time went on, surprise and curiosity gave way to annoyance, and then finally to a grudging respect. After all, I was living among them, eating their food, walking the same streets and even making a serious attempt to speak to them on their level in their language. It was in this environment, after several months at post, that a certain level of trust and cooperation truly began to develop.

Sometime in the spring of 1993, the phone call finally came from Peace Corps in Riga. The project had been approved! Flush with victory, I phoned Helgi at the *Maavalitsus*. She was genuinely pleased that we were getting the money, but I could tell from her voice that she knew there were still some obstacles to overcome. The next day at work, I placed the order for the signs and carried the finished version of the guidebook to the print shop. It was encouraging to see how both the printers and the woodworkers immediately set to work. In a surprisingly short time I had five hundred guidebooks and a warehouse full of signs, all right on budget. I paid for the work done by the private sector and then turned my sights on the *Maavalitsus* and the Department of Roads. The deal was that the *Maavalitsus* would pay the Department of Roads, a state entity, to put up the signs. Fairly simple, but bickering developed over when payment would actually take place. The Department of Roads wanted cash up front, but the *Maavalitsus* wanted to wait until the job was done. All I cared about was that the signs were up by the time the tourists started to arrive in June.

After several weeks, I managed to break the logjam and soon found myself riding on a Department of Roads dump truck full of signs and chain-smoking road workers. With shovel in hand, I helped the laborers put up the signs in the tough, rocky soil conditions in the south, as well as the soft sandy conditions of the north.

On the second day, we were on an empty gravel road installing an identifying English-language sign. The sun was quite hot and as I wiped the sweat from my brow I saw an old couple approach on bicycles. I sensed the coming of the elusive Peace Corps Moment. I was sure the old couple would stop, shake my grimy hand and heap praise on me for my vision and determination. The laborers would look at each other in approval, nodding their heads, and my purpose would be affirmed. As the pair drew closer, I leaned on my shovel and smiled at them. Unfortunately, they didn't stop. They just looked suspiciously at me as they drove slowly past. Then, when they thought they were out of earshot, the old woman leaned over and said to the man. "I told you it was happening, Juhan. We just got rid of Russian and now English is already invading."

Shot down hard, I nursed my wounded pride that evening with a few shots of vodka.

The next day, I went to the *Maavalitsus* building to see Helgi and report that the signs were up. I found her poring over a long fax in English. She looked up when I came in and handed me the fax with a worried look on her face.

"Douglas, can you help me with this?" she said apologetically. "I'm afraid I don't get it."

"Sure," I said and took the fax. "What is it?"

"Well, the governor has told me that we must open a TIC, a tourist information center."

That sounded promising. "Great! But what's in the fax?"

"I had a friend in Denmark send me the international standards for a TIC."

"International standards?"

"Oh, yes. In order to use the official green and white sign you must meet certain standards."

I shrugged. Sounded logical enough. "Well, okay. Let's have a look."

I went over the four-page fax, which consisted mostly of specs on how the international tourist information sign—the large green and white "I"—should be displayed, how big it should be and what the exact color specs were. The documents also contained language requirements for TIC workers (English plus local languages) and a minimum number of hours the center was to be open per week. I handed the fax back to Helgi and explained the contents.

"Nothing too difficult," I said. "Where is the TIC going to be?"

"A travel bureau said we can use their office. It's near the central square."

"Good location, but who is going to work there?"

"Well, that's something else I wanted to talk to you about."

And that's how I became a tourist information center worker on the island of Hiiumaa. I had no problem with the foreign tourists, but I felt sorry for the poor Estonians. They just couldn't figure out who this person was speaking bad Estonian and handing out tourist pamphlets on one of their remote islands. More than a few just turned on their heel and walked out when I started talking to them.

I tried to take it all in stride. After all it was great language practice and the few that did stay and talk were amazed that a foreigner was taking the time to learn Estonian. It was clear they were sensitive about the former occupiers' disdain for their language and pleased that a guest in their country was showing the native language the respect it deserved. I can't count how many times I heard someone berate the Russians who had lived there twenty (or thirty, or fifty) years and didn't speak a word of Estonian.

Weekdays or weekends, there was never a dull moment at the TIC. People came from all over the world, even in the off-season. Sometimes we were amazed at how people had actually found their way to Hiiumaa. I enjoyed explaining to visitors where they could go and what they could see. In return, I received more than a few compliments on my good English. Things got so busy that I decided to rent an apartment in Kärdla so I wouldn't have to commute from Tarmo's place in Putkaste every day.

One morning, a portly Finnish man came in and, in a particularly arrogant way, started spouting off how talented he was in languages and how we could speak in any language I preferred–except, of course, Estonian because "nobody who's anybody speaks Estonian." Yeah, right. And Finnish is the next "world language". Usually, I took such arrogance in stride, but it really annoyed me that some of the foreign tourists treated me in such a condescending way. They only did it because they thought I was an Estonian and, therefore, a second class citizen in their eyes. When they learned I was American, then it was "How nice!" and they would start treating me as their equal. Most times I simply let such affronts slide, but this guy was so obnoxious I thought I would have a little fun.

I told him we could speak in English and started explaining about the island. He watched me for a while and then interrupted to say that my English was "pretty good." He asked me where I had studied and I thoroughly enjoyed watching his eyes widen when I said I hadn't formally studied English, that I'd just picked up the language from watching MTV. The poor man was so amazed, he went out and gathered up his whole tourist group to come and see this "miracle."

European tourists, though often clueless, provided endless entertainment. Sometimes, when I was having a slow day, I would go with small groups and show them around the island myself. I ran tourists up and down lighthouses, took them through the forests, and visited the museum and handicraft shops until they begged to be allowed to rest.

People asked all sorts of questions, ranging from the insightful ("How has Estonia changed since regaining independence?") to the absurd ("Are you sure they will let us off the island?"). Some just didn't quite understand that Estonia was really no longer a part of the Soviet Union. Two backpackers from Switzerland asked me to take them deep into the forest and then, looking around anxiously over their shoulders, asked about "the real story on Estonia" and whether it was "really a free country."

My favorite form of self-amusement was to take small groups to the forest where I had hidden the unexploded artillery shell I found with Tarmo. I would drive down the road, telling them about the battle that took place fifty years ago. Someone in the group would invariably ask if there was still evidence of the battle in the forest. I would reply, "I don't know, let's take a look" and pretend to just stop the car at random. I would randomly kick around in the moss-covered forest floor until I made my discovery. When everyone gathered around real close, I would make big show out of slowly uncovering the shell and gently lifting it up for them to see. After getting the group's rapt attention by explaining how thoroughly dangerous a find like this was, I would abruptly end the show by pretending to drop the shell, causing everyone to scream and either dive for cover or run back to the car. I got more mileage out of that unexploded shell than I ever could have hoped.

Another way I kept tourists interested while driving from place to place was to tell then some of the local legends I had learned. Most of the time I held pretty close to the original story, but sometimes I just couldn't resist embellishing details a little bit. I didn't really consider it lying. I thought of it as helping people have a more "complete experience." For example, near Kärdla were the ruins of an old church that had burned down early in the twentieth century. During the Soviet occupation, the soldiers had used the church grounds as a shooting range. Apparently they either had very bad aim or were a little reckless with their weapons because the whole outside of the church was pockmarked with bullet holes. I usually took people there as an example of the darker side of the Soviet Union's relationship with religion, which was more geared toward destruction than rebuilding. For shock effect, I wouldn't tell them about the shooting range until we arrived and they could see the damage for themselves. This usually produced quite an effect on my audience, but one time a Swedish woman jumped out of the car as soon as we stopped and ran over to the church. Before I could explain anything, she looked up at the church with wide eyes and then down at the ground littered with shell casings. "My God," she said in awe to her friends, "think of the battle that must have taken place here. Think of those poor, poor Hiiumaa people trying to save their church."

I know I should have just corrected her and gotten on with the tour, but something in the way she and her friends looked at the church with tears in their eyes made it irresistible for me to play along. While the group gasped and wrung their hands, I told them about the legendary "Battle for Paluküla Church." Yes, it was a fierce battle, with the local villagers hopelessly outnumbered but determined not to give up their church. At first, the farmers with their shotguns and hunting rifles repelled the Russian invaders, but they were soon surrounded. The Soviets then began their final assault from the forest after nightfall. Yard by yard they advanced, with the Estonians' losses mounting at every step. Finally, it was hand-to-hand combat with pitchforks against bayonets. In the melee that followed, the church caught fire and all that was left the next morning was the burnt-out, pockmarked shell you see today. The villagers had fought to the last man. When I finished, the Swedes sighed, wiped the tears from their eyes and scooped up handfuls of shell casings as souvenirs.

Aside from my occasional yarn weaving, my new job in tourism had given me cause to feel useful on the island. I had the guidebook done, I was helping at the info center and I was beginning to establish myself as a tourism advisor and guide. A young reporter I knew at the local newspaper did a couple of interviews with me during which I talked about tourism on the local radio station (a whopping ten-watt transmitter). People started to greet me in the store and folks waved as they drove by. Some even stopped to offer me a ride as I trudged from place to place in Kärdla. Although I had yet to experience the elusive Peace Corps Moment, it sure felt great to be able to give at least a partial answer to the question "What on Earth are you doing here?"

Then, just as tourism season was in full swing, all hell broke loose. It started with a few editorials in the newspaper. It seemed some people were upset at all the signs that had suddenly cropped up. The English-language ones especially drew their ire. People wrote letters that decrying how "Yankee imperialism" had come to Hiiumaa. They wrote of their fear that if they let an American come in and put up English language signs, then soon a German will come and put up German signs and the Finnish people . . . etc., etc. In retrospect, I understand their feelings.

The *Maavalitsus* had assured me there was no problem. Upset at the negative press the project was getting at the hands of a small but vocal minority, I went to speak with the Deputy Governor. I was hoping he would write a rebuttal and explain more of the details of the project, especially how the Hiiumaa government officials had participated in the decision-making process. The response I received when I presented my concerns was "Ah, don't worry about those stupid people. They will quiet down soon."

In part, he was right. The articles eventually stopped, but then the battle moved from the pages of the press onto the streets. People started tearing down the wooden road signs—not many signs, but there were certain localities where the activists chose to take action. Though the representatives of the four municipalities on Hiiumaa had agreed to take responsibility for the signs in their district, they were slow to respond when a sign was down, if they responded at all. It got to the point that when I was driving around with Tarmo and I noticed a sign on the ground I would stop, take a shovel and put it back. A week or so later it would be down again, or sometimes even just turned around backwards. I would drive by, stop, and put it back. This game continued well into tourist season and became quite a joke for the islanders, who had seen me resolutely digging by the side of the road.

Then, one day about mid-summer, Helgi came into the info center with a worried look on her face. She looked worried most of the time anyway, but on this occasion she was particularly distressed. She approached the desk where I was sitting, adjusted her glasses, wrung her hands and took a deep breath.

"Douglas, I am afraid there is a bit of a problem," she said in her best British English.

"What problem?" I asked.

"It seems the language board is here from Tallinn."

"Language board? What's that?"

"Well, they're responsible for ensuring compliance with Estonia's language laws."

"You mean, sort of like a language police?"

"Well, yes, I guess you should say that."

I shrugged. "Okay, what do they want?"

"They uh…well . . . they are upset with your signs."

"*My* signs? Don't you mean *our* signs?"

"Yes, of course but I . . . " She fought for the right words. "They are concerned about your project violating the law."

"Now wait a minute. We talked about all this beforehand and you said no problem."

"You are absolutely right and that's what I told the governor, but I was just wondering…"

"What?"

"Well, do you think your Peace Corps would pay for Estonian signs also?"

I couldn't believe it. I had already aroused the ire of some of the locals and now I had the National Language Board breathing down my neck. The situation had to be taken care of, but it wasn't going to be the U.S. taxpayer footing the bill. I sent Helgi back to the governor with the message that there was no way the Peace Corps would give more money for this project. The *Maavalitsus* could just as well come up with the funds. It wouldn't be that expensive, we could even use the same posts that the English language signs were on. The woodworking shop could just carve out some Estonian language signs and we'd nail them up. Problem solved.

As you might have already guessed, the rest of the tourist season went by with no movement towards correcting the trouble. I endured a fair amount of teasing and chiding from not only Estonians but also arrogant European tourists displeased with the "inexorable spread of English as the lingua franca." By the end of tourist season, I actually welcomed the quiet solitude of fall.

Oh, the Estonian language signs were finally made, but then I couldn't get the *Maavalitsus* to put them up. No amount of pleading, reasoning or cajoling could get them to move. The signs just sat out by the garage, and for the whole winter lay covered with snow. Months passed until I started worrying that I might have to face another tourist season with an island full of illegal monolingual signs. I could just hear what the Peace Corps bosses in Riga would say if they caught wind of my transgression: "So, Wells, violating the law in the name of Peace Corps, eh? And with U.S. taxpayer dollars to boot!"

As it turned out, I was saved by an act of God. Actually, it was an act of God's servants in the form of eight young U.S. missionaries who traipsed into the info center one spring day, complete with twelve-string guitar and numerous pamphlets. When they found out that I was an American they were truly amazed. One of them was even from Nebraska! They praised me for undertaking my mission with Peace Corps, and I reciprocated by praising them for bringing religion back to the Baltics after the fall of communism. We praised and praised until finally they prepared to leave. That's when they made their big mistake.

"You know, Douglas, we'll be here for a few days. Let us know if you need any help."

"Uh-huh," I said, eyeballing the large van outside and gauging its cargo-carrying capacity.

At nine o'clock the next morning, I had them show up with their shiny van, sans guitar and pamphlets. We drove over to the *Maavalitsus*, grabbed the signs and some tools out of the garage and off we went. I also grabbed one of the journalists from the Hiiumaa newspaper. The next issue showed a group of grinning young missionaries brandishing Estonian-language signs. The head-line read something to the effect of "Hiiumaa Tourism Saved by Divine Intervention." Harsh tactics maybe, but I think the point was made.

17—THE CROSSING

Living day after day on Hiiumaa, I sometimes forgot it was an island. First of all, it was flat and so heavily forested you only saw the sea when you were very close to the shore. Also, I was so busy learning about the island and doing my Peace Corps business that I sometimes didn't ride the ferry for weeks at a time. People on the mainland asked me often about whether I felt isolated or cut off, to which I would reply that most people spend weeks on end inside a relatively small geographic area anyway. It was no different for me, just that my space was surrounded by water and nearly twenty miles off the coast of Estonia. The only times when it really hit home that I lived on an oversized rock in the middle of the Baltic Sea were when I was trying to get home from the mainland and couldn't, or when I absolutely had to get off the island and the weather wasn't cooperating. Fortunately, neither situation came up very often.

The ferry was really the only feasible means of transportation on or off the island, but it wasn't always the only choice. When I first arrived on Hiiumaa, there were Estonian Air flights that cost only three dollars. The planes were small forty-seat Russian jets (YAK-40's) that flew out and back from Tallinn on a daily basis, morning and evening. The planes were never full, and once I even had the unique experience of being the only passenger on board an evening flight from Tallinn, with only the two pilots and a stewardess to accompany me. Although I'm not an MBA, I was pretty sure the Tallinn-Hiiumaa line was losing a boatload of money. Sure enough, shortly after Estonian Air was privatized, the flights ceased. Some time later, a small ten-seat prop plane started making the run, once on Monday and once on Friday, but only during the winter months.

The main advantage of the plane was that, despite its limited schedule, it flew no matter what the weather–and it was fast. You were in Tallinn in thirty minutes, as opposed to four hours by bus if the ferries were running on schedule. I rode in the small plane a few times and it proved quite convenient, but it could be a pretty scary experience. I was convinced the Russian pilots were veterans of the Afghanistan conflict because they always circled the airport, shouted at the tower a few times, and then dove down to the runway as if trying to avoid Stinger missiles.

On one of these white-knuckle approaches, we hit the runway extra hard and the plane started weaving violently back and forth as the pilots cursed in Russian and grabbed at the controls. It looked like we were headed for disaster, but the plane screeched to a halt still quite some distance from the terminal. The pilots gave no explanation as they brushed past me. (The pilots always exited first.) At the door, one of them turned around, shrugged his shoulders and said in heavily accented English, "We walk." After I exited the plane and thanked God for his boundless mercy, I saw that we had actually blown a tire when we pancaked in. As we walked down the remainder of the runway, the young director of the airport came running out of the terminal, his face portraying a mixture of relief and concern. After making sure everyone was okay, he took me inside and bought me several drinks at the small airport bar.

So, despite the four-hour journey, when the weather was nice the ferry was really the best option. In good weather you could stand outside on the deck as a gentle breeze blew through your hair and the small islets in the strait slipped by one by one. There were always gulls flying around and sometimes seals could be seen alongside the ship, keeping track of our progress. At night, the blinking of lighthouses on the various reefs and shoals guided our way. Quite idyllic, but when a storm kicked up, all bets were off for sea transport. Normally there were several ferries making approximately seven runs a day, but once the winds reached thirty-five miles per hour the ferries simply remained moored at the pier.

Sometimes they stopped for just a few hours, sometimes for a few days. It didn't matter who you were or where you wanted to go–if the ferry wasn't going, you were stuck. In that respect, the ferry was the great equalizer. Everyone from the Governor of Hiiumaa on down to the lowly local Peace Corps Volunteer could be seen waiting their turn to be a passenger on one of the hulking converted troopships.

The trip usually took ninety minutes, but as winter set in and the ice started to form in the seventeen-mile strait between Hiiumaa and the mainland, the time it took to make the crossing grew longer and longer. The first ferry of the morning had it the worst, since it was the one that had to break a new channel for the others to follow. The vessels were tough-hulled and powerful icebreakers, but as the ice pack thickened to one foot, two feet and even more, their progress slowed to a crawl. Sometimes the ferry would actually back up, take a run at the ice, then repeat the process. It was quite a sensation to feel the huge craft rear up onto the ice and then break through like some floundering elephant seal. Once in a while the ferry became stuck in a vice between ice floes and had to wait until the ice pack shifted enough to give the captain enough sufficient room for another assault.

In the winter, trips of two and three hours were common, but everybody had their own ferry horror story to tell. I had been relatively lucky, with my longest crossing being a little over three hours, and there was always the bar to supply drinks and sandwiches and the television to reduce boredom. I had heard stories of excruciating ten, fourteen, eighteen-hour ferry rides in the days before the bar and television were put in the passenger compartment. The best ferry tale I ever heard was from one guy who said that his ferry left Hiiumaa and battled its way out for twelve hours before getting stuck and having to fight its way back another twelve hours. The whole ordeal lasted an agonizing twenty-six hours and the poor guy never even made it off the island. Despite the yearly hardship, the Hiiumaa folks always seemed to take such setbacks in stride. "After all," they would say, and shrug their shoulders, "what to do?"

This second winter for me in Estonia, as the ice grew thicker, I noticed that Tarmo was beginning to act strangely. When we were driving around, he would often go out of his way to get close to the shore. Sometimes he would stop the car in order to stand and gaze longingly toward the mainland. I attributed his behavior to some kind of cabin fever, but I was to learn the real cause soon enough. One quiet weekend afternoon, I was at Tarmo's place reading a magazine when he suddenly walked over and gave me a slap on the knee.

"Hey, do you want to drive to the mainland?" he asked with that familiar glint in his eye.

"Nah. The ferry takes too long these days," I said and went back to my reading.

"No. I mean, let's *drive*," Tarmo responded, trying to be matter-of-fact.

"What are you talking about?" I glanced up. "There's no road to the mainland."

"Oh yes, there is," said Tarmo with a note of triumph. "The Ice Road!"

"Ice Road?" I put down the magazine and looked closely at my mischievous friend.

"That's right! We can get across in forty minutes."

"You mean, drive across the whole way on the ice?"

"Sure! Lots of people do it."

"Look, I'm not driving seventeen miles across the open sea, solid ice or not."

"Ah, come on. Don't be scared." Tarmo was in full stride now. "It's pretty safe."

"*Pretty* safe?"

"Well, they do lose a few cars every year, but I'm careful."

I raised my magazine again to block him out. "No way, I'm not going."

"Douglas, you said you were here to experience Hiiumaa life and this is it."

"Look, I didn't come here to die, so forget it."

"Okay, okay," he relented, and appeared to drop the subject. "Tell you what. I have some Vana Tallinn Liqueur. Let's have a drink."

We stepped into the kitchen and Tarmo pulled out a bottle of the syrupy Estonian drink that he knew I had a weakness for. Most Estonians turned up their noses at this mix of roughly 50% sugar and 50% percent alcohol, but I was crazy about it. We (mostly me) did shots while Tarmo continued talking about the wonders of the Ice Road. He was absolutely set in the idea that I had to go across on the ice. I resisted, but as the alcohol began to take its toll my protests became weaker and weaker. Tarmo assured me that it was not like in the old days when you drove completely at your own peril. I wondered aloud who would have been the first guy to try to cross. I pictured it this way: A bunch of Hiiumaa guys would go down to the shore and start drinking the dreaded homemade Hiiumaa beer. Then, when everybody got good and sauced, they would load the drunkest one into an old Lada and send him on his way. The rest would stay behind and watched with binoculars. If the poor guy made it, then the rest would follow. If not....well, they could try the next day. Come to think of it, that's probably the reason why there are more women than men on Hiiumaa. Every year, a few men would be sacrificed to the Ice Road.

Nowadays, Tarmo explained, the Department of Highways went out and tested the ice, marking out a safe route by pounding small pine trees into the surface. Still, there was no guarantee that the ice wouldn't shift or crack, so you were definitely driving at your own risk. There was also the problem of sudden storms. More than one unfortunate individual had become disoriented in the blowing snow and missed the island completely, driving on and on until the car dropped off the edge of the ice pack on the way to Sweden.

I was still pretty hesitant about going, but Tarmo kept up the pressure, sometimes teasing, sometimes earnestly appealing to my sense of adventure. Finally, my judgment thoroughly impaired by alcohol, I stood up and banged my fist on the table. "Ice Road! Let's do it! Yeah!"

We jumped into Tarmo's little blue pickup and drove down to the ferry harbor and through the parking lot, then bumped down a snow-packed path behind the harbor building. There, on the edge of the sea ice, sat a small booth with a policeman standing outside. He was holding a clipboard and talking to each driver that passed through. Tarmo explained that this was a control system to help determine if there was need for a rescue mission. The cop at one end would write down the license numbers of all the cars that passed. He would then call his colleague on the other side and give him the list. They would check cars off the list as they came through and then compare notes at the end of the day. If there was a car that went through on one end and didn't show up at the other, a rescue mission might be necessary. I felt somewhat reassured that at least someone would know that we were embarking on this risky adventure.

We pulled up to the booth, gave the policeman our license number and then rolled out onto the ice. I grabbed reflexively at the door handle as we rolled out onto the smooth surface. Tarmo saw this and laughed, but I didn't care. I wanted to be ready to abandon the vehicle if we broke through. It was some comfort to see that there was a good covering of snow, which obscured the fish swimming just inches below us. If I concentrated hard enough, I could imagine that we were driving across a snow-covered field back in Nebraska. I shielded my eyes against the sun's glare and picked out a line of small pine trees, one every 100 meters stretching out to the white featureless horizon. Tarmo gradually accelerated and, with me clutching the dashboard, we began our crossing. I noticed that he had unbuckled his seat belt, probably to enable a quick escape, so I did the same.

As Hiiumaa grew smaller in the rearview mirror, I began to relax. Like a desert caravan heading for an oasis we followed the other cars along the line of pine trees leading to the other side,. When Hiiumaa was no longer visible, we were surrounded by unbroken whiteness, horizon to horizon, with nothing to disturb the icy surface as far as the eye could see. It was so bright that I could only look out the window with one eye shielded by my glove. The beauty of the barren landscape held me in a kind of trance and I almost forgot that under us was nothing but cold seawater. I felt some safety in our little wagon train. After all, if there was a hole somewhere one of them would go through first, giving us plenty of warning. I slowly released my grip on the dashboard and door handle and sat back with a sigh. I was actually on the Ice Road. What a story to tell!

Tarmo glanced over at me and, apparently unhappy with my inner peace and tranquility, decided to stir things up a little bit. With little more than a "Watch this," he cranked the wheel to the left and the little pickup leaped up out of the wheel ruts and sped across the pristine surface away from the safety of the established road. I grabbed the dashboard and protested loudly, the last warmth of the moment (and the Vana Tallinn) vanishing into the crisp winter air. As the speedometer reached unbelievable heights, I looked back to see that we were leaving an enormous plume of powdered snow behind us. It rose up and swirled around like a snowy dust devil, reaching high into the blue sky before falling back to the surface a quarter mile or so behind us. It reminded me of those films of cars breaking the land speed record at Bonneville Salt Flats. Terrified of the speed and the likelihood of us taking an unexpected dive into the Baltic Sea, I begged Tarmo to slow down. He gave me one of his puckish looks, let off the gas and pulled hard on the emergency break.

The effect was immediate. Without any discernible reduction in speed, the rear end of the pickup broke lose and launched us into a slow spin. I resumed gripping the dashboard as the centrifugal force pressed me against the door. I had cut some "cookies" in my old car during high school, but they paled in comparison to the maneuver we were engaged in now. We made one sweeping quarter-mile pirouette after another until I lost count of the number of spins. The whole time, Tarmo whooped with glee and I hung on in grim silence. When we slid to a stop we were immediately engulfed in a cloud of snow that invaded the cab of the pickup in such quantity that for some moments I couldn't even see Tarmo sitting next to me. When the snow settled, the first thing I saw was Tarmo's grinning face. He was thoroughly pleased with himself, having once again managed to give me a near-heart attack.

"Well, how did you like that?" he said with palpable pride.

"Get–get back on the road!" was all I could manage to sputter.

"No hurry," Tarmo responded calmly. "The ice is just as thick here."

"How in the hell do you know that?" I responded, getting my breath back.

"I can just tell. Watch this."

I dreaded those two words more than any others that ever sprang from Tarmo's mouth. They always boded some feeling of discomfort or fear on my part–and this time was no exception. As I watched in horror, Tarmo jumped out of the door and began jumping up and down on the ice.

"See, it's strong," he said, trying to reassure me

"Tarmo, get back in the car! Are you crazy?" I asked, as if I actually needed a response in order to ascertain his level of sanity.

"This is great, isn't it? Think what you can tell your friends!"

"If I live to tell about! Please, get back in the damn car!"

"It's almost like we're not *on* the sea," Tarmo continued, as if he hadn't heard me.

"Yes, yes!" I said hastily "Now, let's get going."

"But we are on the sea, Douglas. Watch this!"

There it was, that dreaded phrase again. And as I watched in helpless disbelief, Tarmo went to the back of the pickup, pulled out his ice auger and began chewing a hole through the ice just a few feet from my door. I scrambled out the driver's side and stood a safe distance away while Tarmo happily ground his way down through two feet of ice. Suddenly, he broke through and a geyser of water burst from the hole. As the water began spreading across the ice, he jumped back in the pickup and drove over to where I was standing. "Pretty cool, huh?" I got in and looked back warily at the rapidly expanding pool.

Just as the water started lapping at the tires, Tarmo slipped the pickup into gear and we were under way. At a more reasonable speed this time, we headed back towards the Ice Road. Eventually, my heartbeat slowly returned to normal and my adrenaline stopped pumping. Tarmo was visibly pleased, tapping on the steering wheel and humming to himself. He had done it to me again.

Then, like a mirage, a ferry appeared ahead of us. A stranger sight I had never seen before and will probably never see again: car and boat meeting in the middle of an icy wasteland. We actually drove by the ferry close enough to wave at the passengers on deck. The ferry was hard at work lunging up onto the ice and breaking through. In the process, it sent huge cracks shooting across the surface of the ice towards us. Fortunately Tarmo gave the ferry a wide enough berth and soon we were back on the marked road. Twenty minutes later we were giving our license number at the booth on the other side. When we finally bounced back up onto dry land, I breathed a silent prayer of thanks.

We decided to grab something to eat and visit the medieval castle in the coastal town of Haapsalu. It was mid-afternoon but the light was already starting to go. I also detected a shift in the wind, which worried me a little bit. Storms came up fast in the winter, and I couldn't afford to be trapped on the mainland. I had to be at work the next day and attend a few meetings.

A little food, some shopping, and a walk around Haapsalu castle and it was already time to head back. I noticed that some gray clouds were building up on the horizon and the wind had picked up considerably. Tarmo noticed this too, and drove a little faster than usual through the town and down the coast to the ferry harbor. We were anxious to beat the storm, but by the time we reached the harbor darkness had fallen and the snow was starting

to fly. We sped over to the booth by the seashore, but the policeman waved us off with his baton. The Ice Road was shut down.
Cursing under his breath, Tarmo jumped out and engaged the
policeman in an animated conversation. They talked for a good
ten minutes, but when Tarmo got back into the cab I could tell by
his face that there was no chance of driving across. Our only hope
was the ferry, and in the strengthening wind that possibility was
less and less likely. Other disappointed drivers began milling around
the policeman's booth. At one time there were so many crowding
around that all I could see was the officer's baton waving emphatically in the air. Everyone was trying to convince him to open the
Ice Road.

Tarmo, however, saw the writing on the wall and drove over to
the harbor building. He knew that as soon as it became clear that
the Ice Road wasn't going to be opened, there would be a run on
ferry tickets. We checked the schedule and found out we had arrived a half-hour before the departure of the next ferry, as was
required. We purchased our ticket and sat in the café next to a
large picture window where we had a great view of the harbor and
would be able to line up quickly once the loading started.

By now it was completely dark and the snow was really starting to fly. There was a sense of uneasiness in the harbor as the
dockhands glanced warily up at the sky and lashed down equipment on the ferries that were idling at the pier. A half-hour went
by with no movement from the harbormaster, and the wind continued to increase. I could tell that the wind was nearing the point
where it would preclude any ferry traffic. After an hour, there was
an impromptu conference on the pier with the harbormaster, the
captains of the two ships in port and some of the waiting drivers.
When the conference broke up, a couple of the drivers came into
the bar and gave us the news. We were going for it.

The café quickly emptied and people scrambled for their cars.
As we lined up, we learned the plan was to take two ferries at once
for safety, which was almost unheard of. By the grim looks of the
crew and the other drivers, it was obvious that the decision to go

had not been made lightly. Our group of cars was formed into two lines and we began to load. Our line boarded the ferry *Ahilaid* while the others loaded onto the *Vohilaid*. After about twenty minutes the loading was complete and the *Vohilaid* struggled away from the pier and set out through the ice. The *Ahilaid*, with us on board, slipped in behind and began the tortuous journey through the ice pack and the blinding snowstorm. I sat with Tarmo in the warm passenger compartment where we shared a cognac and coffee. The grinding sound of the ice on the hull was reassurance that we were making progress. A few of the passengers were already settling down to sleep and it looked like we were in for an uneventful, albeit unusually slow, journey.

About half an hour into the crossing, our ferry suddenly cut its engines and we drifted to a halt. I went to the window along with some of the passengers, but we could see nothing through the driving snow. The others sat back down and started chatting, but I still wanted to see what was going on. I bundled up my coat and went out onto the deck. I walked up as far forward as I could go, leaned out over the rail, and peered through the driving snow. I could just barely make out the reason for our delay and also the reason for us traveling in tandem: the *Vohilaid* was stuck fast, her running lights barely visible about a quarter mile ahead. The *Ahilaid* paused several minutes, then backed up a few hundred meters. She then revved her engines, surged forward, and broke out of one side of the channel cut by the *Vohilaid*. With a great grinding and cracking sound, we began to break our way around the imprisoned *Vohilaid*, finishing the maneuver by cutting closely across her bow and breaking the ice that was holding her fast. I watched in awe as our straining ship tossed up chunks of ice close to a meter thick. Then, as we waited, the *Vohilaid* struggled free and forged on towards Hiiumaa. The *Ahilaid* then backed into the channel cut by the lead ship and we pressed forward once again.

We repeated this maneuver several times, and each time we successfully freed the *Vohilaid*. Although if was bitterly cold standing out in the storm, I was fascinated by the drama playing out in the icy Baltic Sea. This was real man-against-nature stuff—

our two ferries struggling alone against a raging storm coming out of the North.

For a while we seemed to be winning the battle, but then the worst-case scenario happened. As the *Ahilaid* bravely forged out of the channel once again in an effort to free her sister ship, she herself became stuck. The powerful northerly wind was shifting the ice and we were now both caught in its vice-like grip. After straining for several minutes, we shut down our engines and the ship fell silent. The *Vohilaid* was stranded about three hundred meters off our port side, also helpless.

When nothing happened for several minutes I went back inside, ordered a cognac and coffee to warm up, and sat down next to Tarmo. A few of the sleeping passengers stirred and asked what was going on, but for the most part we sat in silence and waited. An hour dragged by, then two.

As we got into the third hour of waiting, a strange thing started to happen. The passengers, who had been sitting in glum silence, started stirring and talking to one another. One man went up to the bar and bought drinks for all the folks on his bench. Another followed suit and a line quickly formed at the bar. It was as if everybody had come back to life all at once. A couple of older men came and sat down with Tarmo and me and started sharing with us their own nightmare ferry stories. Somebody flipped on the television and the room started taking on a real party atmosphere. I was amazed how the normally reserved Hiiumaa folks seemed magically transformed by this inconvenient and possibly dangerous situation. We continued on with our drinking and talking until one of the men took a look out the window and called out that the *Vohilaid* was getting closer. We crowded to the window to see and, sure enough, the *Vohilaid* was now clearly visible, not more than a hundred meters away. Thinking she had freed herself, we crowded onto the deck to take a look.

We expected to be greeted by the sound of straining diesel engines and cracking ice, but there was nothing but the sound of the wind. The laughing stopped and a chilling silence came over us when

we realized what was happening. The shifting ice pack was pushing the two ships together, slowly but surely. If we were to collide,
there would be no hope of rescue in the driving storm. In addition, both ships were probably being shifted out of the shipping
lane, maybe into shallower water where we would be grounded on
the rocks, which was also a pretty bleak scenario in this kind of
weather.

We watched quietly as the *Vohilaid* drew closer and closer. Strangely
enough, the lyrics of the song "The Wreck of the Edmund Fitzgerald"
were running through my head. I realized this might be the end of my
Peace Corps career. I once again found myself wondering how many
Volunteers had been lost at sea. Maybe I would receive some kind of
posthumous medal. Then again, probably not.

When the distance between the two ships shrank to about fifty
meters, we could clearly see the passengers on the deck of the *Vohilaid*
staring back at us through the driving snow. I noticed that their
passenger compartment was dark. Weren't they also partying? As we
drew even closer, one of the other passengers recognized one of his
friends on our ship.

"Hey, Mart," he called out. "You got a beer?"

"Get your own, ya mooch!" Mart called back, and we all
laughed, breaking the tension.

"Can't," replied his friend. "Our bar's not open."

"Well, that's real sad. Ours is open for business." We all made
sounds of mock sympathy.

"Really? *Kurat!*" came the reply, as we on the *Ahilaid* raised
our glasses in a toast.

"Not to worry, we can help you out," somebody from the
drunker crowd on our side yelled.

A few of our group went back up to the bar and returned with
several bottles of beer. As I watched in amused disbelief, one of the
burlier guys hauled back and flung a beer in the direction of the
other ship. It fell well short and broke on the ice as the passengers
on the *Vohilaid* jeered. Our man calmly lit a cigarette, waited several minutes until the ship was closer, and then launched another

missile. This one fell just short and the mocking laughs echoed once again from the deck of the *Vohilaid*.

Some of the others on our ship took up the challenge and bottles began flying. They had the distance, but it was nearly impossible for those on the other side to catch the flying bottles, which ended up either smashing on the deck or against the wheelhouse. Probably six beers fell victim to this ill-fated scheme before the old captain of the *Vohilaid* came sputtering out of the wheelhouse, calling us all a bunch of "crazy bastards" and herding his passengers back inside. Now we had nothing to do but wait.

The distance closed and once again we fell silent. There seemed to be no way out of our dire situation and no sign the storm was letting up. The deckhands on both ships started making preparations for the seemingly inevitable collision. We were nearly close enough to jump from one ship to the other before our captain decided to make a final last-ditch effort. He revved up the diesel engines one more time and the ship strained against the ice holding it captive. When there was no progress forward, the captain shut the engines down and tried in reverse. After two more unsuccessful tries, we finally detected some movement. We were breaking free.

I breathed a sigh of relief and a cheer went up from both ships as we edged slowly away and gained valuable running room. The *Ahilaid*, engines at full throttle, valiantly struggled to break a channel around the front of her sister ship. After much back and forth motion and thrusting of huge chunks of ice, we were both free and back on our course towards our destination.

At least two more hours passed before the lights of Hiiumaa's harbor came into view. As we pulled up against the pier, I noticed the *Hiidlased* reverted back to their stoic quiet selves. Nobody crowded up against the rail to wave at loved ones on shore. There was no backslapping or congratulations as we filed down the stairs to our cars. It was if nothing unusual had ever happened. The cars filed off the ferry in an orderly manner and I took a look at my watch, which read 2:30 a.m. It had been almost eight hours since we had left the ferry port on the mainland. All I wanted to do was go to bed, but I was happy knowing that I would have real story to tell the next day. Then again, maybe I would just keep quiet.

18—THE HIIUMAA CHRISTMAS BELL

One beautiful spring day, just as the first tourists began to arrive, I was at my usual post in the TIC, looking forward to the second tourist season since my arrival as a Peace Corps Volunteer. Actually, it was only the third tourist season for Hiiumaa ever, now that Estonia had regained independence and the islands were no longer closed border areas in the Soviet Union.

I had run across my share of interesting characters during my time on the island. Hiiumaa's closed conditions had, over the years, produced a unique and fascinating local culture. However, nothing could have prepared me for the next guest who burst through the door to the info center. The man, who looked to be about seventy, was bald on the top of his head with great shocks of white hair bursting up on both sides like smoke coming out of his ears. His piercing blue eyes quickly took in the room before focusing straight on me. He was rather tall, and after he approached the counter he had to look down slightly to speak to me. He gripped the edge of the table and spoke in an excited voice.

"Are you Douglas Wells?" he said in Estonian and raised one bushy white eyebrow.

"Yes," I replied. "How can I help you?" He glanced quickly from side to side before lowering his voice and bending down slightly. "My name's Jetter Tull. Do you still have that metal detector?" Now this was a strange question for a tourist to ask, so I didn't answer right away. I did still have the metal detector, but I was wary about making that public knowledge, especially after the Energy Triangle debacle. Needless to say, having to go to the armory to check out my detector had cut back on my forays to the forest. All I wanted now was for the whole thing to blow over. I didn't want more rumors circulating that the local Peace Corps Volunteer was a pillager of ancient local culture.

When I finally answered the old man's question, I did so slowly and in a guarded tone. "Yes, I still have it. Why do you ask?"

The man's arm shot out and grabbed my wrist. "You've got to help me! We must find the clock!"

"What clock?" I said. I pulled back a bit, but the man held on and pushed his face closer to mine.

"The church clock!" he said, his voice low and husky. "The church clock that they buried fifty years ago. You have to help me. We're running out of time!"

I was becoming nervous by how worked up the stranger was becoming. I couldn't imagine it could be about some old clock.

"Where is it and what is it made of?" I asked, still skeptical.

The old man released my wrist but stared at me strangely. "Bronze, of course. Solid bronze. It is somewhere in the forest near Emmaste village. Please come. My car is outside!"

My paranoia raised some suspicion in my mind, but the old man was so earnest, his piercing blue eyes so intense, that I could no longer doubt his sincerity. He was obviously a man with a mission. Against my better judgment, I agreed to accompany what appeared to be a relatively unstable old man to an unknown location in the forest, where the National Guard cronies just might be waiting to "protect" the local culture from unsavory characters like me.

First we went to the to the armory where, after a brief interrogation, the duty officer unlocked the gun locker pushed aside a few Kalashnikov machine guns and ceremoniously handed over my fearsome metal detector.

Then, as we drove toward the south side of the island, Jetter seemed to relax a little. He pushed back in his seat, took a deep breath and began to talk. I sat spellbound as he told a story that could have come from a best-selling adventure novel.

It all started in the summer of 1943. The tide of the war had turned and the Germans were being pushed back from Russia. With raw materials scarce, both sides had taken to scrounging for metal in the countryside. Hiding or hoarding metal was an offense punishable by a firing squad, so countless antiques and other objects of value went into the melting pot. Particularly sought after, the man told me, were large objects such as solid bronze church clocks. Already a few churches in Hiiumaa had been relieved of their clocks and now the small village of Emmaste was worried that theirs might be next. Their clock was the pride of the village. It was made in Tartu of solid bronze, weighed about 400 pounds, and had been in the tower since 1925. Although I couldn't imagine a clock made of solid bronze, the story captivated me and I let him continue.

One warm summer night in June, six men in the village gathered secretly to work out a way to save this important part of the heritage of Emmaste's church. The young men had thus far managed to escape the ravages of war. After much deliberation, they agreed on a plan. Late the next night they went to the church and, avoiding the occasional German patrol, carefully took down the pride of Emmaste. They carried the clock to the forest where they buried it, the plan being to return it to the tower when the war had quieted down.

But things didn't quiet down. The war took its course and scattered the group of six young men that were in on the secret. One was taken prisoner and sent to Siberia where he died in a prison camp, three tried to escape to Sweden ahead of the advancing Soviet army (only two succeeded), and two found their way to Canada after slipping away from Hiiumaa in a fishing boat. Only one made it back to Hiiumaa at war's end. When the Soviets reestablished their control over the island, it was immediately clear that this was not a religion-friendly regime, so the clock stayed put for over forty years until Estonia began taking steps to reestablish its independence.

In 1987, one of the original conspirators decided it was time to take stock of the situation and see if something could be done about restoring the lost treasure of Emmaste Church to its rightful place. Only three members of the group remained alive: one still on Hiiumaa, one in Canada and the one in Sweden who had decided the time had come to put things right. All were quite old so they sent my friend, the old man, from Sweden to find the clock.

Not surprisingly, the people of the village had pretty much given up the clock for lost. While the other locals had searched without success, the member of the group still on Hiiumaa kept quiet, fearing repercussions from the Soviet authorities. After all, if you get right down it, they burglarized the church and their noble motives would have been hard to explain, especially if the bell remained missing. The villagers had eventually decided that one of them must have sold it, taken the money and escaped. In fact, they blamed the member of the group who was still alive in Sweden and had even "found out" the price that he had received. For a loyal Estonian exile on his deathbed in Sweden, the accusation was too much to bear. This is what had brought my friend to Hiiumaa. His mission was to clear his friend's name before he went to his grave.

After hearing the man's story, I agreed to look around in the forest, but there were complications. No one from the group had been back to Hiiumaa since the '40s, except for the one member who had stayed. Unfortunately, time had fogged his memory to the point that he was no longer able to remember the clock's exact location. On top of that, a road and some buildings that had been constructed during the 50 years since the clock was buried had made the landscape almost unrecognizable. It was under these unfavorable circumstances that we started our search.

We arrived in Emmaste and Jetter directed me to a spot near an old farm where he said we would find our church treasure. There our search began. Back and forth, back and forth, I went with the metal detector. The old man followed close behind. At every beep of the detector, he jumped ahead with his shovel and started to dig. But alas, our search was in vain. At dusk I decided to give up.

"Look," I said, trying to be diplomatic, "maybe you've got the wrong place, or somebody else dug it up and sold it. At any rate, it's not here."

Jetter had a strange look of puzzlement and resignation on his face. "I don't understand it," he said at last. "It has to be here somewhere."

We drove back to my apartment without exchanging a single word. When he dropped me off, he said goodbye and shook my hand, but his mind was clearly elsewhere.

I wanted to write him off as a senile lunatic, but as I lay in bed that night my mind kept picturing the old man going back to Sweden and telling his sick, unjustly accused friend that the search had been fruitless. I recalled the old man's piercing blue eyes as he gripped my wrist and begged for my help.

As the next few weeks passed, I tried to forget about the strange encounter. Perhaps he was crazy or perhaps the clock really had been sold. Perhaps it was just plain lost. At any rate, I was glad to be through with the affair, and the rest of the summer and fall passed uneventfully. With the coming of bad weather, the metal detector sat undisturbed next to the machine guns in the armory.

One December day I sat in the info center, watching the rain and sleet fall outside. Although the current weather didn't evoke thoughts of the season, the announcer on the radio kept assuring we would have a white Christmas. The tourists had long since left, so I was a little surprised to hear the outside door open and some-one stamping their feet on the mat. A head poked around the corner and a hand pulled off a wool cap to reveal the unmistakable bushy eyebrows and white hair. Jetter bounded into the room and squinted at me with his blue eyes.

"Still here, eh?" he said. "I've got new information! The other living member of the group visited Sweden, and he told me we were looking in the wrong place."

I knew full well what he would soon be asking of me and, as I glanced at the rain and sleet falling outside, I felt a sinking feeling come over me. I tried politely to beg off without hurting his feelings. "Could you come back?" I asked hopefully. "The weather's kind of bad and I don't think the clock is going anywhere. Besides, the local National Guard has been kind of uppity about me using the metal detector."

I thought the last part would surely do the trick, but the old man would have none of it. "You *must* help," he went on, those blue eyes boring into me. "A man's on his deathbed with his honor at stake!"

He had me there. With a sigh of resignation I took my coat, which the old man had already retrieved from the coat rack, and headed out into the cold December rain. As I locked the door to the info center, I thought about how I would probably catch pneumonia over some stupid clock.

We rode in silence as the windshield wipers beat out a steady rhythm. Though it was only about one o'clock, the light was already fading and I figured that, at the most, I would have to run around in the forest for maybe two or three hours before I'd be back in my warm apartment, practicing Christmas songs on my guitar.

Jetter interrupted my thoughts. "First we get the metal detector out of the armory. Then we go to another old farmstead about one kilometer south of where we first were. According to the new information. That's where it should be. The group member from Canada was absolutely sure."

I highly doubted the memory of an elderly man who hadn't even stepped foot on the island in over fifty years. "Sucker," I said to myself, as I hunched down in the seat for the ride.

By the time we finally stopped on a gravel road, the rain had let up a bit. Just twenty feet away I could see a grove of trees, an old abandoned car wash, and what looked to be a grain-drying facility. It seemed pretty unlikely that anyone would try and hide something valuable in this particular spot. Apparently, my partner didn't share my skepticism. The old man jumped out of the car, grabbed a shovel from the trunk and motioned for me to follow him. I stuck my head out of the car door and squinted up at the sky, hoping to see a break in the clouds.

I sighed and grudgingly got out of the car, shouldered the metal detector and followed the old man towards the car wash.

There was no sound but the tone of the detector and the rain dripping off the leaves. With the old man accompanying me, I walked back and forth through the brush. I tried to maintain an organized search pattern, sweeping the detector around trees and through the ditch by the roadside, but Jetter kept calling, "Try over here! Try over there!"

After about two hours of this I had reached the limits of my patience. This is ridiculous! I thought as the light slowly faded and the wetness seeped through my clothes. As the old man watched me silently, I think he read my thoughts. He pointed at a small cluster of trees barely fifteen feet from where the car wash had been built.

"Please, just try that one last place," he said plaintively.

I crawled out of the ditch and mumbled aloud to myself. "If this is really some sort of church icon and if God wants us to find it, we will. It is in His hands, not mine. When I'm done here, I'm going to go home and forget about the whole thing!" Not thirty seconds later the metal detector gave a loud chirp. There was something really large buried between the small trees.

The old man saw me stop and came running over. "What is it?" he asked breathlessly.

I studied the detector's display. "I don't know, but it's big and pretty shallow and. . . . damn! It *is* some kind of bronze or other light metal."

The old man swept the leaves and ground clutter away, then rammed the shovel into the ground. Thunk! The blade hit something solid before it was even six inches down. Jetter dropped to his knees in the muddy soil, digging with his bare hands and throwing dirt from between his legs like a crazed gray-haired fox terrier. I stood watching in amazement as he uncovered a ring about three feet across, certainly nothing that resembled a clock.

"Ah, that ain't it," I said in disgust and started to turn away.

Jetter reached up and grabbed my collar. "What are you talking about? We've found it! Get back here and help me!"

Mostly out of fear, I joined in the digging. As we dug down in the center of the exposed ring and hit metal again, it finally dawned on me what we had found. This was no clock, but rather a huge church bell resting upside down only a few inches under the soil, mere feet from major construction.

I suddenly recalled learning that the Estonian word for "clock" was the same as that for "bell." The former usage was so common that I, with my fledgling Estonian, completely misunderstood the old man.

After we uncovered about half of the bell, my fellow treasure hunter sat back. He looked up at me and said with quiet determination, "We need help, and we need to tell the old pastor of the church. He was here when the bell was buried and he has to be told." His wet scraggly hair drooped down over his blue eyes as we silently looked at each other and then at the bell. The only sound was the light rain hitting the leaves and dripping onto the concrete pad of the car wash. After some moments, we gathered up our things and went to the car.

The pastor lived a couple of miles up the road in an old farmhouse. He had come to Hiiumaa after serving early in the war as a German officer. He had seen so much death and destruction (he himself was injured in the leg) that he joined the seminary after his discharge and retreated to this little island to do God's work.

A little dog barked excitedly as we pulled up, and an enormous yellow cat gazed at us through the window. The pastor's wife already had the door open by the time we reached the porch and we went straight inside without more than a few words of greeting.

"Where's Guido?" the old man said excitedly. "I have great news, wonderful news!"

The pastor's wife gave us a puzzled look. "He's in watching TV but what...?"

She didn't have a chance to finish as Jetter shot by her and into the living room with me close behind. There sat the bald elderly pastor holding a cane upright between his knees and resting his chin on his hands as he watched television through thick glasses. When we burst into the room he gave a start and squinted up at us. Without a word of explanation, the old man grabbed the pastor by the shoulder and started shaking him so hard that the poor man's glasses almost fell off. "Guido! We found the bell!" he shouted into the pastor's ear.

Pastor Guido Reinvalla shrank back in his chair with a look of confusion on his face. "Why are you yelling? What do you want?" he said in a quavering voice.

The old man sat on the floor in front of him and looked the pastor straight in the eyes. Slowly, he repeated his words. "Guido, we found the bell, the lost Emmaste Church bell!"

After a few short seconds, a look of comprehension swept over the pastor's face and, as it progressed, the years seem to melt away from his body. Almost magically, the pastor appeared to transform. As he straightened up and squared his shoulders, a fire came to his eyes.

"The bell!" he said, and suddenly leaped from his chair. Dropping his cane, he headed straight for the front door and would have made it outside had his wife not grabbed him by the shirt collar and pulled him back. She was larger than he was, and it was quite humorous to see the pastor trying to pull open the door while his wife held him back.

"Not without your coat and boots," she said firmly. "You'll catch your death of cold!" As his wife pulled on his boots and placed a cap on his head, the pastor looked like a child trying to escape out into the season's first snow.

"Let me go!" he said, and finally broke free. His wife followed us out, holding his cane, but the pastor never even slowed down. He jumped into the car and literally bounced up and down with anticipation in the back seat. I looked back to see his wife framed in the light of the open doorway, tears in her eyes and her hands folded in a silent prayer of thanks.

As we drove back, I think the pastor noticed me for the first time. I explained who I was and why I was helping to look for the bell. He didn't respond, only nodded thoughtfully. We rode the rest of the way in silence.

When we slid to a halt on the muddy road near the bell, Pastor Reinvalla was the first one out of the car. He held on to Jetter's arm as they made their way to where the bell lay half-uncovered. At the edge of the hole, the pastor stopped and peered down. He looked for a while, then slid his glasses down on his nose to peer over them. Several silent seconds ticked by before he fell suddenly to his knees. Tears rolled down his cheeks as he whispered a prayer of thanks. I could only stand there and watch, my mouth wide open.

A couple of old women rode by on their bicycles and stopped to see why the former village pastor was kneeling next to a hole in the ground. They walked up, took one look at the bell, and were off like a shot towards the village. I have never seen anybody pedal a bicycle so fast! Soon others from the village came, along with the director of the island's museum. After quite a crowd had gathered, four or five of us tried to pull the bell out of the hole. It wouldn't budge. We tried unsuccessfully until somebody brought a front-end loader, at which point the bell was lifted up and carried about a quarter mile to the church. I marveled again at how it had escaped detection in such a shallow hole, especially with the construction work done all around. It seemed a miracle.

When the bell had been placed on the floor of the church, the pastor held a short service to bless and welcome it back to its home. With night now fallen, I asked Jetter to give me a ride home. A crowd still stood about, pointing at the bell, then at the old man and me.

* * *

A few days later I went back home to Nebraska on Christmas leave. The flight path out of Tallinn took me right over Hiiumaa and I looked down at the cross-shaped island. "Merry Christmas," I said softly to myself, and imagined the beautiful sound the bell would make ringing in its first Christmas service in fifty years. With the cold crisp nights, the sound of the bell would reach to neighboring villages, beckoning people to come and see the miracle in Emmaste. I felt a surge of Christmas spirit like I hadn't felt since I was a kid.

With all the excitement of being back home and the holiday season, I didn't give much thought to the bell until one day I received an e-mail message from Tarmo in Estonia. "Douglas, you're not going to believe this," it started out. He went on to tell me how every major newspaper in Estonia had picked up the story of the Emmaste bell. The President of Estonia had thanked me personally during his Christmas speech to the nation:

> *"As a result of the occupation of Estonia, the Emmaste congregation took down their bell and hid it in the bosom of the earth, that it would survive until the restoration of the Estonian Republic. Months and years turned into decades. The hidden one's exact location faded from memory, but the memory of the bell waiting for its time to come burned bright. The national memory of the Estonians was only made stronger by the iron grip of the occupiers.*
>
> *Let the wondrous return of the Emmaste Bell to its tower be a present-day Christmas present to all Estonian people. Let the peals of the bell bring peace, loyalty, and love throughout Estonia, bringing news of the Christmas miracle that has been born among us.*

President Meri had his Chief of Staff call the Peace Corps office in Tallinn to say thanks. He even offered a percentage of his salary to restore the bell and put it back in the church tower. The Lutheran Bishop of Estonia also mentioned the bell in his Christmas address. I hadn't realized how important the bell had been to the rest of the country.

Back in Nebraska, my brother did a feature on the bell during the radio news show he hosted at a local radio station. He put it on the AP wire and the Omaha paper called to ask me to do an article. The story was picked up by several major papers and even made it to the English-language newspaper in Moscow. Needless to say, Christmas 1994 was a very special one for me.

Despite it all, one small fact bothered me. If the President was giving money to restore the bell, then it wasn't in the tower for Christmas after all. The thought saddened me because it seemed that all this had happened with just that in mind.

The holidays passed quickly and soon I was on a plane back to Estonia. Then, by bus and ferry, I made my way to Hiiumaa Island. I went to the church that Sunday to talk to the current pastor. He greeted me warmly and asked if I had heard about all the fuss.

I nodded. "Yeah, but it's too bad the bell wasn't up in the tower for Christmas."

The young pastor gave me a strange look. "Of course it was in the tower for Christmas!" he said. "We hosed it off and six guys from the village put it back up."

I thought for a moment. Six guys had taken the bell down, six friends who had never been able to return to finish their work. Now only three were still alive. How would the member of the group in Sweden react, the one who had been accused of selling the bell? I'll bet he had a great Christmas, perhaps his last.

"But what about the President's money?" I finally asked. "He was supposed to give a portion of his salary to help restore the bell."

The pastor looked at me for a moment and then laughed. "He did say that. And when we heard that such an important person as the president wanted to pay for putting the bell in the tower, we went right up and took it down again!" We both laughed and went inside the church. I walked over to where a thick rope was hanging down through a hole in the ceiling. I reached out to touch it, then turned to look at the pastor. He read my thoughts and, with a smile, nodded his head. I turned back, grabbed the rope with both hands and pulled as hard as I could.

19—THE THIN BLUE LINE

It is always nice to see someone who really enjoys his work and who is really well-suited for his job. Officer Karjamaa was one of the handful of police officers responsible for keeping order on the island, which was about fifteen by twenty-five miles in size. Hiiumaa was pretty sleepy most of the year, with some excitement in the summer when the tourists came to enjoy the few months of long days, sunny skies, and warm temperatures. The tourists also served as amusement for locals, as they often got drunk and did stupid things, or just generally tried to show how superior they were, coming from the mainland and all.

Aside from the tourists and visitors who came and went, the police pretty much knew everyone on the island, and all the locals knew who the police were. This familiarity among the island's population was for the most part charming, but it did have its downsides and often created unusual situations you would never see on the mainland. For example, there was no car theft on Hiiumaa. If someone were to steal a car, the police would just go down to the ferry port and wait for the thief to try and leave with it. Or they would just park somewhere by the main road that circled the island and wait for the carjacker to drive by, which he would have no choice but to do at some point. If some petty crime did occur, people on the island would ring their hands and worry that this new democracy would turn Hiiumaa into a "Chicago," the place they used to denote complete chaos and utter lawlessness.

It was in this placid realm that Karjamaa fearlessly did his duty. The Terror of Hiiumaa, as everyone called him, was responsible for traffic safety, a job he took very, very seriously. Drivers feared him. No one was safe from Karjamaa, regardless of their station in life. Rich or poor, young or old, all were equal in the eyes of Karjamaa. He was so notorious and diligent in enforcing the law that if someone would leave a late-night party to go drive someplace, people would look at them with sympathy and say, "Karjamaa in your path," much like actors tell each other to break a leg.

Pretty much everyone had been stopped and lectured by Karjamaa at one time or another, and as a passenger I had witnessed countless traffic stops. The scenario was almost always the same: Karjamaa would step out from the side of the road somewhere and flag you down, sometimes for no apparent reason, which is legal in Estonia. He would walk up to the driver's window, pull himself up to his full height, and introduce himself as "Traffic Police Inspector Mihkel Karjamaa." This was required by law, so he did this even though we all knew exactly who he was. After he completed his official business he would salute, wish you a good day, and wave you off down the road. The last thing you would see in your rearview mirror was the good inspector standing in the middle of the road, arms folded, holding his little black and white police baton with the red reflector on the end.

My first run-in with Karjamaa as a motorist was shortly after I had purchased my first vehicle in Estonia. I wasn't really supposed to drive, but with the infrequent public transportation, I found it impossible to do my job properly without some kind of vehicle. I settled on an old black Volga, which in its glory days was the car of choice among the Communist Party elite. People made endless jokes as I drove the beat-up former taxi around, but for me the important thing was that it was cheap and parts were plentiful. I think every Estonian male had some Volga parts behind his garage and these guys always wanted to tweak something or replace something on my Volga when I came to visit. It was all I could do to keep them from going at my car with a wrench or screwdriver, sometimes even at stop signs.

It was on a day when I was cruising along near the edge of Kärdla that I was stopped for speeding. The speed limits were in kilometers, but I think I was doing like forty-something in a thirty-five zone. Karjamaa stepped out from beside his car and waved me to a stop with his little baton. He came over, smartly introduced himself as always, and asked me to present my documents. Throughout the incident, the officer kept one hand behind his back, which I found a little strange. I also noticed a certain spring in his step and—could it be?—a little mischief in his eyes. He spent some time poring over my Nebraska driver's license before handing me back my papers. He then drew himself up to his full 5'8" of height and proudly announced that I had been speeding.

"Vells," he began, pronouncing my last name with an Estonian accent, "you were going forty-four in a thirty-five zone!"

"Um, okay. I'm sorry, sir."

He seemed perturbed that I had not grasped his point. "No, you don't understand. I mean you were going *exactly* forty-four kilometers."

"All right," I said, not getting what he was driving at. "That's a little fast. Right, sir?"

At this point, he was visibly shaking with anticipation. "Don't you even want to know how I knew you were going exactly forty-four?" he asked hopefully.

"Okay, I'm game. How did you know I was going exactly forty-four?"

"Because, Vells," he said triumphantly, "I have…this!"

He pulled his hand out from behind his back and proudly showed off his new toy. The look on his face was priceless, like that of a child who had finally received the perfect Christmas present. As he twisted his new possession in his hand and regarded it admiringly in the glow of the setting sun, I realized that a new era had begun in Hiiumaa. Police radar had arrived.

But that wasn't all. Karjamaa then leaned down to show me the blinking blue digital numbers and thumped his finger emphatically on the manufacturer's nameplate. He could barely contain himself as he delivered the coup de grâce.

"Vells, look at that. This little baby is from America. It's made in Texas! That's where you're from, right?"

"Actually, sir, I'm from Nebraska."

"Doesn't matter! You have been caught with foreign aid from your own country! What do you think about that!"

As he laughed heartily, I slumped down in my seat and sighed. No place was safe from change. Before this, the police would just stop you, say you were speeding, and collect some fine based on how fast you seemed to be going. At first, it was hard to get used to handing a cop a handful of cash, but at least they gave you a receipt—no court costs either. Now Karjamaa had radar, and he was like a kid in a candy store. He regained some semblance of a business-like expression and addressed me sternly.

"Well, this has been great, but I am afraid you're still going to have to pay a fine."

"Sure, I understand. How much?"

"75 kroons." This was the rough equivalent of about six American dollars.

I rummaged through my pockets but came up short. "I've only got sixty-three with me."

"All right, all right," he said impatiently. "Just give it to me and we'll call it even!"

I handed him all the money in my wallet. He wrote me out a receipt, then turned briskly on his heel and walked backed to his car without so much as performing his customary send-off routine. For the next three days he sat on the edge of town clocking people. After being stopped three times myself, I started riding my bike to work. Even when I was safely home in my apartment, I could still see his car out of my window. I began to think that the Terror of Hiiumaa didn't even sleep. He was there when I woke and he was there when I went to bed. I don't think he was even writing tickets, just showing off his new toy. I could see him walk over to the hapless driver's window and wave his radar gun excitedly for a while before the car drove off. Word spread fast that the Terror was now equipped with modern technology, and people muttered behind my back in the grocery store line that it was thanks to those "meddling Yankees" and the "new world order."

The last time I saw Officer Karjamaa it was Midsummer Night's Eve. It was at this time that people really cut loose. They would build bonfires, sing, dance and often drink themselves senseless. On the Summer Solstice in Estonia, the days were so long it never got completely dark at night. For just a few hours, an enchanting twilight descended on the island, which seemed to add additional energy and mystique to the partying.

The band had a full schedule at this time of year, so as usual I was driving home in my black Volga from a late night (early morning) party on the other side of the island. I wasn't drunk but I had put down a few of the infamous Hiiumaa beers and definitely would have failed the no-tolerance limit for drivers in Estonia. As I came around the curve on the highway into town, I spotted a police car up ahead by the side of the road. A glance down at my speedometer confirmed that I was a little over the speed limit. Damn.

Sure enough, the Terror stepped out into the middle of the road and waved his baton. I noticed he had a new recruit with him this time, probably breaking him in on the mean streets of Hiiumaa. My biggest worry was that they would make me do a breath test, which, if I failed, would cost me a good piece of change. Plus, it would be hard to explain a DWI to the Peace Corps office when I was officially only supposed to be riding a bike.

I pulled to the side of the road and Karjamaa stepped up to my window while his fresh-faced rookie watched intently from the car. He snapped to attention, went through the introduction and asked for my license and registration, which I figured he would have already memorized. He took them back to the car and showed them to his trainee, who seemed quite interested in my Nebraska license, turning it over and over in his hand and holding it up to the dome light. After they talked for a while, Karjamaa leaned out the window and yelled for me to come over to the car. I got out and walked across the road, expecting the worse. As I drew closer, Karjamaa nudged his new partner and gave a "watch this" kind of wink.

"So, Vells, you were going a little fast there."

"Yes, sir. I'm sorry. I just crossed city limits and hadn't slowed down yet."

"Do you want to know how fast you were going?"

I played along with his little game. "Uh...okay."

"You were going exactly sixty-two. Do you want to know how I know that, Vells?"

"Well, I imagine it's because–"

"Because I have this radar gun, Vells."

"Yes, sir."

"Look, it says right here that you were going exactly sixty-two."

"Yes, sir."

"And do you know where this radar gun was made, Vells?"

"Texas, sir."

"That's right!" he said and looked triumphantly over at his partner.

I was getting a little tired of this cat and mouse game, and I wished he'd just get on with it. Karjamaa seemed to read my thoughts. He looked at my license and registration again, then scratched his chin thoughtfully. He then looked over at his rookie partner, who sat up straighter in his seat and watched with anticipation. Finally, after a long pause, Karjamaa spoke.

"So you were speeding. Eh, Vells?"

"Yes, sir."

"Well, what do you think we should do?"

"Excuse me?"

"What do you want to do?"

This caught me completely off guard and I was at a loss for words. I had never in my life been asked by a police officer what I would like to do, and I wondered if it wasn't some kind of trap. Karjamaa and his partner waited patiently while I mulled over what the correct answer to this question should be. My future as a Peace Corps Volunteer probably depended on it. Finally, at a complete loss, I decided to just take the direct, honest approach.

"How about this: I walk back over to my car, get in and verrrrry slowly drive away."

I took a step back and waited for a response. Karjamaa thought for a minute, then turned to his partner. "That okay with you?" he said gruffly. His partner just shrugged and looked the other way, seemingly disappointed by this strange turn of events. Karjamaa thrust my documents into my hand and motioned for me to go.

"Okay, Vells. Have a good holiday. Slow down and drive carefully!"

I thanked him and walked back to my car in a daze. What the heck had just happened? I couldn't believe my luck as I started the Volga and drove away. I kept looking in the rearview mirror expecting them to take off after me but all I saw was Karjamaa, standing by the road and thumping that black and white baton into his palm.

I never saw the Terror of Hiiumaa after that. Rumor has it he was reassigned to a desk job, a severe punishment for him considering how much he had enjoyed his role as a traffic officer. What could he have done to deserve such a fate? Karjamaa stopped the Estonian Prime Minister during an official visit and tried to ticket the entire motorcade–or so the legend goes.

20—GETTING THE WORD OUT

The more I experienced on Hiiumaa Island, the more I liked it. The more I liked it, the more I wanted people to come and visit my new exotic island home. Sales of the guidebook were off to a good start and there was no shortage of people wanting to come for a visit. My workload was such that I spent more and more time in my Kärdla apartment. In particular, my Peace Corps colleagues wanted to check out the place that I had been raving about. Naturally, in addition to reading about the points of interest, they also wanted information (in English) about where they could eat, sleep and shop. This was perfectly reasonable and I should have been able to just hand out brochures or drop something in the mail. Problem was, there was no English-language source of information listing shops, lodging places and restaurants. We at the TIC were reduced to scribbling names and phone numbers on Soviet-era Hiiumaa maps and passing them out to tourists in search of food and lodging. Not only was this a little embarrassing and time-consuming, this meant we had nothing to send to travel agencies and potential tourists who called or wrote. In my opinion, this revealed a serious flaw in Hiiumaa's developing tourism industry, so I approached the local government officials for help.

In a letter, I asked the four Hiiumaa municipalities plus the town of Kärdla to put together a list of businesses that tourists could patronize, including their addresses and phone numbers—nothing fancy, just lists that I could compile into some kind of comprehensive information sheet. The response was . . . well, let's just say that it was less than enthusiastic. My explanation that more tourists equaled more revenue for businesses, which in turn equaled more tax revenues, seemed a little bit too convoluted for them to buy into. I think only one of my letters was answered with any kind of useable list. When I telephoned to follow up on the letters, the responses ranged from the charmingly typical ("Oh yeah, we should do that sometime") to the indignant ("If the businesses want tourists, let them type up their own list!"). I was even treated to the characteristic fatalism I heard so often when I was trying to pitch an idea: "All local businesses cheat on their taxes anyway, so we won't benefit one bit!"

What really drove me up the wall was that every time I found myself in one of these conflicts of ideas, I came out on the losing end. Despite my exhaustive Peace Corps training in cross-cultural communication, instead of me "helping" them, which I felt was my duty, the encounter always turned into them patiently trying to teach me "how things really were," which they evidently felt was their duty. There was not even an inkling of the give-and-take that we were told would be such a critical element in a successful Peace Corps venture. The Hiiumaa folks were maddeningly confident, believing firmly that they knew exactly what was going on and exactly what needed to be done (or more often, not done). It was as if they thought I was there for two years to study the Hiiumaa way of doing things, as opposed to me sharing my knowledge and skills with them. Things began to follow a familiar pattern: I would approach them with an idea or request and they would smile patiently as they shot me down, reducing my visions to rubble. So much for those Peace Corps posters at the recruiting office, which showed smiling natives gathered around a Peace Corps Volunteer, waiting for another pearl of wisdom to drop out of his mouth. This was ideological war!

I realized my efforts to put a brochure together were going nowhere fast. As I went from place to place to pitch my idea, a system of blame-shifting became apparent. The local governments pointed their fingers at the *Maavalitsus,* who in turn bemoaned the lack of activism in the private sector. Small businesses pointed the finger at the local governments.

And so the vicious cycle was formed. Each party was excellent at creating compelling arguments as to why somebody else should be responsible for doing whatever needed to be done to attract tourists but were suddenly tongue-tied when it came to talking about what they themselves could do to help tourism. I just wanted to accomplish something and I couldn't see spending the rest of my Peace Corps service running around in circles. Clearly it was time for another project.

If I could land some project money for a brochure, then I could use this as a carrot to entice the various parties on Hiiumaa to cooperate. The only problem was that Peace Corps wanted all the cooperating parties to be on board in advance. Furthermore, they wanted signed statements of interest that would show there was "buy-in" by the local people. Fortunately they only wanted these in English, so I put together the statements and went around asking the government folks and small business owners if they thought it was a good idea to have a brochure. If they agreed the brochure was a good idea, then I had them sign a statement saying they supported it and would provide some unspecified "assistance." Since most of them doubted I would receive the money or felt they could later get out of the deal, they weren't too concerned about their stated part in the project and signed happily on the dotted line.

In this way, I was able to persuade a talented local nature photographer to provide some pictures. I also managed to convince the local Small Business Association to promise an overview of Hiiumaa's economy and the Adult Education Center to help with layout on their computers. I thought I was pretty clever, taking advantage of their willingness to say yes just to be rid of me. It was heartening that some, such as the biosphere reserve folks and the local museum staff, were genuinely interested and helpful (their English was too good for me to fool them anyway). I really felt that I was building some credibility among the small business proprietors who owned the lodging places, shops and restaurants. This was a refreshing change after the Agricultural Advisor debacle with the farmers. It took very little convincing to get my new associates on board. After a more protracted effort, the *Maavalitsus* agreed to throw in some cash for printing–provided they received credit in the brochure.

In order to bolster the project's chances in front of the Peace Corps committee, I next added an educational element. I knew that if I just asked for money to make a brochure I would probably be turned down. The Peace Corps wanted projects that wouldn't simply "give people grain, but give them a plow" so that after Peace Corps was gone, the learned skills would live on. I decided to bill my latest project as a "Marketing Seminar" for local small business owners. I would do a half-day presentation on advertising and marketing, followed by one-on-one sessions in front of the computer where I would help them put together a four-color ad about their company using the latest software. The brochure, which was really my main goal, was presented in the project proposal as an end result of the educational progress, a sort of "learning by doing" that would provide valuable experience for all participants and still produce something practical. For this phase of the project, I had no trouble finding support among the proprietors of the island's few lodging places, bars and restaurants. They all seemed eager to participate in my seminar and happily signed a form stating their interest.

The pieces were starting to come together and I worked late every night, typing up the project proposal and preparing the various documents requested by the Peace Corps project committee. As I drifted off to sleep the night before submitting the project, I had a vision of smiling officials from the municipalities and the county governor himself standing hand-in-hand with local businessmen in front of a big stack of glossy Hiiumaa brochures. They would be the first of their kind in rural Estonia, and journalists would come all the way from the mainland just to snap pictures of me, the volunteer from America, and my new partners from both the public and private sector. It would be an almost unheard of instance of cooperation between government and private business!

Considering the publicity, my boss might even come from far-away Latvia to participate in the festivities. The elusive Peace Corps Moment was at hand–I could just feel it!

The next day I rushed to the post office just as it opened and sent my project package off to the Peace Corps office in Latvia with double postage, just to make sure. Then, the weeks of waiting began as another short summer faded into fall.

Finally, I received word that the project had been approved. I was a little surprised because the standards had been toughened. I had also already received some project money and others had been left out of the previous round of funding allocation. However, I didn't waste much time pondering this. I quickly set about visiting the folks who had signed cooperation agreements and prepared myself for some serious arm-twisting. I expected a big hassle, but to my surprise most agreed to fulfill their obligations without much of an argument. However, there was one person I knew was going to give me trouble. By the time the project was finished his name would come to be like bile on my tongue.

Mr. Urmas Tuulik was the head of the Small Enterprise Development Center and a studied master of the "yeah yeah, sure sure" routine. You would think by his job title that most of his time would be spent with the struggling entrepreneurs on the island, but his main focus seemed to be getting invited to expense-paid seminars in Europe and attracting funding from various Nordic government agencies. He had already learned that if you can walk the walk and talk the talk of consultants you can have lots of money thrown your way without doing a great deal of real work. I suppose you can't really blame people for going from one provider (Moscow) straight to another, but the sad thing was he was supposedly one of the "Young Turks" who were supposed to free Estonia from the morass of its Soviet-dependent legacy. I knew that Tuulik was going to be trouble, but I really wanted a section on Hiiumaa's various fields of economic activity for the brochure. So I convinced him to commit to giving me six English-language pages about the structure of Hiiumaa's economy and an overview of what the local small businesses had to offer. I told him that he was a part of a much larger project and many people were depending on him fulfilling his commitment. Maybe I just wanted to believe too much, but this time his "yeah yeah, sure sure" sounded a little more convincing than usual.

I next started working on the seminar, which, I figured I could do with the help of a translator and maybe one or two guest speakers. It would be a half-day of lecture followed by some hands-on computer work with the various small business owners in attendance. I definitely needed some publicity so, with Tarmo's help, I ground out a short article for the newspaper. I then went to the local ten-watt radio station and arranged to do an interview. The article came out, the interview went off without a hitch, and soon the local people were talking about another of "Douglas' projects." Just as I seemed headed for surefire success, the glorious sandcastle I had built in my mind began to crumble.

First the printer called and told me that with my budget and the number of color pictures I wanted, there would only be room for twenty pages of advertisements. When I protested, he informed me that it had been four months since I had asked him for an estimate and that "times had changed." In all fairness, inflation was indeed high at that time and prices always seemed to be edging up. I had to think fast. After all, I had just broadcast all over the island that I was going to provide free advertising space in the first-ever full-color English-language brochure that Hiiumaa had ever known. I had said that anyone who wants to participate should let me know, and if they attended the seminar they would receive a half page of color advertising. Certainly there would be scores and scores of interested people, and with a mere twenty pages I could do no more than forty ads. After much deliberation and consultation with my friends and colleagues, I decided that the only fair thing to do would be to give out space in the brochure on a first-come, first-serve basis. I went back to the newspaper and the radio station and did another round of interviews, this time saying that only the first forty people who signed up would have an ad in the brochure.

At this early stage of my relationship-building with the locals, it was critical that I do nothing to damage my credibility, so I felt good about coming up with a seemingly fair resolution to my problem. Everyone would have a fair chance and only the most pro-active local entrepreneurs would receive a place in the brochure. So on Tuesday morning I went to the info center a half-hour early. I was practically alone as I walked through the town square in the bright morning sunshine. The only other life forms stirring were a few old women on bicycles delivering milk, their metal containers swinging from the handlebars and a few cats chasing after to lap up whatever spilled. I half-expected people to be already lined up outside, but I wasn't too surprised to find the TIC quiet and undisturbed as usual. *Hiidlased* weren't the kind to rush in and crowd around. They would quietly show up one by one until a long orderly line would form around the building.

I set about making a pot of coffee and getting my paperwork in order. I was in high spirits as I readied myself for the first phase of the Hiiumaa Marketing Education Project. As the clock ticked toward nine, I sat down at my desk, arranged my paperwork for the tenth time and nervously fiddled with my pen. As the big hand hit twelve, I took a deep breath and braced myself for the onslaught of project participants. The bracing went on for quite some time.

Nine o'clock came and went, marked only by the sound of the clock ticking on the wall. At 9:03, I checked if the door to the info center was unlocked. At 9:10, I was still alone in the info center, tapping my pen in time with the wall clock and gazing nervously out the window. At 9:15, I called the radio station to confirm that I had indeed given the correct time and date in the interview. Then I pulled out the local newspaper and looked over the article about the project. Sure enough, the time and place were correct, and it was clearly written that only the first forty in the door would be able to participate. Come late and you miss out!

I was becoming nervous. I had talked personally to maybe fifty people about this once-in-a-lifetime opportunity, done everything possible to create a "buzz" in the community and stayed up all hours typing project proposal documents for Peace Corps. People seemed genuinely excited about the idea of the first-ever full-color English-language brochure about Hiiumaa. Plus, there was that critical educational element, the coveted "skills transfer." I was personally going to help the entrepreneurs with the computer graphics for their ad–proof of Peace Corps interest in the little guy. It had all the makings of a great project! Still, there I was twiddling my thumbs and staring at the clock as it moved slowly towards ten o'clock.

At eleven, I could stand it no longer. I locked up early for lunch and headed out to find some of the people I had talked to. It didn't take long to find some of the small business owners amongst a group of men standing in the open-air market. I went up to them and politely waited for a chance to interrupt their conversation. One of them, a bed and breakfast owner named Aarne, finally turned to me with a smile.

"Hey, Douglas!" he said with a little bow and shook my hand. "How's Peace Corps life?"

"Not bad," I responded cautiously. "Didn't you remember about the project for today?"

"Ah, yes, your project. How did the registration go?"

"I don't know. Nobody's shown up yet."

"Nobody?" said Aarne, his eyes wide at first, then narrowing as he shook his head emphatically. "You know, Douglas, we are still living with the legacy of communism. People are not used to thinking for themselves and they are too afraid to ask for help. That is our curse. The *Hiidlased* just don't appreciate the wonderful things you are doing. Don't let their apathy get you down. Someday you will triumph." The rest nodded in solemn agreement.

"Well, I was thinking more about today," I responded. "Where were you, for example?"

"Oh, you know," said Aarne, scratching his chin. "This morning I had to dig potatoes."

"How about you, Marek?" I said to a shop owner in the group. "Don't you want an ad?"

"Ah, Mr. Wells," Marek said with a wave of his hand. "I am not in need of any fancy advertisement. Who doesn't know where my store is. It's right next to the post office!"

"And you Toomas?" I asked hopefully of the owner of a local café.

"Bah, English! Everything has to be in English!" he groused. "*Kurat*, I don't need any damn foreigners!"

We fell silent and the men slowly drifted away. Soon I was standing alone in the market, my bank account full of Peace Corps cash and no takers.

Just then, I saw one of the most successful men on Hiiumaa speeding through the town square. He was a former member of Parliament who was making a fortune selling logs or metal or something from Russia to the outside world. Nobody was quite sure exactly what his business entailed and he didn't seem to feel any obligation to explain, at least to me anyway. I flagged him down in the slim hope that perhaps he just hadn't heard of the project and would be willing to participate. He was a real trendsetter and always busy doing something. If I could bring him on board, others would surely follow. Luckily, he stopped and stuck his hand out the window.

"Mr. Douglas!" he said in his jovial way. "Let me shake the hand of the great American!"

"Yeah, right," I said sarcastically, accepting his hand. "Listen, have you heard about the marketing brochure I'm working on?"

"Yes, of course! The whole island has been talking about it."

"Well, why haven't you signed up?"

"Oh, Mr. Douglas," he said sadly. "I would so much like to help you with your little project. I know what it means to you, but the fact of the matter is that I don't need any more customers. I have plenty!"

"Come again?"

"Yes, yes!" he said emphatically. "I also have plenty of money!" With that, he roared off.

I didn't go back to the info center that afternoon. I made one stop at the liquor store and then headed home, a defeated man. I think it took the better part of a liter of vodka before the words "I would so much like to help you with your little project" stopped ringing in my head. The Hiiumaa folks had done it again!

The next day, nursing a hangover and a shattered ego, I pondered my fate. I had said that people must come and register, and they didn't. If the businesspeople were going to be so apathetic then they didn't deserve a brochure. The right thing to do would be to announce that the project was off and send the money back. Of course, I would be skinned alive by the Peace Corps and barred from submitting further projects, but this was a matter of principle. After much deliberation, I came to a solemn conclusion. I would have to go out and beg shamelessly until I had enough participants to hold the seminar.

After much pleading, cajoling and prodding, I finally lined up twenty entrepreneurs. I cut my lecture in half and then herded them into the computer room. I had asked everyone to bring a picture and some text about their business, but only one person did, so my one-on-one teaching sessions had to be postponed until the next week. After those were done, I collected the photos and text from the museum and made an appointment with the printer. There was only one thing standing in my way: Mr. Urmas Tuulik.

Mr. Tuulik had promised me several typed pages in English about Hiiumaa's economy. From time to time I had checked in on him, and he always claimed he was "thinking about it" or "working on it." Funny thing was, when I asked to see what he had done so far, he could never produce so much as one typed page for me to look at. I had ignored him for a while because I was tied up with the seminar, but now I started to hound him mercilessly. He kept dodging me and making excuses until things went down to the wire. It was the day before I was to turn the material over to the printer when I finally cornered him in his office.

"Urmas," I said evenly. "Do you have the text? I meet with the printer tomorrow morning."

"It's almost done, really!" said Urmas, the look of a trapped animal creeping into his eyes.

"You know," I said and went for the throat, "you *are* the Small Business Development Center. How do you think it would look if you blew a chance at six pages of space in a brochure that's going to be distributed internationally? Will your Europartners like that?"

I knew I had struck a nerve. I turned on my heel and left Urmas stuttering a promise to have the completed text by five o'clock. Then, as I found out later, he promptly went home sick. With no text about the economy, the whole project was in jeopardy. I had negotiated with the printer for a particular number of pages and Peace Corps knew that. I couldn't just skip the small business section, yet the printer had other deadlines to meet. I had to give him the finished product the next day. Still thinking about my dilemma, I went to my Kärdla apartment and fell asleep.

About midnight, I awoke to hear somebody jiggling the latch on my apartment door. I usually left it unlocked, as did most others on the quiet and relatively safe island. As I listened in the darkness, I heard the door open a little and then shut quickly. Fearing some drunk had stumbled into my apartment, I crept through the darkness towards the door. I stopped and listened but didn't hear anything, so I went into the foyer and turned on the light. No one was there and I breathed a sigh of relief. Evidently, whoever it was had realized his mistake and left. As I turned to go back to bed, I noticed some papers on the floor, as if someone had thrown them there. I bent to gather them but almost dropped them again when I realized what they were. In scrawling penmanship, written as though in a panic, were six pages of rambling Estonian text. Mr. Tuulik had come through at last. Well, sort of.

I spent the better part of the night cursing his name and translating the nearly illegible text into English. I knew it wouldn't make six typewritten pages so I augmented it a little bit and finally went to bed about five in the morning. At ten, I met with the printer and handed over the entire package. I headed back to the info center, swearing I would never, ever submit another project proposal. And I didn't . . . for a while.

21—THE ADVISORS AND HIIUMAA BEER

Being a Peace Corps Volunteer and the only foreigner on the island definitely had its ups and downs. On the up side, I never tired of meeting people who had never before talked to a foreigner, and it was fun surprising them with my ability to speak Estonian. Most people were very friendly and hospitable, despite the fact that for so many years they had been told Americans were the enemy. During my entire time on the island I never encountered a single soul whom I would consider a dyed-in-the-wool Communist. I had come prepared to engage in at least a few ideological arguments over the benefits of capitalism vs. communism, but strangely enough, considering we were in the former Soviet Union, the situation never materialized.

That is not to say that relations were always smooth between the local residents and me. Most days I could find common ground with the people I worked with, but some days I just couldn't figure out why the people on Hiiumaa acted the way they did. On those occasions, it was nice to know that there were a few people on Hiiumaa that I could turn to when things got really weird. And when I say weird, I mean weird to the point that I sometimes doubted we were even from the same planet. Tarmo, of course, was always there to take my mind off things. But there were a couple people who really tried to help me understand the psychology of the island folk—more specifically, why the *Hiidlased* seemed to enjoy acting in exactly the opposite way I'd expect.

One of my good friends was Riho Maripuu, director of a grade school in a small village not far from Putkaste. Riho, a big bear of man, was a former wrestler for the Soviet Union's national team who I would never want angry with me. Fortunately, he was one of the most even-tempered people I had ever met. I ran into Riho during the first few days that I was on the island when Tarmo took me to see the beautiful manor house where the school was located. In addition to his duties as director, Riho also taught English to the children in grades five through eight, so he was delighted to see a native speaker on the island. He asked me to come to some of his classes and talk to his students in English. I agreed, and we became good friends. We spent many a long dark winter evening at his house, talking about Americans and Estonians and how they were both different from the folks on Hiiumaa.

What I especially liked about Riho was that he was always honest with me. If I had an idea for a project, I could always tell when he thought it wasn't going to work. Riho would merely listen, then start to shake his head with a bemused smile that meant I was way off the mark. "These are just simple country folk," he'd say kindly. "You expect too much from them." We often argued about when it was necessary to push an issue and when to back off. I'll never forget a speech he gave me one night when I was pouring out my frustration about how people never seem to want to take initiative or work together to make changes.

"Douglas," he said, "I have some pen pals in America who remind me of you. They are Estonians who fled to the West near the end of the war. They are always asking, 'Why don't you do this or that for Estonia, why don't you fight the system!' What you all don't understand is that all the movers and shakers in Estonia are gone. They are all dead or living in the West. First, the Russians came in 1939, and deported all the rich and powerful in cattle cars to Siberia, where many of them died. The entire officer corps of the Estonian army simply disappeared. Then the Second World War came and the Russians took most of the young active men into the army. When the Germans came in 1941, they took more men. And when the Russians returned in 1944, everyone who remembered the deportations and purges of 1939 did everything they could to escape to the West. Many died in the process. Then came Stalin and more terror. For the next fifty years, every person who stuck his or her head up had it cut off. Every person who spoke up was silenced. And every person who had the courage to fight was either shot as a partisan or put in prison. Brave and ambitious men are usually the sons of brave and ambitious men. We simply have none left. It will take an entire generation living in a free Estonia to restore what we had in the thirties: a well-developed European country."

I agreed with most of what he said but, in my view of the classic nature-or-nurture argument, I believed that the people could still learn and change, that they weren't condemned to live out whatever their genes passed down to them. After all, on the mainland there were plenty of examples of young men being very successful in business and politics. I felt that the same could happen on Hiiumaa, that it was just a matter of time and the right influences. Over strong Estonian coffee (Riho never drank alcohol) we argued these points late into the night. His valuable insights weren't a magic key to getting my way all the time, but he helped me at least understand why I was getting stymied at almost every turn by the friendly but maddeningly stubborn Estonians.

My other friend who always gave me good advice was Dr. Aivar Pruul, the scientist at the Hiiumaa Center for the West Estonian Archipelago Biosphere Reserve. Despite his fancy title, he was very down-to-earth and never turned me down when I wanted to talk over a glass of beer. His take on the Hiiumaa psyche was more complicated and focused on how the paradoxes of Hiiumaa's environment created the paradoxes that could be found in the *Hiidlased's* character. "Hiiumaa is an island," he told me one night after several beers, "and the sea that surrounds it both isolates Hiiumaa and makes it open. That's why they are so friendly but at the same time so reserved and inward looking. The sea both threatens Hiiumaa and offers it opportunities. The people of Hiiumaa look at the outside world in the same way as the sea, something that both entices and at the same time threatens. That is why they resist change so much. They fear the results of straying too far from what is familiar to them, too far from the shore. That's also why they treat you the way they do."

He downplayed the effects of the Communist occupation on the Hiiumaa people's behavior, but he did have some interesting insight as to why the Estonians weren't so jubilant and enthusiastic about their restored independence as I would have imagined. "When you think of Estonia regaining its independence, you are looking at things through American eyes," he said. "If there had been a big war, like you had with the British, and the last Russian was chased across the Narva River and out of Estonia, it would be different. But it didn't happen that way. The Soviet Union just fell apart and Russia just gave up any claims to Estonia. Think of it as a fairy tale where the prince puts on his armor and rides out to save the damsel in distress from the dragon. But in this case the dragon said 'Ah, you can just have her,' and then left.

"Sure, there was the singing revolution and people pushing for more freedoms, but there was no housecleaning, no great purge of the leaders that were in power during the Soviet times. Most of the people in power just took off their communist hat and put on a democratic hat, even on Hiiumaa. Those people you deal with at the *Maavalitsus* are all former party members. It is hard to find anyone in Estonia who will admit to being a communist in the ideological sense. Almost everyone says they simply played along. Plus, there are still many Russian troops in Estonia and that makes it difficult to get too excited about Estonia's freedom. What free country still has another country's troops on their soil against their will?"

Dr. Aivar was always the source of great insights, but he also performed another valuable service. When things got too philosophical one night, he introduced me to Hiiumaa Beer. This wasn't just any beer that you drank out of a bottle. This was home-brew, made by the locals in large vats deep in the forest, with myriad recipes that had only one thing in common: the combination was lethal. The beer looked innocent enough. The finished product was a mocha coffee color since it was unfiltered and not pasteurized. It had a sweet nutty flavor with no hint of alcohol, and it lured you into thinking that you could drink glass after glass, especially on a hot summer day. But woe to the unwary tourist who dared to drink more than a few mugs of the concoction! Suddenly, like the hammer of the gods, it would strike and you could kiss your judgment, and sometimes your consciousness, goodbye. The effect was more like some kind of drug than a simple homemade beer, and rumor had it that with enough indulging you would have visions of "little devils." The island was rife with stories about mainlanders who had disappeared during a beer party and were found two days later wandering in the forest with no idea of what they had been doing for the previous forty-eight hours.

I had tried a glass or two of the brew with Dr. Aivar, but my first real experience with the power of Hiiumaa Beer was when I witnessed the mystical beer-brewing process. Actually, it was more like a secret ceremony than a process. What I witnessed took place in a dark outbuilding on an isolated farm in the forests of southern Hiiumaa. The farmer, a thin middle-aged man in stained overalls, had a huge wooden vat into which he put all the usual stuff that you would expect to see in beer-making: yeast, hops and water. Then he started muttering to himself and went outside, returning with an armful of prickly juniper branches that he cut into pieces and threw into the vat. All the while he chanted and uttered what could only be described as prayers to the Beer Gods. After that stage of the ritual was finished, he carefully stirred the bubbling mixture in the vat, still humming to himself, and then hustled me outside so I wouldn't witness the final process that made his beer unique. Everyone who made beer had some special step to make a brew different and supposedly better than everyone else's and they jealously guarded their secrets. What this particular farmer did I don't know, and I was probably better off not knowing. I had heard rumors of brewers using such ingredients as sheep's urine, rancid cheese and healthy portions of spit. Finally, the farmer called me back in and proudly gave me a glass of beer from a previous batch that had sat for a sufficient amount of time.

I emptied the wooden mug of sweet frothy mixture and the farmer poured some more. We sat outside and chatted until suddenly I found that my Estonian was becoming markedly better. I was able to describe and expound on concepts I had never before been able to verbalize in Estonian. I mentioned my newfound skill to the farmer, who nodded seriously and said, "Yes, another name for the beer is 'the liquid dictionary.'"

After a few hours of shooting the breeze in my newly fluent Estonian, it started to grow dark and I knew I should grab my bike and head home. I had originally planned to stay the night at Tarmo's, which was nearby, but I suddenly felt inspired to ride all the way to Kärdla, about twenty kilometers away. The farmer helped me onto the bike and I wheeled unsteadily down a dirt road and onto the asphalt highway. It was a straight shot to Kärdla and barring an encounter with a crazed moose or wild boar, I had it made.

Things went pretty well for the first kilometer or so, at which point I noticed a strange phenomenon. The earth began to tilt to the left, as if the island was developing a list. I didn't feel dizzy or disoriented, so I didn't attribute it to being drunk. I just pedaled onward and watched in fascination as the right side of the horizon kept rising, until finally the angle became so steep I was forced off the road into ditch.

I lay on the ground for a minute until the island came back to a level position. Then I got up, brushed myself off and continued on my way. After another kilometer the island began listing again, only this time to the right. Again I tried to hold my position on the road until the island tilted so steeply, I had no choice but to ride into the ditch on the other side. I rolled to the ground and lay there, looking up at the stars and trying to figure out what was causing Hiiumaa to move like that and wondering what chaos it was causing in the populated areas. At any rate, I decided to forego the long journey to Kärdla.

Things were probably a mess there anyway and, at one kilometer per tilt I could look forward to crashing into the ditch at least twenty more times. Better to hang out at Tarmo's place until the island settled down.

22—TALKING TRASH

"Douglas, your trash cans are full." said the voice at the other end of the info center's telephone. I politely thanked the caller for the information, hung up the phone and gave out a loud groan. This wasn't helping my hangover one bit. My two newly hired colleagues at the info center, Peeter and Merle, looked over with concern.

"What's the matter, Douglas?" said Peeter, as he put down the paper he was reading.

"It's starting again!" I said and slapped my hands to my head.

"What's happening?" asked Merle.

"Why did I do this project?" I continued. "After the brochure fiasco I promised I would lay off."

"Ah, the environmental project," said Peeter. "That went off pretty well, I thought."

"Yes, but the follow-up, the buy-in!" I stopped short as I realized my Peace Corps-ese was making no sense to my friends. It was my mess. I would just have to deal with it.

Yes, I know that after the marketing brochure disaster I swore I was never going to become involved in another major project. I did receive a little money so we could reserve a booth at a four-day Swedish tourism fair, but that nearly turned into a situation comedy. First of all, I had the words "Hiiumaa Island" printed in large letters above our box. Little did I know, the word "Island" meant "Iceland" in Swedish, so I had to spend the first few days desperately trying to explain to people who took our brochure that Hiiumaa Island was indeed in Estonia. I think I got through to most of them, but I have no doubt that more than few ended up wandering around Reykjavik looking for the famous Kõpu lighthouse. Secondly, I had to fend off all sorts of questions about Serbia and Croatia, as most people couldn't make the distinction between "Baltics" and "Balkans." It wasn't a complete disaster, but after four days of endless explaining about Hiiumaa to people with a questionable grasp of English, I was anxious to get back home and return to the basics of Peace Corps life: one-on-one skills transfer and cross-cultural communication. I would have been perfectly happy to serve out the rest of my time without any more "big ideas."

Then the buzz started. On Hiiumaa, news spread not by radio, television or newspaper articles, but by gossip. The joke on the island went that if you woke up and drove from one side of the island to the other, by the time you arrived the people there would know what you had for breakfast. So when people started grumbling that the tourists the "Peace Corps Man" had brought were leaving their trash lying around, I didn't read about it or hear it on a local talk radio show. Instead, somebody would say something like "A friend of mine heard there are some people upset about the increase in litter being left around the island"–nothing direct or that could be traced, but efficient and effective nonetheless. Even though I knew I had consulted with all the proper authorities and won their blessing and participation, I began to feel guilty about the perceived litter problem. In reality, I didn't even know if there was a problem or if it was the tourists who were causing it. More than once, I had seen the remnants of parties Hiiumaa people had held on the beach, and their beer bottles and sardine cans looked the same as those supposedly left by the tourists. But in the end, it really didn't matter. The perception was there. Peace Corps had brought environmental ruin to the island and the blame was being placed on me, left on my doorstep like an anonymous package in the night.

I knew Hiiumaa well enough that I couldn't fight the buzz, so I did the only thing I could: try to figure out another project that would repair the damage I caused with the first three. (Ah, the life of a Peace Corps Volunteer!) Thus the "Keep Hiiumaa Beautiful" project was born. It was another blend of education and practical assistance that I figured would go over well both with Peace Corps and the residents of Hiiumaa. This time, my partner was the Biosphere Reserve Office. They would be responsible for giving a traveling seminar, one day in each parish, that would educate people about the impact of human activity on the island's delicate ecosystem. In return, part of the project money would go to producing a map showing the environmentally sensitive areas on the island, copies of which would be distributed to schools and the local governments. The hands-on part would be a beach cleanup in each parish, with the local governments providing transportation for participants and the Peace Corps providing money for trash bags and gloves. The crowning element of sustainability would be provided by the placement of twenty-five heavy concrete trash containers in spots where tourists were the most numerous. Liners and the job of emptying the containers were the responsibility of the local governments, a point I made sure to put in writing so there would be no mistake as to who was responsible for what. I was still smarting from the sign fiasco.

Working with the Biosphere Reserve scientists was a breath of fresh air. They generated ideas, gave me advice on the style and color of the trash containers, and overall were extraordinarily supportive and pleasant to work with. Even the local parish governments seemed excited about the beach clean-ups and they set about mobilizing school kids and other local resources. The only difficulty I had was with the maker of the trash containers. As usual, I wanted to keep most of the money on Hiiumaa, so I made a deal with a small contractor deep in the forested central region of the island. I doubted if I could ever even find the place, so I completed the deal by phone and made an agreement with Tarmo for him to pick up the containers when they were finished. I talked to the guy for almost an hour and faxed him the dimensions of what I needed. I told him that I needed the containers done by April 27 and he agreed. That taken care of, I busied myself with other details for the next few weeks. A few days before the first seminar and beach cleanup, I called back.

"Hi, is this Ago?" I said cheerfully.

"Yes, who's this?" came the voice over a crackling phone line. (I always marveled at how calls to Nebraska were clearer than calls across the island.)

"Douglas Wells. You remember, the Peace Corps Volunteer?"

"Oh yeah," said the voice, a little hesitantly. "How are you?"

"Well, fine. I wanted to ask if the concrete containers were ready to be picked up."

"No, I haven't even started, why do you ask?"

"Uh, because we had agreed that they would be done by the 27th."

Ago seemed a bit surprised. "Oh, you mean you really wanted them by the 27th?"

"Yes, Ago," I said and gritted my teeth. "We have seminars starting the day after tomorrow."

"Oh, damn, that's a problem," he said in a voice that seemed to direct blame at me. "I can only do two or three a day. How many did you need?"

"Like I said before, twenty-five," I said evenly. Yelling would get me nowhere.

"Hmm, let's see," he mused. "You need five trash cans for every seminar, a seminar every day starting the day after tomorrow, I can make maybe three a day, Damn! Where's a pencil?"

"Look, Ago" I interrupted, "Just do as many as you can, as fast as you can, all right?"

I hung up the phone and called Tarmo about the change in plans. Luckily, my friend was very helpful and he agreed to swing by Ago's place before each seminar and pick up what was available. The rest we would put up ourselves in the places indicated by the local governments or the Biosphere Reserve. All systems were go, and finally the long-awaited seminar week began. Conditions were hectic at times, but the events went off like clockwork. The level of interest was higher in some places than others, but that was to be expected. The high point of the whole series was when the governor himself came out to pick up trash in his parish and the local press was right there to snap the picture. It made for a nice article I could send to the Peace Corps office.

Tarmo and I made sure all of the remaining trash containers were in place for the beginning of tourist season. I even had the local woodworking shop put together some nice signs to put by the containers that said "Keep Hiiumaa Beautiful, Place Your Trash Here" (in both languages, of course). I was feeling pretty good, having addressed the concern and tapped the protective instinct that *Hiidlased* had about their island. People greeted me with smiles on the street and I was quite proud to have pulled off a good project without any negative repercussions. The feedback from Peace Corps headquarters was also quite positive. As a matter of fact, they gave me a one-year extension to my tour. As the days went by and things died down, I turned my attention to the info center and started preparing with Merle and Peeter for the busy summer season.

Then, right after the beginning of tourist season, the phone calls started. At first I tried to explain to people that it wasn't my responsibility to empty the trash containers, but I could tell by the sound of their voices that they weren't buying my excuse. When I tried giving them the number of their local governments, that didn't work because no one at the local governments professed to know what the callers were talking about, so people just called me back. I finally started calling the local governments myself to find out what was going on, but the person I needed to talk to was always out to lunch, or on vacation, or planting potatoes or whatever. The people I did talk to always assured me that the proper person would receive the message, so all I could do was hang up and wait.

The results of my phone campaign were decidedly mixed. The containers in some of the parishes were emptied, others were not. Unfortunately, the parish that was giving me the most trouble happened to be the one that contained the top two tourist spots

on the island. Things got pretty ugly. And smelly. Trash over-
flowed in the parking lots where tourist buses arrived, angry phone
calls were made to the newspaper, tourists who visited the info center
made snide remarks. I couldn't blame the locals and the tourists for
being upset at the situation. I had put the fallen Lighthouse Tour
signs back up myself, but this time I was determined to make the
local governments follow through on their promises.

After one particularly long and arduous call from a scolding
old women, I'd finally had enough. I picked up the phone and
dialed Tarmo, my friend and partner-in-crime.

"Hey, Tarmo. Are you busy?" I asked when he picked up the
phone.

"No, what's up?"

"Just drive your pickup over and get me."

"Uh, sure." Tarmo was puzzled. He was usually the one who
thought up the schemes.

"Thanks." I took his usual role even further. "We're going to
go get something."

"Get what?"

"Revenge on those worthless idiots who've been making my
life miserable."

This went completely over his head. "Huh?"

"Just come on over. I'll explain in the car."

Tarmo picked me up and I pointed out the direction I wanted
to take. When we were outside the city limits, I explained my
plan. We were going to empty the containers at the two locations
that were causing the most problems, take the trash to the local
government building, dump it on the lawn and then leave. My
eyes gleamed at the thought of it, but Tarmo wasn't so sure it was
a good idea. After all, it was technically illegal and could backfire.
I didn't care and became increasingly excited as we drove along. I
had gone over the edge and nothing was going to stop me from
engaging in a little payback. Tarmo, clearly disturbed by my ranting
and cursing, finally gave up trying to talk me out of completing
my mission. We continued on in silence as I gripped the dashboard

and peered out the windshield, looking for the first overflowing container.

We found the two offending sites, which were indeed awful to look at. It was easy to see why the overflowing cans, surrounded with nasty, rotting, maggot-infested trash, had caused such a stir. It was an obscenity for them to be scarring the beautiful scenery of the island. At each site I jumped out, put on some gloves, grabbed some trash bags and started gathering up the fetid mess. At the first location, Tarmo just watched from a safe distance away from the smell, but at the second site he finally sighed, shrugged his shoulders and pitched in. In no time we had a pickup load of the most evil-smelling refuse you can imagine. I examined our load and smiled as I gingerly picked up a used diaper with worms crawling out of it. Tarmo just shook his head.

Our next destination was the local government building. Tarmo tried one last time to talk me out of going, but I would have none of it. After a short drive, we pulled up onto the grass in front of the small but stately municipal building. Tarmo stayed in the cab while I jumped in the back and started tossing off the bags, some of which broke open on impact, spewing their foul contents on the lawn. Tarmo gunned the motor and prepared for a fast departure, but as I was about to toss the last bag I stopped. I couldn't do it. Unlike the gossipmongers, who had no problem talking behind my back, I wanted my insolence to be face-to-face. As Tarmo watched in disbelief, I jumped out and loaded the truck back up.

"So," said Tarmo, "are you ready to stop this craziness and drop this stuff off at the dump?"

"No," I replied, my voice hard-edged with determination. "I'm going in."

"What, are you crazy? Get in the truck!" Tarmo said and glanced around nervously.

"No, I'm going to go make them see first-hand what their promise-breaking does."

"But you don't have an appointment. You haven't even called!" Tarmo pleaded "Let's go!"

"Nope. You wait here," I said, and marched up the steps of the building.

I went inside the foyer and turned left into the secretary's office. I marched up to her desk and asked to speak with the head of the local government. The secretary gave me a startled look and informed me that there was a parish council meeting going on.

"Good," I replied, and walked toward the council chamber with the secretary in hot pursuit. Before she could stop me, I pulled open the heavy door, stuck my head in and smiled broadly at the stunned participants of the meeting.

"Hi! Excuse me, but I'd like to show you guys something," I said cheerfully.

There was long silence as everyone looked at each other, then back at me.

"Come on," I said, motioning toward the door. "There's something outside I want you to see."

"Uh, Douglas, we're having a meeting," one of the councilmen finally stammered.

"I know," I said brightly, "but this is rather important. Please come *now!*"

Startled by the change in my tone of voice and the wild look that was beginning to creep into my eyes, everyone quickly shoved back their chairs and followed me outside onto the steps. As they nervously studied the pickup truck, the women in the group crinkled their noses at the smell. When Tarmo saw us coming, he quickly hid his face and ducked down in his seat. I felt enormous satisfaction at having Tarmo be the panicked one for once. When the group had assembled, I cleared my throat and swept my arm dramatically towards the pickup full of trash.

"Do you see that?" I said in my best lecturing voice. "That is the trash from just two containers that were placed in your parish, just two of the five that were placed there and, by agreement, were supposed to be emptied by you. Now no one appears to be emptying them, do they? The situation has gotten so bad that today I left my office, drove all the way out here and emptied two of the containers with my own two hands. Now, I ask you, do you think that is right?"

The members of the council stared at their shoes like scolded children and were silent.

"Is that my job?" I asked again in righteous indignation.

"Of course not, Douglas. We just haven't had time," a councilman said quietly.

"So? Does that mean I'm supposed to do it instead?" I said, my voice rising a little more in pitch.

"It is our job. We just don't have a truck we can use," offered another.

"You mean in the whole parish you don't have a single truck?" I asked incredulously.

"We'll organize a meeting to talk about it," said one woman and everyone else nodded.

"Please," I said as I struggled to control myself, "no meeting. Just promise me that you'll empty the containers next time. Figure it out somehow, okay? Promise?"

"Douglas, you know what the problem is?" said the parish economic counselor calmly.

"What? What's the problem?" I said impatiently, noticing how they dodged my question.

"The problem is simply this, Douglas," said the young woman, straightening up and adjusting her glasses. Like a student who knows she has the right answer, she was clearly enjoying the attention being focused on her. She took a deep breath for effect. "You see, when we empty the trash containers they just fill up again."

I stared at her in stunned silence. Eyebrows raised, mouth open, I looked at the others to see if the absurdity of this statement had registered. On the contrary, everyone was smiling and nodding in approval. Like a leaking balloon, I deflated. My shoulders slumped as I mouthed the words to myself: "When we empty them they just fill up again." I was defeated and I knew it. What could I say to a statement like that? What could I say that would do any good? I weakly waved goodbye, turned, and walked down the steps as if in a trance. I blindly grabbed at the door handle of the pickup and plunked down on the seat as Tarmo slammed the truck into gear. As we departed for the village dump, I stared blankly out the window at the group still smiling and talking on the steps. They had done it again. I was sure this time I had them, but they did it again.

We drove for a while in silence before Tarmo looked over at me and gave me one of his famous grins.

"You sure told them, didn't you, Douglas," he said, stifling a laugh.

"Shut up, Tarmo." I said wearily, "Take me home. And stop by the liquor store, will you?"

23—STAYING LEGAL

One day I noticed that my living permit was about to expire. It was a strange feeling when I realized I had been on the island over two years. I hadn't really thought much about the time passing by and I hadn't received any reminder from Peace Corps. I did a little checking and, to my delight, found out that there was actually an office of the Estonian Immigration Board on Hiiumaa. This saved me a trip to the mainland and standing in the now infamous lines at the offices in Tallinn where most of the non-Estonians from the former Soviet Union had to go. At the same time, it was a little surprising because Hiiumaa was almost one hundred percent Estonian. In Tallinn I would hear Russian spoken everywhere as soon as I got off the bus, but on the island I could go for weeks without hearing anyone speak Russian. It was probably because of Hiiumaa's status as one of Estonia's fifteen counties that it rated an office.

So, one day I stopped by the Office of Immigration and was happy to find, instead of some faceless bureaucrat, a nice young man in his twenties named Raivo who was part of the new Information Technology Department at the *Maavalitsus*. I had worked a little with him recently, since the *Maavalitsus* had just acquired a computer server and Internet access. When I walked through the door of the small office, Raivo stood up to greet me in a friendly way, but with a formality unusual among people who knew each other on the island. He was easygoing, but it was clear right then that he took his new part-time job very seriously. He leaned back in his chair and spoke in an official, but not unfriendly, voice as a representative of the government.

"So, Mr. Wells," he said with a shy smile. "How can I help you?"

"Well, Raivo," I replied, "I need a new living permit, since mine's nearly expired."

"I see," Raivo said thoughtfully, scratching his chin. "Let me check the manual."

"My first time I just got one of these and it was good for two years," I said, hopefully eyeing his collection of rubber stamps.

Raivo ignored me and pulled out a huge book from one of the desk drawers. He began methodically leafing through the manual, pursing his lips and running his finger down the pages. Finally, after several minutes, he slammed the book shut and pushed it aside.

"Douglas," he said slowly and carefully, "I understand you need a living permit."

"That's right." I replied, wondering why I was having to repeat myself.

"Well, according to the manual, to get a living permit you now need a work permit."

"Well okay," I said, not understanding the problem. "Give me a work permit then."

"I'm afraid it is not that easy"

I sighed. Of course it wasn't. "What do you mean?"

"You have to be either a student, have relatives here, or work for an Estonian company."

"But I'm a Peace Corps Volunteer," I protested. "Your government invited me here."

"Does that make you a student?" Raivo replied calmly.

"No."

"Do you have any relatives here in Estonia?"

"Raivo, you know I don't. I'm an American."

"Are you employed by an Estonian company?"

"No, I'm a Peace Corps Volunteer."

"Well then," Raivo sighed, "I can't see how I am supposed to give you a work permit."

"Wait a minute," I said after thinking for a moment. "I do help out the *Maavalitsus*."

"But do you work for them?"

"Well, yes, you could say so."

Raivo opened up the book again and perused the lines of regulations. He flipped back and forth between several chapters, his expression alternating between that of cautious optimism and deep concern. After a few minutes of this he closed the book and straightened in his chair. I also straightened up and waited expectantly for his decision.

"I can give you a work permit if you work for the *Maavalitsus*," was his verdict.

"Great, then I can get my living permit also?" I replied, anxiously handing over my passport.

"But first," said Raivo as he pushed back my passport, "I need to see your work contract."

"Work contract?"

"Yes, if you work for them you must have a work contract. I need a copy of it."

"But we don't have a contract. I just help them because I am a Peace Corps Volunteer."

"I'm sorry, but it says here I need a copy of the contract. Maybe they'll give you one."

"Come again?"

"Go to the *Maavalitsus*," Raivo said calmly, "and ask them for a work contract."

"But I don't actually work for them as an employee."

"You just said you did work for them," Raivo said smugly, folding his hands on his desk.

"Yes...but I..." I broke off as I realized the futility of further argument.

I headed out the door, jumped on my bike and rode over to the *Maavalitsus* building. Of course, the governor was too busy to see me, but a nice young woman named Maire, who held the position of County Secretary, saw me hanging around. She asked me what I needed help with and I explained my dilemma. Maire furrowed her brow and thought for a moment before speaking in that precise grade school British English I heard so often when Estonians spoke to me in my native tongue.

"Douglas," she said, "the problem, as I see it, seems to be that we don't actually pay you."

"I know and that's what I told them." I said helplessly.

Maire thought a little more before her face suddenly brightened up. She picked up the phone to call the bookkeeper. After another long round of explanations she cupped the phone and looked over at me.

"We are going to make you up a work contract with zero as the salary," she whispered.

"Fantastic!" I gave her a conspiratorial smile.

It seemed my journey was almost at an end, but suddenly the smile disappeared from Maire's face and she began arguing with the woman on the other end. They were talking too fast for me to understand, so all I could do was wait. Maire finished the conversation and hung up the phone with a sigh.

"What's wrong?" I asked

"You see, Douglas," Maire said, searching for the right words, "the work contract is fine."

"All right."

"We can also write the contract to show zero salary. But," said Maire, rolling her eyes, "we can't employ you."

"Why not?"

"Because you are not unemployed."

"Huh?" was all I could manage to say.

"If you aren't registered as unemployed," Maire explained, "then we can't employ you."

Maire and I looked at each other silently. We both knew what I had to do.

Without a word, I marched out of the office and down the hall to the Work Office. I walked straight in the door and declared to the startled women inside that I wanted to register as unemployed.

"Oh, Douglas! What happened?" they said with great concern, and asked if my American government had deserted me there on the island. Once again, I went through the whole story and everyone had a good laugh as they marked me down on the rolls of the unemployed on Hiiumaa Island (non-citizen, of course).

I took the unemployment registration papers back to Maire, who had the bookkeeper make up a work contract with "0" marked as the salary, thus ending my one hour of official unemployment in the Republic of Estonia. I then took the work contract back to Raivo who looked it over and pronounced it satisfactory enough for a work permit stamp on my passport (in stylish blue ink, the same color as that of the Estonian flag). The work permit, in turn, allowed him to grant the treasured and elusive living permit, good for another two years. As I was leaving, I looked over the stamps and noticed that I was the proud owner of work permit #1. My living permit, however, was #3. I almost went back and asked who the other two unfortunate individuals were and what they had to go through, but I decided to quit while I was ahead.

24—THE DUCHESS

The times I had on Hiiumaa Island were dear to me and I gained many things from the experience. Before arriving, I had been adrift in Nebraska, working for my parents as an accountant and living only for the next payday. Coming to Estonia as a Peace Corps Volunteer gave me a chance to do something completely different and perform a job that was personally fulfilling. In many ways, my time there was a test, and I treated it as such. I sincerely felt that if I could make something out of the difficult situation I was put in, as one of the first Peace Corps Volunteers to come to Estonia, then it would mean I had proven myself. I wanted to show others–as well as myself–that I was able to handle things on my own. Plus, it just felt good to do something not just for my own benefit, but for others and for a cause. The little island of Hiiumaa had become my cause, but in the end I gained more from Hiiumaa than it gained from me. The biggest gift I received from Hiiumaa came to me by sheer chance. Actually, it was because of fried chicken.

I was doing my usual work in Kärdla when somebody told me that there was a place nearby that was serving fried chicken for lunch–not just chicken, but *American* fried chicken. Now this may not seem like a big deal, but you have to understand that I hadn't been anywhere near real American fast food in almost a year. True, there were chickens in Hiiumaa, a great deal actually. Even in the town of Kärdla I could hear them crowing and clucking as I walked around. But these were Baltic chickens, a scrawny poor cousin to those big fryers we have in the States. With a drumstick off a Baltic chicken, the meat ended about a third of the way down the leg, the rest was just bone. What little meat there was on the emaci- ated bird was tougher than anything I'd ever eaten. One of my

Peace Corps colleagues was convinced that Estonians held chicken drives, much like the cattle drives of the Old West. He believed they herded the chickens for miles and miles to market, and that's what made them so sinewy.

So I had to check out this rumor of American fried chicken. That day, it felt like eternity until lunchtime came. At twelve o'clock sharp, I bolted out of my office and headed across the street to a little bar that I hadn't even known existed. In true entrepreneurial fashion, the bar was made in a converted garage next to a charming wooden frame house. These sorts of start-ups came, and unfortunately went, with some regularity on the island as everyone tried their hand at small business under the new market economy.

With my mouth watering, I crossed the street, walked up to the little bar and pushed open the door. As my eyes adjusted in the dim light, I took in my surroundings. It was a small place, just four tables on a tile floor. A serving counter about the size of a breakfast bar was on the left and standing behind it . . . I held my breath as I took in the presence of a gorgeous young woman. I had never seen her before. She looked to be about eighteen or nineteen (too young for me, I thought) with ash-blond hair, pouty lips and a lean, well-proportioned body. She was not the classic Scandinavian type, but had a drop-dead model look about her. Her high cheekbones and seductive brown eyes made me weak in the knees. I quickly collected myself and did what any red-blooded American male would do. I tried to hit on her.

In retrospect, I should have been a little bit cooler in my approach. I knew, despite what Peace Corps told us, that Estonian girls weren't just waiting for some American to come and take them away. We actually had lectures in Peace Corps training where they cautioned us about locals hitting on you simply because you were from the States. The way they painted the picture, the girls would flock to you, just hoping that you would choose them so they could have a chance to become a citizen of our great country. In theory, this sounded pretty good, and I was rather looking forward to the prospect of being hit on all the time. But, alas, nothing was further from the truth. As it turned out, being from America was quite often a disadvantage. First off, many Estonian girls thought of American men as arrogant and overly confident. They fully expected you to hit on them, so they lay in wait, relishing the chance to shoot you down. Secondly, they were openly suspicious about our real motives as Peace Corps Volunteers: what were we doing there anyway? Did we really expect them to believe that we gave up our friends, family, cars, apartments and jobs just to come to Estonia and *help*?

Despite all this, I still went for it. I used the ace-in-the hole that I knew would spark her interest. I would speak to her in Estonian and, impressed with my language skills for a foreigner, she'd be smitten and off we'd go for a whirlwind romance.

I took a deep breath and stepped up to the bar. She was absently wiping a glass and occasionally holding it up to the light coming in through the small window. Here goes, I thought as I got ready to lay my Estonian language on her, she's going to melt like butter!

"*Tere, kuidas läheb?*" I began with the Estonian version of "how's it goin'".

"*Hästi,*" (fine) she said casually, and glanced at me before turning back to her glass.

I admired the way she turned her body with even the most ordinary moves. "My name is Douglas."

"Hmmm."

"What's your name?"

"Kairit," she said in a bored voice while attacking another spot.

I had already come to the end of the dialogue I had envisioned. "Um, nice bar you have here."

"Did you want something?" she said somewhat impatiently, and tossed her hair back, all the while rubbing the glass and checking it against the light.

I could see things were not going well. My foreign-sounding name and accent hadn't sparked any interest. Also, she was getting that "Oh, just go ahead a try to hit on me" look on her face. I was sure that many had tried and probably failed, but I had to at least take my best shot. I decided to pull out my secret weapon; a long complicated sentence in Estonian that would leave her mouth hanging open. That would show her that I wasn't just some stupid tourist!

"I am really happy to meet you because I know you have chicken and I like chicken especially because I haven't had it in a while so I came over to eat and it is nice to talk to you and maybe get to know you better though that is not why I came here it was because of the American chicken and I am also from America are you from around here?"

The glass rubbing stopped. She calmly put down the glass, turned towards me and gave me a long look, her head tilted down slightly and her lips parted. The only expression on her face was a raised eyebrow as she digested my massive sentence. This is it! I said to myself. Now she would certainly compliment me on my language, then ask about the United States and I'd be off and running. I smiled patiently and awaited her reply.

"Uh, maybe we better just speak in English," she said in an annoyed voice as she disappeared through a swinging door into the kitchen. I just stood there with my mouth open, shot down in a big way with engines pouring smoke as I spun into the ground. Boom! Smash! Ouch! Did she really mean that?

Soon she returned from the kitchen and set the plate of chicken firmly on the counter. "Here you go," she said in English. From her tone and the resolute look on her face it appeared as if she did indeed mean it. This was no ordinary girl! I humbly paid for my meal, slunk off to a table in the back, and studied her surreptitiously while gnawing on a leg. The chicken was plump, tender and evidently from America, but I hardly tasted it as I chewed absently and watched this apparition named Kairit. She never once looked at me as she moved around behind the bar. Even when she came out and wiped down a table next me, she kept her eyes averted. With her back to me, I stole my first real good look at her from top to bottom. No, certainly too young for me. She could have been in high school and I was already thirty! Just leave it! I tried to tell myself, but I couldn't help staring.

When I finished, I set my plate on the bar, said goodbye in English and slipped out the door. She said goodbye and I took a quick look back. I wasn't sure, but I thought I detected a faint smile.

Back at work that afternoon, I asked around but nobody seemed to know anything about this Kairit, which was pretty unusual for the small island of Hiiumaa. I just couldn't get this mystery girl out of my mind and, though I felt I should stay away, I soon found myself hungry for chicken again.

I think that maybe Kairit felt a touch of guilt about the thrashing she gave me. Maybe she just felt a little sorry for me. At any rate, when I returned a few days later using the excellent fried chicken as an excuse to come back, she was still a bit cold, but at least gave me a half-smile when I came through the door. Feeling a little encouraged, I hung around the bar a while after I finished and tried again to talk to her in Estonian—this time in smaller sentences.

In a standoffish, unsmiling but polite way, Kairit carried on a brief conversation with me, during which I found out that she was actually twenty-one. Good news! However, I found out that she was not overly impressed with Americans or their attitudes about the Russians. Bad news! For example, she couldn't understand why with most Americans it was always "Russians bad, Estonians good." This was a little hard for me to believe, considering the havoc the Soviets had wreaked on Estonia. When I brought up the subject of deportations and killings, she pointed out that most of these horrendous acts had been committed by Estonians against other Estonians. Her own grandmother had been deported to Siberia but held no grudge against the Russians.

Kairit then proceeded to recall her summers on the Black Sea in Russia and how friendly the Russian people were. This was really too much for a Nebraska-born Cold War baby to handle, and I launched into an explanation of how people were oppressed under Communism, deprived of basic freedoms and so on. Kairit didn't give an inch and finally I left, shaking my head in amazement and frustration. Frankly, I didn't really mind so much. I was just happy she was talking to me.

Even after the chicken supply ran out, I kept finding myself in the little bar during lunchtime. We would spend the hour going back and forth with these Cold War arguments and even got into discussions about religion–or the seeming lack thereof–in Estonia. I sensed I was making a little headway with Kairit so I asked her over to dinner, luring her with the promise of some homemade Mexican food. She accepted and I spent the entire afternoon shopping all the different markets so I could make good on my promise. I had some spices I had brought from the U.S. and figured I could make the tortillas from scratch. Cheese and onions were readily available, so the big challenge was finding lettuce and tomato at that time of year. It was getting dark when I finally hurried home with my plastic bag of goodies.

The evening went rather smoothly. Kairit helped me roll tortillas in the kitchen while we talked about our families. Through this discussion I gained some valuable insight into the possible cause of Kairit's seemingly "aristocratic" manner. She actually had some royal blood in her! Her great-grandfather was a Polish count who had married a countess from Germany. This seemed to explain a lot about Kairit's beauty and the way she carried herself. If it weren't for the chaos and destruction of the twentieth century, she could very well have been a countess herself. After that, I nicknamed her "The Duchess," a promotion she didn't seem to mind. She was an only child and was amazed to find out that I came from a family with sixteen children. This fact only seemed to add to the differences between us that made me enjoy her company so much.

Of course, I was trying to hard to make myself look good, so I told her about the band I played in before I joined the Peace Corps. This seemed to impress her, at least a little, and after we ate I showed her my guitar and played a few tunes. Later, she insisted I help her learn a few chords. So, I ended up sitting behind Kairit, my arms around her warm body, showing her where to put her fingers on the guitar neck. Unbelievable, I thought, this is going too well! The evening passed like a dream.

Then, all too soon, the time came for her to go. I was torn about what to do. I felt I should play it cool, but I wanted to let her know that I cared about her, that I wanted to be with her. So, I asked her to stay the night. I couldn't have made a worse move. She just looked at me, standing there in the doorway, and I could see the disappointment in her eyes. She didn't say it, but I could see what she was thinking: typical arrogant American who thinks he can get everything with the wave of his hand. Without another word, she turned and went down the stairs. A silence descended on the stairwell, a silence broken only by the sound of me banging my head in frustration against the doorjamb.

After she left I cleaned up the dishes, put away the guitar, and cursed my bad timing. I had blown my chance and there was probably no hope of getting in good with Kairit again. Still, I decided I wouldn't give up. I figured that when I saw her again, I'd know if there was still a chance of getting to know her better. It was hard to get to sleep that night.

I showed up the next day to apologize, pleading cultural differences. At first Kairit would have none of it, but eventually she relented and a sort of détente was achieved. Unfortunately, she also dashed my hopes by informing me that she had a boyfriend on the mainland–a Russian guy, no less! He even visited a few times from the big city and made a point of being right there when I was in the bar. He was tall, dark and didn't smile much–the typical dour-looking Russian from my point of view. He gave me a lot of hostile looks from the kitchen but remained silent. I had no idea what Kairit saw in this sullen-looking young man. I decided I had to show her that we Americans presented a much better choice. She just needed more time to get to know me, at which point she would drop this guy like a hot potato. After all, I was here on the island and he was way over on the mainland. The stage was set for a Cold War conflict as I resolved to win Kairit over.

25—WINNING THE COLD WAR

After the debacle at my apartment, I didn't see Kairit for a while. I stopped by the bar a few times, but she never seemed to be there. Her mom, who lived in the house next to the bar, said she was on the mainland but wouldn't give any more details. I gradually started to lose hope, figuring she was back in the arms of Ivan or Igor, or whatever his name was. So, I went back to my Peace Corps business. I don't know how many weeks went by before I ran into Kairit at a local restaurant. I was sitting there drinking beer with two of my friends when I noticed her talking to some guy a few tables away. This guy had to be about forty, and as I watched it seemed by their behavior that they were on a date, or at least he seemed to think so. While they talked, the guy would smile and reach for Kairit's hand, but she kept pulling it away. My heart sank as I realized Kairit was probably a lost cause for me. Maybe she had dropped the Russian guy, but she had probably hooked up with one of the new rich, the "businessmen" who could offer her cars, travel, nice clothes–everything I couldn't offer on my $200 a month salary (up from $100).

I pretended not to notice as they stood to leave, but to my surprise Kairit spotted me and came running over to our table.

"Hi! Why haven't you called me?" she said with a bright smile.

"Uh, well, I didn't know you were still around," I managed to stammer.

She gave me a teasing look. "Well, I'm around!" she answered, and was gone.

I couldn't help noticing that her date had stopped at the door to shoot me a dirty look. I didn't understand what I had done to prompt such a reaction. Now I was really confused. Was she just being friendly with him? Was she still interested in me? We hadn't even kissed, but it appeared I already had at least two enemies in Estonia because of her. A million thoughts spun around in my head as I walked home.

Luckily for me, it turned out I had an unforeseen ally: Kairit's mother. We had talked a few times when I visited the bar and found that Kairit was off somewhere else. A cheerful woman of about forty, Kairit's mother had recently moved to the island with her new husband to try to build a bed and breakfast. So far, they had only established the small bar, but she delighted in showing me the plans for the future B&B. She was extremely patient with my badly flawed Estonia and we seemed to hit it off. Most importantly, she had always encouraged me to keep up my relationship with Kairit, but I shrugged off most of her suggestions on how to proceed–mainly because she was especially vague when I inquired about Kairit's "status." I figured she was just being polite, so I didn't really expect much help from her.

Then, in a memorable event, Kairit's mom invited me to the weekly family sauna. This was no small thing as the sauna is a very important and very personal aspect of Estonian family life. Only family and close friends were invited. There was always good food and drink to be had, and this was one of the few times when Estonians really loosened up. Of course I showed up, but I was surprised to find Kairit's date from the restaurant sitting there also. Usually all the men entered the sauna first, followed by the women when the men were done. In the sauna everyone was buck-naked on a bench, sweating like crazy. I did the first round with the men and then we sat around in towels next to the fireplace, drinking beer and swapping stories while the women took a turn. The guy I saw with Kairit kept glancing over at me with a not-too-friendly look on his face. Kairit was nowhere to be seen and I was starting to become a little worried. After all, I hadn't come just to drink beer with the boys!

Then, just as the women were coming out, Kairit showed up. She was shivering from the cold and wanted to go into the sauna right away, even though it was the men's turn. To my surprise, her mom calmly suggested that Kairit and I take a turn together. To my profound and boundless disbelief, Kairit agreed to this with little more than an annoyed glance. I didn't even dare look at my apparent rival as I numbly followed her into the sauna room and just stood there in my towel, unsure of what to do. Kairit, without missing a beat, stripped completely naked right in front of me and stood waiting.

After a few excruciatingly long moments, she turned and went into the sauna, glancing back over her shoulder at me before she closed the door. What did this mean? What should I do? The most important thing was that I shouldn't blow it this time, as I already had two strikes against me. I resolved to play it cool. I dropped my towel, calmly sauntered into the sauna room and sat on the bench next to Kairit. I kept my eyes down the whole time and made polite conversation, even though my mind was racing. I was determined not to stare or get, well, too excited. This worked well for a few moments until she went to shower off, at which point I had a clear view out of the sauna window. Oh my God! The whole affair served to reinforce my determination to win Kairit over from the Russian. Something that good had to be in American hands!

I resolved to ask Kairit out on a date. I hoped that this would finally clear things up and I would at last know where I stood. I learned from the folks at the *Maavalitsus* building that the whole foreign diplomatic corps was planning a retreat on Hiiumaa Island. This meant that fifteen to twenty ambassadors and ministers would be coming from the mainland to stay in one of the local hotels. I quickly finagled myself an invitation for two from the governor's secretary and headed over to talk to Kairit. I was interested to see what would happen, as Estonian girls were notoriously shy, especially around foreigners. This would be a real test for her, as diplomats and prominent folks from the island would attend this event.

To my surprise, Kairit agreed without hesitation. She actually seemed excited about the prospect of meeting a lot of important foreigners. In an effort to find out if this was really a date from her point of view, I inquired about the guy I had seen her with at the restaurant. "Oh, him," she said nonchalantly. "That was a relative of my mother's new husband. He works for the *kaitsepolitsei,* the Estonian Secret Police." What I really wanted to know was if they were seeing each other, but I didn't pursue the matter further. One thing was certain, this guy seemed awfully possessive. The last thing I needed was a run-in with a member of the *kaitsepolitsei.* But wait a minute, what about her Russian boyfriend?

I picked Kairit up at her house in my beat-up old Volga. When she came out, all I could do was stare. Up until then, I had seen her dressed only in casual clothes, but now she was wearing a long sexy evening dress, just transparent enough to show off her gorgeous legs that led down to black high-heeled shoes. I was always amazed at the types of terrain the Estonian girls could negotiate in heels. Kairit gracefully maneuvered across the rutted gravel driveway as if it were a ballroom floor, then hopped lightly across a ditch and came up to the car. When I opened the door for her, she smoothly pulled up the hem of her dress and slipped into the passenger seat, one long beautiful leg at a time. She made herself comfortable and looked up at me expectantly. "Shall we go?" she said.

I suddenly realized I was staring right down the front of her dress. "Oh sure!" I said hurriedly, and shut the door. I could see already that this was going to be a rough night. My main goal was just to make it through the evening without saying or doing anything stupid. I figured that by the end of the night I would know if we were dating or not. The good night kiss would say it all. Finally, I would know where I stood!

When we arrived at the hotel, I could see all the fancy European luxury cars pulled up front. Feeling a little self-conscious in my Russian beater, I maneuvered around back and helped Kairit out of the car. Together we walked into the reception and started to mingle. At first we stood side by side, but as we became involved in different conversations we became separated. It became apparent fairly quickly that Kairit was the center of attention. I hated making small talk at cocktail parties, so I hung back near the wall with my drink and watched Kairit work her way around the room. She looked unbelievably beautiful, and I admired the way she carried on a conversation, smiling and laughing at the right moments. I noticed she held a drink in her hand the whole evening, but never took more than a sip from it. Finally, I got close to her again and led her out onto the porch.

We stood looking out over the Baltic Sea with the moon reflecting off the water. It was the perfect romantic situation, but I was too worried about making the wrong move to try anything. I tried to make her laugh with some dumb jokes, and she told me about what it was like to be in high school before Estonia regained its independence. As we talked out there on the porch in the moonlight, I found I wasn't even listening to what we were saying. I just wanted to be with Kairit, to be close to her and have her smile at me. It was then that I realized I was falling in love with this beauty from behind the Iron Curtain.

When Kairit was a little girl she had been a "pioneer," a Soviet version of the Boy and Girl Scouts. For her, the Soviet times had been mostly a game. Of course there were inconveniences, but with nothing else to compare them to, things didn't seem so bad. In addition, the Soviets fed their people with a steady diet of propaganda about how terrible conditions really were in the West. Unemployment, racial tension, and crime were almost unheard of in Estonia during the '80s.

It was only when Kairit was allowed to take a trip to Sweden that she realized the truth. She realized, along with many others, that the Soviet system was doomed to failure and started to prepare for the day that Estonia would be free again. In Estonia, tens of thousands of people gathered in Tallinn's main stadium for a song festival and suddenly, spontaneously, they began singing old patriotic songs that had long been banned. Kairit was there, and she remembered the power the people's voices held. Without arms or violence, they showed their desire for independence, and all the Soviet authorities could do was watch. It was the first time that I had seen her become emotional about Estonia's drive to regain independence. Her eyes shone as she talked about the "Singing Revolution." She had seen the famous Baltic Chain, where people linked hand for hundreds of miles through Estonia, Latvia and Lithuania to show solidarity for Baltic independence. I studied her closely, the breeze blowing back her hair, the moonlight shining on her face. Do I dare try for a kiss?

"It was wonderful!" she said softly and looked out to sea. "My mother was working for Estonian television, so we got to ride in a helicopter with a crew from ABC."

"Weren't you afraid of a crackdown?" I asked.

"Sure, we were all a little scared, but we really believed that the time had come. Even when the coup in Moscow happened and tanks started moving toward our capital city, we didn't lose hope. We all gathered at blockades near the Parliament building and waited for whatever would come."

"What an exciting time," I said. "That must make you proud to be an Estonian."

Honestly, I had not intended to do it but just as surely as if I had planned it, I had stood in the batter's box and swung for strike three. Just as suddenly as the dreamy look in her eyes had come, it was gone. A look of bitterness came to her face and she disgustedly threw the contents of her drink into the bushes. When she turned toward me, the contempt in her eyes was such that I actually backed up a step.

"Yeah sure," she said with a sarcastic smile. "I should be proud of what? What Estonia is today? Sure, we all held hands and sang and talked about working together, but it was all an illusion. As soon as independence came everyone just turned back to grabbing whatever they could for themselves. Stealing, corruption, old people without food, ex-party members with Mercedes Benzes, drinking, prostitutes–that is what has become of our Estonia! It was a nice dream, but I should have known not to expect so much from our people. We are a nation of small thinkers. It's impossible to go back to the glory days of the first republic. My grandmother has told me about the heroes that lived then, but they are all gone, sent away to Siberia or escaped overseas or just shot…like her husband!"

Before I could say anything more, Kairit turned and went back inside. She resolutely made her way through the crowd and headed out the front door. I quickly followed and found her sitting in the Volga, dabbing at her eyes with a handkerchief. I wanted to say something, but I didn't know what. When I tried to give her a reassuring pat on the shoulder, she only pulled away. I started up the car and we drove back to her house in silence.

As soon as I pulled up to Kairit's house she hopped out, shoes in hand. She said a quick thank you and goodnight, and by the time I had even opened my door, she was gone. I just sat there for several minutes, both hands grasping the steering wheel. How could I have blown it again? Why did I always seem to step in it? Finally, I started up the Volga and headed for the seaside, where I spent the next few hours going over the night's events and plotting out different ways it could have ended. Most of the versions ended up with Kairit in my arms and us kissing in the moonlight by the sea.

I stayed away from the bar for the next few days and plotted my next move. I wanted to know where I stood, but I had to figure out how to bring up the issue of other boyfriends without sounding as if I was rushing things. As it turned out, we got together a little sooner than I had expected. On the first really warm summer day, I was driving past Kairit's bar when she came running around the corner of the house and beckoned excitedly for me to come over. I pulled quickly into the driveway of her house, a little extra quickly because I noticed that she was wearing a very nice two-piece swimsuit that I definitely wanted a closer look at. I didn't have to wait long as she ran up to the car and stuck her head, shoulders and her . . . well, the upper part of her body in the passenger-side window.

"Douglas, come here! You have to see!"

"See what?" I said and set the parking brake.

"Just come and look at my new boyfriend!"

"Wait a minute, I…"

"Just come, just come!" she pleaded, and all but pulled me out of the car.

"Okay, okay!" I laughed and let her pull me around the back of the garage.

We rounded the corner and I was hit squarely in the shins by a squirming, yapping little ball of black fur. I was a little startled at first, but quickly realized that this bundle of pure energy was a puppy. It was amazing the way it wiggled every appendage it had, each with its own direction and tempo. Another mystery, "the boyfriend" comment, was also resolved when the little mutt lifted up his leg and proceeded to relieve himself on my shoe.

"Oh, he likes you! Isn't that cute?" Kairit squealed and clapped her hands with delight. Actually, for that single look of happiness on Kairit's face at that moment I would gladly have let a whole litter of puppies relieve themselves on me. I found out that his name was Tan-lan and that Kairit had brought him from the mainland to keep her company. I made a mental note to myself: get in good with the dog.

We finally got the puppy settled down, and as he snoozed in the mid-day sun, Kairit stretched out on a recliner for some sunbathing and closed her eyes. Looking at her in that swimsuit, I figured it was now or never. It was time to figure out just how she felt about me. Damn the torpedoes! I would just have to ask her straight out. I took a deep breath and waded in.

"Uh, Kairit?"

"Yes."

"I wanted to…uh…ask you something."

"What?" She continued to sunbathe without even glancing towards me.

"Well, not really ask you something. I just wanted to…you know…find something out."

"What?" Kairit said and looked up at me, shading her eyes with her hand.

"Well, I am not sure how to ask this. I.... uh...don't want it to sound bad."

The anticipation was killing her. "What? Ask me!"

"Well, I thought that maybe...you know.... that I...I mean we...uh..."

"Douglas, what is it?" Kairit said, and sat up with a smile on her face.

"Can you...do you...is there...." I stammered. It was going worse than I had imagined.

"Douglas, what's wrong? Tell me!" Kairit said pleadingly, and grabbed hold of my arm.

I took another deep breath. "Kairit, would you be my girl-friend?"

Kairit's jaw dropped and she stared at me. Oh man! I thought, and turned quickly away. "I can't believe I just said that! I should have just asked how her boyfriend was, or some other indirect question. You know, use some tact! The way I asked sounded like some love-struck seventh-grader. What a bone-headed move! Blush-ing bright red, I turned back towards Kairit, expecting the worst. Would she laugh out loud? Or worse, would she politely tell me to get lost and then run to tell all her friends what an idiot I was? The story would be all over the island in minutes!

To my surprise, Kairit did neither. She just sat there with a thoughtful look on her face. Finally she looked up at me and said, "Douglas, I don't know. It would be difficult." That was it. It wasn't a straight no, but it certainly wasn't a yes. I was too embar-rassed to pursue the subject anymore, so I just changed the sub-ject. Before I left, I did ask her out again, just to see if I at least still had a chance. To my boundless relief, she agreed right away.

Over the next few weeks I took her to every romantic spot I could think of on the island. I told her the legends I had learned about the different landmarks and showed her the guidebook I had written. We took long walks by the sea where she shared with me her valuable insights about why Estonians behaved the way they did. I played guitar for her and showed her the songs I had written for

HEPT. I didn't ask any more questions about boyfriends or where I stood. I just took it one day at a time, and after about a month it finally paid off with a goodnight kiss. Shortly after that, she told me she had broken up with her Russian boyfriend. A few months later I asked the beautiful Kairit to marry me. Her acceptance of my proposal filled me with more happiness than I had ever known.

Unfortunately, there was one big problem. I wanted to be married in the church where I had been attending services. It was the oldest church on the island and, in my opinion, the most majestic, a beautiful stone Lutheran structure that had been built in the 1200s. The church had many legends and stories attached to it dating back to the Crusades. Kairit thought this was a great idea and the pastor was very pleased about it, but he informed me that since Kairit had never been baptized, which was not unusual in Soviet times, we couldn't be married in the church. I figured it would be just a matter of splashing some water on her head, but the pastor informed me that adult converts have to attend six weeks of classes before they can be officially baptized and accepted into the church.

So, for my sake, Kairit attended six weeks of classes with others who were converting to the Christian faith. She was baptized in the stone church, wearing a white dress as a very proud (and anxious) Douglas looked on. Now, at last, we could be married.

Of course, there were still more obstacles before us. It turned out that Estonia didn't recognize church weddings. You could do them if you wanted to, but they had no legal significance in the Republic of Estonia. You had to go through a ceremony at the *perekonnaseisuamet,* or office of family statistics. To make things more interesting, you had to hold the ceremony in the town where you were registered to live. This was a leftover from Soviet Estonia that didn't apply to me, but Kairit couldn't be married in Hiiumaa because she didn't "officially" live there. We would have to go the capital, Tallinn, where she was registered as living in her mother's "official" apartment.

I wasn't one to let a little bureaucracy stop me, so one day, we boarded the Hiiumaa-Tallinn bus, which crossed via the ferry and then proceeded on to the big city. We found the right office, a castle-like building with a huge wooden door along a major thoroughfare. Once inside we found ourselves in a huge foyer with a stone floor. The door closed behind us with that familiar resounding boom. When my eyes adjusted to the semi-darkness, I could make out the form of the ever-present coat clerk knitting, as they always did, behind the counter in front of the coat racks. I approached her and asked for directions.

We headed up the stairs to the third floor and knocked on the door of the registrar's office. I told Kairit to let me do the talking. I had a lot of experience dealing with the Estonia government and I felt I could make short work of some marriage bureaucrat. Kairit just shrugged her shoulders and waited. A stern-looking middle-aged woman came to the door and motioned for us to sit on two huge chairs across from her desk. She sat back down in her chair, crossed her hands and peered at us over the top of her glasses.

"Can I help you?" she asked

"Yes," I said, "we would like to get married."

"Are you registered in Tallinn?"

"I'm not, I'm an American. My fiancée is registered here."

"Hmmm, I see," she said. "When did you want to hold the ceremony?"

"Well, we actually want to get married in the church, but I understand we have to come here first."

"That's correct. But to have a ceremony, you first have to see Mr. Sibul downstairs. When he has given his authorization, you must then wait thirty days before you can have a ceremony."

"Well, we really don't need a ceremony," I explained. "Can't we just sign a paper or something and then take it with us?"

The woman narrowed her eyes, gave me a long look and said firmly, "That would be quite impossible!"

"Who is Mr. Sibul? I mean, what position does he have?"

"He is the person you must speak to before you can get married," she said simply.

"Well, okay," I said. " Where is this Mr. Sibul?"

"He isn't here today."

"May I ask when will he be in?"

"His office hours are from three to five on Tuesday, but some-times he isn't there at those times."

"Can we make an appointment with him?" I asked hopefully.

"No, you must come between three and five on Tuesdays, and if he is in his office you can speak with him."

"But, I live on Hiiumaa Island and it is a five-hour trip to get here," I pressed. "Can't I just call in advance and set up a time?" I felt a sense of hopelessness sweeping over me.

"You may do so, but there is no guarantee that he will be in his office at that time."

"Let me get this straight," I said, leaning forward. "I have to get on the bus and make a five-hour trip to Tallinn in an attempt to see a Mr. Sibul. I should arrive at the *perekonnaseisuamet* be-tween the hours of three and five in the afternoon and go to his office where he may or may not be. If he is not there, I must wait, and if he doesn't show up by five then I must simply return the next week and try again."

With that, Kairit giggled and whispered, "Is the big bad Dou-glas putting the bureaucrat in her place?" I looked at her sternly. I really wasn't trying to be a smart-ass. I sincerely hoped the woman would recognize the absurdity of the situation and offer some sort of solution. But it was not to be.

"That's correct," she said coldly and stood, signaling that our meeting was over.

We stepped out into the bright sunshine and headed back to the bus station. I was railing about the stupid Estonian marriage system and what a pain it would be to find this mysterious Mr. Sibul. Kairit was strangely quiet, and every time I looked over at her she nodded sympathetically in agreement. However, a few times I caught her turning quickly away to hide what appeared to be an amused smile. To her credit though, she never said anything about my performance, which I am sure she found very entertaining.

So, for the next few weeks we made the pilgrimage to Tallinn every Tuesday. We always had lunch in the medieval quarter of the city and then we went over to wait for the elusive Mr. Sibul, who was never there. We chatted outside his empty office until five, then caught the six o'clock bus back to Hiiumaa. For Kairit, her experience with the Soviet system had made her a little more patient, and she seemed to take the whole situation in stride. I, on the other hand, was beside myself with frustration and took to ranting aloud about the evils of socialist bureaucracy while we rode the bus or ferry, much to the curiosity and amusement of the local populace.

One day we finally spied a light on in Mr. Sibul's office when we arrived. Filled with hope, I knocked. A gray-haired man with glasses opened the door.

"Yes?" he said, "can I help you?"

"The registrar asked us to meet with you, Mr. Sibul," said Kairit. (We had already agreed beforehand that she would take the lead this time.)

"Oh, come in, come in!" the man said kindly, and motioned for us to sit down.

"We want to get married," Kairit said simply.

"Well, that's nice. Are you both Estonian?"

"I am, but he's American."

"I see, I see. How long has your boyfriend been living in Estonia?"

"About two years," Kairit answered.

"Well, well. That's very interesting," said Mr. Sibul. He leaned back in his chair and rubbed his hands together. We sat in silence for a few moments while he studied us thoughtfully. He finally stood up and extended his hand to me.

"Thanks for stopping in to see me. You need to go back up to the registrar's office and set up an appointment for a ceremony."

"Don't we need a paper from you or some kind of a stamp?" I asked.

"No, no. We try to keep things simple around here. Just tell her that we talked. Goodbye." He led us out and closed the door. "What was that all about?" I asked Kairit. "Who was that guy anyway?" Kairit just shrugged and headed up the stairs to the registrar's office. I paused for a moment, looking back at the mysterious Mr. Sibul's office, then hurried to catch up with Kairit. We knocked and the same woman as before let us in. She smiled briefly at Kairit, but gave me a stern look before showing us to our chairs. We sat down, and this time I did the talking.

"Well, we spoke to Mr. Sibul. Now, we would like to schedule a ceremony."

"All right, it is April 11 today. Would May 10 at two o'clock be all right?"

"Sure."

"Fine then, it is all settled."

I started to stand, but the woman cleared her throat and motioned for me to sit back down.

"Excuse me, but you must pay the registration fee in advance."

"Fine, how much is it?"

"One hundred *kroons*."

"All right," I said and reached for my wallet.

"Oh, I'm sorry but you can't pay here," she interrupted. "You must go pay at the bank and bring me back a receipt."

"Okay, there is a bank right across the street. I'll be right back."

"You can't use that bank branch," she said with a patient smile. "You must go to the one near the center of town. By the way, there are no busses that go there and they close in ten minutes. We close fifteen minutes after that."

I didn't even bother to reply. I grabbed Kairit's hand and we took off down the hall. There was no way I was going to make yet another trip to Tallinn just for some stupid receipt! We dashed down the stairs, past the surprised coat woman and out the door. Through alleys, across courtyards and down the sidewalks we ran until we spotted the sign for the downtown bank branch. With just minutes to spare we burst into the door and took our place in line.

We were both breathing heavily and the other customers regarded us with no small amount of curiosity.

When my turn came, I quickly paid the teller the fee and grabbed the receipt. We ran all the way back to the registrar's office. Triumphantly, I placed the precious receipt on her desk and stood waiting for a response. She looked at the paper and then looked up at me over the top of her glasses.

"Please sit down," she said and fished around in the drawer for some paperwork. We waited silently while she filled in some blanks and then reached for a rubber stamp. She stopped with her hand poised above the document.

"You know," she said, "there is a thirty *kroon* fee for the authorization stamp."

"You mean I have to go back and pay another fee?" I asked in disbelief.

"No, you can pay that to me."

I didn't even bother to ask for an explanation. Resignedly, I fished thirty *kroons* out of my wallet and tossed it on her desk. She calmly counted the money and "thunk!" the stamp came down. She handed us the paper, which we would bring in May for the ceremony. I tried one more time to explain that we just wanted the marriage certificate so we could have a church ceremony, but she would have none of it. With a wave of her hand she dismissed us. Just before the door closed she called out, "Make sure you have the proper permission letters from your respective governments before you come in May!" I turned to ask what she was talking about, but the door had already slammed shut.

Fortunately, the "permission letters" weren't very hard to obtain. Since I was a United States Peace Corps Volunteer, the U.S. government basically wanted to know if Kairit was a terrorist, arms smuggler, drug dealer or if she had planned to overthrow the American government anytime recently. Kairit also had to obtain a slip of paper from the Estonian police saying that she wasn't a known criminal. All the Estonian government basically cared about was whether I was already married back home. I had to go the U.S. em-

bassy and swear out a statement saying that I wasn't married anywhere. Of course, the embassy had no way of checking this and they
even put a big stamp at the bottom of the document saying that they
couldn't guarantee the validity of my statement, but that didn't seem
to bother the Estonians. With all of our papers in order, all we could
do was wait.

The day of our long-awaited ceremony finally arrived. We
showed up at the designated time and went to the registrar's office. The woman carefully looked over our documents then put
them aside and looked at me intently over the top of her glasses.

"All right," she said briskly, "everything seems to be in order.
Did you want to go to the changing room?"

"Uh, we don't need to change," I said, exchanging glances
with Kairit.

"Not going to change?" she said with disbelief, and looked at
us up and down.

"No, we just would like our certificate."

This did not seem to satisfy the woman. "Well, where are the
rings?"

"We don't have any rings," I said with exasperation. "We are
going to do that in church."

"Will you be reserving a ballroom and orchestra?" she said and
pulled out a form.

"No, we aren't celebrating today. We'll do that later."

"Not celebrating?" she said and looked sympathetically at
Kairit. "Surely, you want some champagne."

"No champagne!" I said, desperation creeping into my voice.
"Please, can we just get on with it!"

"A violinist, perhaps?"

"No!"

"Very well," she said, shaking her head and putting the form
away. "Follow me."

She led us to an ornate round room, which had a wide bench
lining the wall. We sat down and the woman left without a word.

We sat for several minutes before a man burst into the room with a camera hanging around his neck.

"Photographs?" he asked hopefully.

"No, thank you. We'll do that at the church ceremony," I said wearily.

"Oh, come on. Just a few for the big day."

"No!"

The man shrugged his shoulders and left. We waited several more minutes, and then two huge doors on the opposite side of the room swung slowly open. On the other side of the doors was a long narrow chamber with benches on both sides and a red carpet running down a center aisle. At the head of the aisle, dressed in a long dark gown, stood the registrar woman behind a podium with a huge leather bound book lying on it. She waited silently in her regal robes, her glasses hanging around her neck. Kairit and I sat on the bench and looked at each other, not sure of what we were supposed to do.

Finally, with an exasperated look, the woman motioned for us to come in. Kairit grabbed her purse and we started down the aisle. The woman's eyes widened and she immediately put up both hands, motioning for us to stop. She glared and made a motion for me to put Kairit's arm in mine. I looked at Kairit, who shrugged her shoulders and took my arm. "Can I leave my purse in the other room?" she said to the woman. The woman cringed and whispered loudly, "No, it might get stolen." With that the doors swung shut behind us.

We stood up straight, facing the podium arm in arm. Satisfied with our pose, the woman solemnly reached over and hit the "play" button on an ancient-looking tape deck. The scratchy wavering strains of "The Wedding March" filled the room. Kairit and I had to try very hard to suppress our laughter under the absurd circumstances. Together, we got into the spirit of the moment and marched majestically down the aisle and up to the podium. The woman motioned for us to halt, then put on her glasses and hit the "stop" button before placing her hands across the huge book on the podium.

"Douglas Wells," she said grandiosely, "do you wish to marry Kairit Männiste?"

"Yes," I said simply, and then prompted by her stern look, hastily added, "I do."

As she turned to Kairit, a workman suddenly burst in through the side door. He was staggering under an armload of little plastic bells and, judging from the smell, the impact of a five-martini lunch. "Hey," he slurred, "where ya want these bells?"

The woman drew herself up to her full height, raised an eyebrow and hissed icily, "Leave here immediately! Can't you see we are having a *ceremony*?" The workman mumbled an apology and staggered back out the door, dropping a few bells that rolled across the floor and up against the podium. The woman gave an exasperated sigh, straightened a stray lock of hair, and turned to Kairit.

"Kairit Männiste," she said solemnly, "do you, of your own free will, agree to marry Douglas Wells?"

"I do," said Kairit, and the woman smiled in satisfaction.

"Please sign here," she said and slowly opened the enormous "Book of Life." We put our signatures into the book where she indicated, and with that we were officially married in the eyes of the Republic of Estonia. Now we could finally prepare for the real ceremony where we would make our vows before God, family and friends.

And what a fairy tale wedding it was! Folks came from all over the island, some in national costumes. My mother and brother came all the way from Nebraska for the event. The poor old church, which the Soviets had closed and neglected for fifty years, probably hadn't seen so many people since before the Second World War, and it was definitely the first ceremony of its kind since then. Kairit wore a stunning white dress, which left me opened-mouth in amazement when she entered the church. Her mother and grandmother, who both worked so hard to make the wedding the best for Kairit, stood smiling in calm satisfaction. Thinking of the sauna incident, I gave her mother a sly wink, which made her laugh.

So, on that July day in 1995, Kairit and I were married. Some friends who raised horses surprised us by bringing a beautiful old carriage, pulled by a mare with her young foal running alongside, as was the Estonian tradition to ensure fertility. To the cheers and applause of the onlookers, we boarded the carriage and made a triumphant exit through the church gate. As we rode with our escort down the tree-lined parkway to the old German manor house where the reception was to be held, the villagers held up a huge rope across the road and forced us to stop. Laughing, they made us get out and perform a whole battery of "tests" to make sure we were suited for each other. I had to chop a log in half with one hand and Kairit had to roll a ball of yarn as quickly as she could. We passed those tests, plus some others (though I really botched the waltz) and we received our "official" Hiiumaa wedding certificate, hand written and tied up with a bow. The whole wonderful event finished with a party by the sea, where I played a few tunes with HEPT. No one, not for all the money in the world, could have planned a better wedding day for us.

26—THE ELUSIVE PEACE CORPS MOMENT

Living with Kairit, the woman of my dreams, made the time simply fly by, and before I knew it my Peace Corps stint was drawing to a close. It was the summer of 1996, and I had spent nearly four years on the island, longer than anyone else in our group of volunteers, and had seen three Peace Corps Country Directors come and go in the Baltics. Now my time was up and I would finally have to leave my new friends and adopted home that bore scant resemblance to the seemingly bleak and deserted island I first encountered a few years ago. It was truly amazing how many things had changed on Hiiumaa since 1992 and the place showed the effects of rapid progress.

When I first started working with tourism, there were about fifty beds for tourists on the island. Now there were over five hundred. There was a gleaming new harbor building to replace the old police shack where I had almost been turned back on my first visit. The waits at the post office for phone calls were a thing of the past, and with one of the new phone cards you could call anywhere in the world from a public phone booth. The *Maavalitsus*'s IT Department had long taken over and improved the first simple website I had created for Hiiumaa, and now the island was leading the country in Internet development and per capita connectivity.

One of my favorite moments in Hiiumaa's development was when the first automatic teller machine (ATM) came to Hiiumaa. Its arrival caused quite a stir and there was even an article in the newspaper in the days leading up to its installation. Never one to miss a grand opening, the mayor came to the ceremony held outside the wall of the grocery store. He gave a heartfelt speech and wished the ATM "long years of operation and many customers" before solemnly cutting a ribbon held by two young female bank tellers. The crowd politely applauded.

When I thought about the projects I had organized and what they had accomplished, I had to admit the results were decidedly mixed. The guidebook and beach cleanup had been glowing successes, but there had also been the sign debacle and the unresolved fight over the overflowing trashcans. Plus, people always talked about "my" projects, which were really the cooperative effort of many people and should have been considered "our" projects. I definitely didn't just come, see and conquer like the legendary volunteers I read about in Peace Corps Magazine. My experience was more akin to that of the Hiiumaa ferries breaking the ice in winter. I charged in until I encountered too much resistance, then backed off and made another run at it. Sometimes I got stuck until somebody helped me out, sometimes I even had to turn back for a while, but in the end, I made it through.

Did I ever experience the elusive Peace Corps Moment? I can't say for sure, but I think it may have happened during my farewell party, held my last day on Hiiumaa. The *Maavalitsus* had arranged a large celebration at one of the holiday resorts and told me I could invite fifty friends. Tarmo and his family were there of course, plus my farmer friend, my advisors, the guys from HEPT, and my co-workers from the tourist info center. Kairit was right by my side, looking radiant as ever.

Given my choice of food and drink that was to be served, I naturally chose wild boar meat, smoked fish and Hiiumaa Beer as the main staples. After lots of food and drink, we all sat round by the sea and talked about the amazing changes that had taken place over the years, and laughed at our missteps and mistakes that we made while getting acquainted and learning to work together. There was no talk of "who will do this now" or "what will we do without your help" and there were no tears or sorrow at my departure. At first, this struck me as odd since no one was coming to replace me.

I would be the first and last business volunteer the island would ever see. Who would continue the work I had started? Then I remembered what our first Peace Corps Director had told me: a good volunteer doesn't work himself into a job, he works himself out of one. If you've done a good job, when you leave everything will just continue on without a hitch. They won't even notice you're gone, except when there's a party.

There was a sudden commotion over by the grill and I looked over to see a bunch of people lining up behind the recently elected Governor of Hiiumaa. He beckoned for me to stand up, and my friends began to come forward one by one to shake my hand. They each gave a little speech about how they knew me and what we had done together, then presented me with a gift of flowers or some other small token to remind me of Hiiumaa. The whole time the governor stood grinning beside two wooden posts that were stuck in the ground about three feet apart and covered with a sheet. Behind the posts was a large car-sized boulder. When everyone had their say, the governor called over the manager of the resort and each stood next to one of the posts.

"Douglas," the governor said, "I have seen the evidence of your work around the island and it is clear how you feel about this place. I have also heard of the Hiiumaa citizens' efforts to keep some of our well-known attractions not so well-known, despite your work to the contrary. So we at the *Maavalitsus* decided on a special gift that would remind you of all your experiences here, both the easy times and the challenging ones. It is my pleasure to present you, as a symbol of our gratitude, with both a piece of Hiiumaa you can call your own and the next stop on the Lighthouse Tour."

With that, the men pulled off the sheet and stood back. There stood an exact replica of one of the wooden Lighthouse Tour signs, right down to the style of the letters in the carved inscription, which read "The Douglas Stone" in both English and Estonian. The crowd burst out into raucous laughter and applause and I joined in with a wry smile. The *Hiidlased* had gotten in the last jab.

"By the order of the *Maavalitsus* of the Hiiumaa," the governor intoned, trying not to smile, "let it be known that this boulder is the property of Mr. Douglas Wells, provided he comes back once in awhile and cleans the leaves off of it. It shall henceforth be known as The Douglas Stone. Furthermore, let no man dare disturb this sign, which is properly and lawfully inscribed in both English and the State Language of the Republic of Estonia. Thank you very much."

The party ended, everyone went home and I departed from the ferry port much the same way as I came. No waving crowds, no speeches and no fanfare save for the persistent barking of that same limping yellow dog I had seen on my arrival.

"Hey, I think that was my moment," I said to myself as I stood at the rail with Kairit and watched the island grow smaller behind the ferry. The success of the guidebook had been wonderful, as was having a hit song. Finding the church bell was an event I would remember for the rest of my life. I had become a part of the local culture, met the love of my life and gotten married in a beautiful ceremony that had the best traditions of Estonia and America mixed together. Still, it wasn't until that last day, that last meeting with the people I had lived and worked with, that I felt like one of those smiling happy people I had seen on the recruiting posters in Peace Corps' offices. Now I knew why they were smiling.

It took nearly four years, but I finally understood that the Peace Corps wasn't about adoration and being irreplaceable. It wasn't about people admiring you so much they'll do whatever you say. It wasn't a competition to see who could be the best volunteer ever. It's about you becoming a part of the society around you and sharing what skills you have in order to make things better. It's about getting down to work, dirtying your hands, and being human like everyone else around you. If you're lucky, you'll make a lasting difference, but more than likely you'll just do your job well, help some people and make a few good friends before you go.

Had Hiiumaa changed because of me? I had certainly changed because of Hiiumaa. Had I really made a difference? I looked up for an answer just in time to see the little island drop into the sea behind the horizon. Like the *Hiidlased* always said, *ootame, vaatame.* Let's wait and see.

Printed in the United States
2975

Printed in the United States
2975